# Mentoring in Physical Education:
## Education:
### Issues and Insights

*Edited by*

## Mick Mawer

 The Falmer Press

(A member of the Taylor & Francis Group)

London • Washington, D.C.

UK      Falmer Press, 1 Gunpowder Square, London, EC4A 3DE
USA     Falmer Press, Taylor & Francis Inc., 1900 Frost Road, Suite 101,
        Bristol, PA 19007

First published in 1996

**A catalogue record for this book is available from the British
Library**

**Library of Congress Cataloging-in-Publication Data are
available on request**

ISBN 0 7507 0564 7 cased
ISBN 0 7507 0565 5 paper

Jacket design by Caroline Archer

Typeset in 10/12pt Garamond by
Graphicraft Typesetters Ltd., Hong Kong.

*Printed in Great Britain by Biddles Ltd., Guildford and King's Lynn
on paper which has a specified pH value on final paper
manufacture of not less than 7.5 and is therefore 'acid free'.*

# Contents

Contents

# Introduction

*Mick Mawer*

This is a undoubtedly a time of considerable change as far as teacher education in the UK is concerned, in fact, others have described this period as 'a significant watershed in the history of teacher preparation' (Tomlinson, 1995, p. viii) in which government interventions have 'transformed initial teacher education in the UK' (Furlong and Maynard, 1995, p. vii). Although many of these changes are also being felt in other countries it has been the speed of change that has characterized the UK context, as a rapid 'stream' of government circulars (DES 1984, 1989a and 1989b; DFE, 1992 and 1993) have transformed a largely higher education-based professional training into a school/university 'partnership' enterprise with two-thirds of the trainees' time being spent in school and the greater responsibility for training and assessment being vested in the practising teacher in school. What is now a largely school-based training for teaching has meant that the role of teachers acting as 'mentors' to trainees has developed in importance.

Many teachers taking on the new role of mentor to a trainee have been enthusiastic about the opportunities provided by a more school-based training, and have welcomed the prospect of not only becoming more involved in the preparation of new teachers, but also in contributing to what they see as a more relevant and effective professional training. However, there are also concerns and uncertainties about taking on the increased responsibility for teacher education without adequate time and funding for the job, and many are naturally a little apprehensive about what has to be achieved. In addition to this there appears to be a certain lack of clarity concerning the role of the mentor in initial teacher education (ITE), and even what 'mentoring' itself actually means. There are also those who believe that we cannot actually conceptualize the role of the mentor in ITE until we understand more fully the processes involved in learning to teach (Furlong and Maynard, 1995). But the issue that is central to these concerns is that if student teachers are expected to develop appropriate forms of practical professional knowledge through a training course in which the bulk of the time is spent in schools, then it is essential that a carefully structured support system in schools is available, and at this point in time such a system is centred around the role of the teacher as mentor.

Most of the literature on mentoring in ITE in the UK has concentrated on a generic view of mentoring in either primary or secondary schools, and very little is known about the school-based mentoring of trainees within partnership schemes in specific curriculum subjects, such as physical education. A greater knowledge of the issues that can influence the effectiveness of partnership schemes in teacher education in PE (PETE) and the quality of mentoring of trainees in schools, will, in turn, affect the quality of the physical education taught and received by pupils in school. That is what this book is about. It attempts to provide information on a number of issues already faced by those involved in partnership ITE schemes in PE, not only to provide an insight into what is happening at the present time and the views of those involved, but to also offer the results of recent research that might help those who are concerned with the planning and implementation of school-based ITE and mentor training programmes.

The book is in four parts. Part One 'sets the scene' so to speak, and includes chapters on the present context concerning 'partnerships' in school-based PETE in the UK, and on the whole issue of what mentoring in ITE is — or is not! As many feel that any planning of school-based ITE schemes and mentor training programmes should start from the trainees' perspective, Part Two therefore includes a series of chapters describing the results of research projects and the issues they have raised concerning the experiences of student teachers of PE during their ITE course. Part Three contains four chapters that discuss issues of particular concern to teachers acting in the role of mentors for trainees in PE. They include not only the results of research that has sought the opinions of teachers concerning their experience of acting in the new role of 'mentor' to trainees and the training that they feel they need to fulfil that role, but also a chapter on two interrelated topics of concern to all involved in the training of the next generation of PE teachers (but of particular importance to mentors in schools) — the issues of 'professional knowledge' and the process of training teachers to become 'reflective practitioners'. The final part of this book takes an International perspective. Not only do the two contributors offer UK readers an insight into teacher education developments overseas, but along with other contributors to this book, they provide a substantial contribution to the building up of a knowledge base about mentoring in PE.

The first chapter by Elizabeth Murdoch and Patricia Shenton raises the kind of issues that are confronting PE departments in higher education institutions (HEIs) in the UK who have spent the last few years developing partnership PETE schemes with schools. They discuss the importance of joint, collaborative planning of the student teacher's learning experiences with the trainee being fully involved in that planning; the need to clarify individual responsibilities of each partner in the training process; and that quality control should be an essential feature of partnership arrangements in terms of the contribution of the mentor, the structure and continuity of the trainee's learning experience, and the opportunities for further professional development to be part of the process. The notion of a trainee's 'entitlement' is central to this chapter, and the authors see sound 'Partnerships in Action' as being the foundation on which such an entitlement may be achieved.

One of the key features of school-based partnership ITE schemes is the vital role played by the teacher as a mentor in the development of the trainee's professional knowledge and expertise. But, what is mentoring? Michael Taylor and Joan Stephenson take us through the difficulties of actually coming to an agreement on a definition of what is true mentoring. Regardless of attempts to empirically investigate what mentors actually do (rather than what they are meant to do), it appears that we still seem to have a lot of uncertainty and lack of agreement concerning interpretations and applications of mentoring across different contexts and settings. The suggestion that effective mentoring may be context-specific does provide support for the view expressed by several authors in this book, that the primary or secondary school physical education ITE context may be unique as far as mentoring and mentor training is concerned, and that taking a generic view of mentoring skills that crosses all subject boundaries may not be the best way of planning partnership courses and mentor training programmes.

There is a view that before one can begin the task of planning the school-based training of student teachers and consider the role of mentors within that training, it is important to have some knowledge of student teachers' experiences, concerns, anxieties and needs — in other words to consider the trainee's perspective (Maynard and Furlong, 1993; Booth, 1993). Part Two of this book does exactly that. Both Sue Capel and Colin Hardy report the results of their research projects examining trainee PE teachers' anxieties, concerns and needs throughout the duration of both BEd and PGCE courses, and they offer suggestions for how mentors and those supporting and planning courses for trainees might help them to cope with and alleviate their anxieties and concerns, particularly in relation to being observed, being assessed, coming to terms with being a teacher, learning to teach and working with pupils, coping with the demands of the course, and dealing with school personnel and working arrangements.

In the third chapter of Part Two, Emma Tait, adopting a phenomenological research perspective, provides a fascinating insight into the 'lifeworld' and experiences of one PGCE PE student teacher, Laura, during her first term of a school-based course. The information that Emma offers about Laura's search for the status of 'being a teacher', her perceptions and experiences of the process of 'belonging', being accepted and being initiated into the work of her school PE department, and the support she received from her mentors, should provide those involved in mentoring trainees with a greater understanding of the process of learning to teach PE.

The theme of gathering evidence on the school-based experiences of trainees is continued in chapter 6, but in this case the subjects are generalist primary trainees and newly qualified primary teachers (NQTs). In this chapter Mick Mawer has attempted to provide an insight into the less frequently researched area of learning to teach PE in the primary school, to identify some of the initial training issues that are leading many primary teachers to feel underconfident about teaching certain aspects of PE to their classes, and to offer the trainees' perspective for what might be done in terms of the planning of their school-based training, the selection and role of their PE mentors, and the kind of support they may need as NQT's.

Kim Yau completes this second section with the first of several reports emanating from the three-year joint research project initiated by Elizabeth Murdoch and Patricia Shenton at their respective institutions and mentioned in chapter 1. In this chapter Kim describes the results of an ongoing investigation of secondary PE trainees' perceptions of the concept of 'partnership' in ITE, their views of the mentoring process and the mentoring they receive in school.

The main focus of Part Three is the mentor — their views about the role of mentor, and the training they need. This section also provides information for mentors and mentor trainers about the importance of the mentor-mentee relationship, and a review of two issues that are of particular interest to all involved in the training of the next generation of teachers — professional knowledge and critical reflection. The section begins with two contributions reporting research related to the mentoring role in PE and mentor training needs. In chapter 8 the joint Liverpool John Moores/University of Brighton project team provide an insight into what secondary PE mentors say and feel about their role, their views on partnerships, resources, recognition by colleagues, on mentoring as an aspect of career enhancement, and on the training they need to do the job well. In chapter 9 Mick Mawer discusses the results of a preliminary investigation examining what primary classteachers acting in the role of mentor supporting PGCE primary generalist trainees feel about fulfilling that particular aspect of their general mentoring role. What do they feel about the part that should be played by the university and school in the training of a primary student teacher to teach PE? What do they see as their supporting role and the skills and knowledge needed to fulfil it? What training do they need for the role and would they prefer to have other staff involved in the support of trainees to teach PE? The views of the teachers and the issues they raise have implications for the planning of partnerships at primary level, the planning of trainees school-based training in PE, and the training of the mentor responsible for planning that school-based training.

The view that mentoring itself may only be defined in terms of the context of the individual mentor-mentee relationship, and that both mentors themselves and those involved in planning partnership ITE schemes need to consider the role of the trainee and their contribution to the mentoring process, is put forward by Joanne Hudson and Ann-Marie Latham in chapter 10. The creation of an autonomous, analytical, reflective trainee, who has the professional knowledge and skills to take part in a mutually active mentoring relationship that not only caters for their individual needs, but also allows them to take part in joint problem-solving and decision-making about the development of their professional skills — is central to this chapter.

The interrelated themes of professional knowledge and critical reflection as important issues within ITE are continued in Tony Rossi's detailed review and thoughtful discussion of the nature of pedagogical content knowledge

(PCK) and critical reflection in teaching physical education. He not only provides the information to enable mentors to understand what the notions of PCK and critical reflection actually mean, but he also offers suggestions as to how mentors might support the development of these important aspects of learning to teach in trainee PE teachers. As with the previous chapter, Tony emphasizes the importance of the mentor working in a close collaborative relationship with the trainee (rather than just see themselves as the expert with 'all the answers') for reflection in the form of action research to be really meaningful, relevant and effective — and also the need for teachers acting as mentors to be 'educational craftspersons' themselves, constantly putting their practice under critical scrutiny.

In order to provide an International perspective on the issues of mentoring and school-based training, three researchers and writers in the field of teacher training in PE in their own countries, Richard Tinning, Deborah Tannehill and Deborah Coffin, were invited to provide UK readers with an insight into the issues influencing mentoring and teacher training in PE in Australia and the USA. According to Tinning, Australian teacher educators are facing similar changes in ITE to that being experienced by teachers and lecturers the UK. In his discussion of the problems that may be associated with these changes he debates the issues that might influence the effectiveness of trainees' school experience (or practicum) as a site for the learning of not only pedagogical skills and curriculum knowledge, but also as a context for facilitating action research and critical reflection. Tinning sees the notion of the mentor (whether school-based or HEI-based teacher educator) as a critically reflective, 'extended professional' as central to this development.

In the final chapter Deborah Tannehill and Deborah Coffin take a wider view of the concept of mentoring and focus on four particular aspects of mentoring within teacher preparation in PE in the USA: peer mentoring within pre-service education; the co-operating teacher as the mentor; recent mentoring developments within collaborative (partnership) initiatives; and mentoring in beginner teacher induction. These issues are discussed in terms of the research based and experimental mentoring programmes being conducted in the US at present, and the authors describe both the formal and informal mentoring strategies that are a part of the mentoring scene in the United States.

It is hoped that the issues raised in this book will not only contribute to our knowledge of, and the ongoing debate about, the complex and difficult task of mentoring in PE, but will also help those who are responsible for the design of partnership schemes of ITE to create coherent, meaningful and relevant programmes of teacher preparation based on close collaboration and carefully structured school-based support. Although a great deal of what has been discussed in this book is concerned with the school-based context of learning to teach, and the vitally important role of the school mentor and the support they provide, it is clear that both the school and the higher education institution working in partnership each have a vital role to play in the initial training of our next generation of teachers of PE.

## References

Booth, M. (1993) 'The effectiveness and role of the mentor in school: The students' view', *Cambridge Journal of Education*, **23**, 2, pp. 185–97.

DES (1984) *Initial Teacher Training: Approval of Courses* (Circular 3/84), London, HMSO.

DES (1989a) *Initial Teacher Training: Approval of Courses* (Circular 24/89), London, HMSO.

DES (1989b) *Articled Teacher Pilot Scheme: Invitation to Bid for Funding Memo 276/ 89*, London, HMSO.

DFE (1992) *Initial Teacher Training* (Secondary Phase) (Circular 9/92), London, HMSO.

DFE (1993) *The Initial Training of Primary School Teachers: New Criteria for Courses* (Circular 14/93), London, HMSO.

Furlong, J. and Maynard, T. (1995) *Mentoring Student Teachers: The Growth of Professional Knowledge*, London, Routledge.

Maynard, T. and Furlong, J. (1993) 'Learning to teach and models of mentoring' in McIntyre, D., Haggar, H. and Wilkin, M. (Eds) *Mentoring: Perspectives on School-based Teacher Education*, London, Kogan Page, pp. 69–85.

Tomlinson, P. (1995) *Understanding Mentoring: Reflective Strategies for School-based Teacher Preparation*, Buckingham, Open University Press.

*Part One*

# *The Context*

# 1    Partnerships in School-based Training: The Implications for Physical Education

*Patricia Shenton and Elizabeth Murdoch*

## Introduction

The impact of the transfer of a more substantial part of initial teacher training (ITT) from university and college departments to schools is now beginning to be felt in both groups of institutions. The interpretation of partnerships is becoming increasingly more sophisticated and there is widespread support for the concept that teachers should be trained in the setting in which they will eventually work.

Much has been written recently about the process of preparing a trainee teacher for entry into the teaching profession but little of this refers directly to the preparation of teachers of physical education. Physical education has earned a reputation for not always fitting easily into patterns of professional practice enjoyed by other subjects, and the development of school partnerships, and all that this entails, is no exception. There is, therefore, a number of important issues which merit recognition as we stand back to review recent innovative practice in physical education both in schools and within ITT in universities and colleges. Reference will be made in more depth to a number of these issues in later chapters but there is value, at this stage, in looking broadly at the major challenges facing the trainers of new teachers.

The setting up of a joint research project between Liverpool John Moores University (IM Marsh Centre) and the University of Brighton (Chelsea School of Physical Education, Sports, Science, Dance and Leisure) has enabled us to collect valuable data from the first two years of operation of the enhanced school involvement in ITT. This chapter offers the opportunity for some critical conceptual issues to be explored. In other chapters, it is hoped that evidence of these issues in practice will be incorporated.

## Partnerships — Are they Working?

The most significant question to be asked at this stage is:

**Do we all share the same view of partnership and what it means?**

The way in which these reforms in initial teacher training were introduced resulted in very hasty and limited planning and implementation in the first instance to allow responses to the Department for Education Circular 9/92 (DFE, 1992) to be made. This central directive with its significant proposals for the future of teacher training set a very short timeframe for its implementation. As a result, early responses were not based on careful and appropriate consultation and planning nor did they allow time for the physical education profession to give systematic thought to the full impact of these changes on the subject as well as on tutors, teachers and students.

The initial reaction of all parties to the proposals was largely one of suspicion born of a level of ignorance that could not be easily rectified owing to lack of joint preparation time. The true potential, and therefore form, of partnerships was still to be considered, realized and appreciated by the partners involved. An early priority in the implementation process, that bordered on the obsessive, was related to the financial implications of transferring appropriate funds from university to schools. This tended to obscure what should have been the main focus — that of building a professional partnership for teacher education in making full use of the relative strengths of each partner in joint, strategic planning. Thus the first cohorts of students came quickly into a system hardly ready for them. It is to the credit of all concerned that they emerged from the experience with positive responses and a remarkable professional confidence.

It is worthwhile at this point to consider briefly the context of teacher training in general within which the changes were to be introduced. Education was going through an unprecedented period of government intervention which had already affected substantially the roles and functions of schools and local authorities. Higher education could not have expected to escape from the radical reforms that were changing the face of education but there was little warning as to the exact nature of the proposals for the shake up in this sector.

Margaret Wilkin (1993) makes reference to three, more specific, conditions in teacher education prior to the advent of Circular 9/92 all of which are particularly relevant to physical education. Firstly, she proposes that there has been, for some time, a reduction in educational theorizing within training courses and that the focus of understanding the process is now much more on personal and reflective experience of the student as teacher than understanding and application of relevant theories. Secondly, she notes a significant change in the balance of theory to practice. A marked reduction in the reliance on the disciplines of education has meant that there is less status given to the student's ability to argue and defend a discipline-rooted viewpoint than to competence in the classroom. Lastly, she recognizes that there has been a 'merging equivalence of status of tutors and teachers' (p. 44) as school-based work came to be valued more and more.

In retrospect, it is interesting to note how these changes have set the scene for and contributed to, the concept of the 'new model of the teacher' that is sought by the Teacher Training Agency. There is neither time nor space in this chapter to pursue in detail the implications of these changes for physical education except to note that, for those who consider physical education to be an almost solely 'practical' subject, the apparent change in balance from theory to practice, with an emphasis on competences, could be seen to be a move in the right direction.

Margaret Wilkin warns that

> Personal theorizing *per se* provides an insecure basis for practice, yet individual interpretation cannot be disregarded if participation and commitment are to be wholehearted. Although reference to the views of other individuals extends one's vision, reference to established research, for all its weaknesses, offers the sounder means of verifying one's assumptions. (*ibid*, p. 50)

and

> it entails engaging the student on an intellectual journey from a particular to a general form of theorizing for the purposes of confirming or disconfirming or clarifying or extending his/her original assumptions. (*ibid*, p. 49)

Setting out together on this journey must be the essence of good partnerships and must challenge the nature of teacher (mentor)/tutor/student relationships and call for a greater degree of joint planning of university courses and school based experience.

To do this, places an emphasis on one of the most critical questions yet to be fully answered:

**Who is responsible for what, in terms of actual practice in schools, professional preparation and subject knowledge?**

The following model based on the interaction of theory with practice may help to clarify different aspects of the approach to producing a teacher, and in particular a teacher of physical education, who is competent and yet at the same time has the ability to be reflectively intelligent

|  | **THEORY** | **PRACTICE** |
|---|---|---|
| **THEORY** | Discipline based theoretical analysis (library based study) | Theory of good practice in teaching (reflection on practice in context) |
| **PRACTICE** | Practical implementing of educational/pedagogic theory (workshop mode) | Teaching in context |

This echoes very closely the work of Maynard and Furlong (1993) in which they propose that professional training happens at 4 levels:

level (a) .............................. direct classroom practice
level (b) .............................. indirect practice
level (c) .............................. practical principles
level (d) .............................. disciplinary theory (pp. 69–70)

All of the above can involve tutor, teacher and student in a contribution to the student's development. The planning of a good partnership must involve the decision about which member(s) of the partnership have the knowledge, skills and resources to make the best contribution at the time.

This will work best when the tutor and mentor share the same subject/ discipline. Where the tutor does not come from the same area of study, the role of the mentor in supporting subject development for the student becomes more critical and the relationship with subject based tutors in the pre-planning of courses becomes even more important.

This could give rise to different models of mentorship in practice. For example, the mentor may arrange workshop sessions where the student could experiment within a teaching episode with pupils while, at another time, the tutor may be engaging the student on reflection on the theoretical principles involved and on the practical outcome.

That the student should be fully involved in the planning of his/her progress and mode of learning is of vital importance and this brings us to another issue within partnership structures. The student should be seen wherever possible as a full member of the team and as such expected to take major responsibility for as much of the partnership as possible alongside the rest of the team. The traditional view of the student as being one who brings nothing or little to the education setting is no longer tenable. Many students bring much experience with them and are capable in many situations of functioning in a fully professional way. This can be particularly true of the physical education student who has many opportunities to gain relevant experience through personal interests such as involvement with children or a coaching qualification, How far this is realized will be dictated largely by the attitudes of the tutor, teacher and most importantly the student.

As the dust settles from the early days of change, it would seem that the time is right for some critical decisions to be made as to what is the real nature of the best partnership for such an important task as preparing for the future of the physical education profession.

In attempting to do this, some assumptions will need to be made that may uncomfortably challenge some long established patterns of practice:

• that this is a real partnership based on collaborative planning, and not merely one partner taking over part of the job of another;
• that the process of training a teacher is a continuum from initial to

continuing professional development and not focussed solely on the traditional undergraduate 'supervised teaching practice' in a school;
- that such a continuum will expect that all teachers will show a steadily developing set of competences appropriate for each stage in the process of their careers;
- that students of physical education (many more of whom are mature) bring with them many personal skills and are capable of taking on an immediate, responsible and active role within a school and thus making a significant contribution to the work of the school and the physical education department while at the same time adopting the more traditional role of the new student teacher.

What are the major issues that need to be addressed if partnerships between schools and HE institutions are going to develop?

Quality assurance and quality control are high on the agenda in all sectors of education. Ultimately, the maintenance of quality in relation to all partners is what will ensure good partnerships. What criteria can be proposed that will allow for a measure of quality control in the partnership between schools (and especially their physical education departments) and the providers of ITT within HE? What factors, if any, militate against the provision of the highest quality of training for students?

It has been recognized that the process of the Office for Standards in Education (OFSTED) inspections in relation to physical education in schools, particularly primary schools, has been less uniformly rigorous than we as a profession would have wished as there are very few inspectors available who have sufficient knowledge of physical education for the subject to be adequately inspected. At this moment a group of physical education advisers and inspectors are meeting with HMI to consider the needs of physical education within an inspection. The group will be addressing, among other areas, the criteria of good partnerships between schools and HE institutions and it is hoped that this will do much to raise awareness of the large variation in standard of the student experience from one school to another, which is the first step towards having a significant improvement.

HMI (1995) recognized this when they suggested that,

Quality control across HE and schools is a major challenge . . . models of good practice involving partnerships of varying numbers of schools were observed. Successful provision usually reflected long established and effective relationships between the schools and HEIs; a great deal of co-operation and flexibility by all concerned; and a willingness to ensure that the combined expertise of school teachers and HEI tutors was carefully co-ordinated and deployed.

One of the expected outcomes of the joint IM Marsh/Chelsea research project will be to devise appropriate instruments for assessing quality in the delivery of ITT within established partnerships.

For the purposes of this chapter, quality and its achievement within good partnerships will be addressed under the following headings. These cannot be considered as independent of each other in practice but, explored separately, will provide a framework that allows for recognition of the significance of the roles of the main providers:

- the contribution of the mentor;
- continuity and relevance of the student's experience;
- continuing professional development.

### The Contribution of the Mentor

From observation of current practice of mentorship in physical education, within an established school/HE partnership, the following would seem to be critical to the assurance of a good and fair experience for students:

(i) **that the mentor has time and status to allow the job to be done well** and this will call for a clear commitment from head-teachers and governors to see ITT and mentoring in physical education as a significant part of the school's work and also recognition of the value of physical education to the school;

(ii) **that the mentor has access to a good personal developmental programme** that is well planned as a corporate exercise and includes knowledge of, and significant input into, university courses experienced by students; awareness of assessment procedures, rules and regulations that pertain in the student's course and how to relate them to the school context; understanding of the Circular 9/92 competences and how to recognize and develop them in a student; an awareness of the competences that are critical for good mentoring and how to improve on these;

(iii) **that agreement is reached between the mentor and the university tutor about the most appropriate model of divided responsibility** that will allow them to address who is responsible for which aspects of content, teaching and learning processes, assessment etc.; how is the integration of theory and practice accomplished; how much content/subject material can realistically be taught in the school during the student placement; who will decide on the underlying philosophy of the placement period with clear objectives or learning outcomes as appropriate.

McIntyre and Hagger (1993), in supporting the strong case for practising teachers being better equipped to provide the 'supervision' of beginning teachers practice, suggest that they must develop to a high level the skills of supervision that tutors in universities and colleges already have, capitalize on the distinctive opportunities available to them and avoid the dangers. Among the distinctive opportunities that mentors have they cite information, continuity and validity. The mentors know more about the school and the people in it; they can provide a much greater consistency, regularity and continuity than a tutor whose visits are infrequent; support for the student does not have the ethos of special occasion about it but is seen as part of normal everyday experience.

McIntyre and Hagger warn us also of dangers. The most significant of these is a combination of arbitrariness and idiosyncrasy. This is a particular danger within physical education where styles of teaching and modes of working have been developed as highly personal and also where areas of expertise within subject knowledge are, in many cases, highly specialist. It has been noted on numerous occasions that young teachers, coming for the first time into a physical education department, with enthusiasm for what was learned in ITT have been firmly told to 'forget all that and realize that this is the real thing!' It is here that negative attitudes to 'all that theory' can be found where practice alone for some is seen to be the nature of the real job. It will be a challenge for many mentors to appreciate the range and width of strategies and styles within which a young teacher must experiment in relation to children's learning and also the breadth of content that has to be mastered.

Another danger cited by McIntyre and Hagger is that of the closeness of the relationship between mentor and student. It is a relationship within which mutual respect is fundamental.

The role of the mentor is one which carries a number of polarities which can lead to tension both for student and mentor.

For example, the mentor is both:

| | | |
|---|---|---|
| TRAINER | and | SUPERVISOR |
| FACILITATOR | and | ASSESSOR |
| TEACHER OF CHILDREN | and | SUPERVISOR OF STUDENTS |

The mentor, in attempting to satisfy all demands, can face difficult decisions. Parents are beginning to ask what effect this new role of mentoring is likely to have on the quality of education that will be received by their children. In some cases, parents feel strongly in some cases that teachers are there to teach children and should not be putting their energies into such demanding tasks as mentoring and where the children may have the student teacher 'experimenting' on them. There is no doubt that this will be seen to be of great significance in the core subjects but there is evidence also of some concern being expressed within physical education also.

### Structure and Continuity of Students' Experience

What is a student's entitlement in preparing to be a teacher of physical education?

An issue that is of significance is the obvious discrepancy in what is offered to one student in one school and another student in a different school. While it is important that schools should have a distinctive ethos and style there is a number of aspects of the student experience that should be found in very similar form from one school to the next. So far, reports from students and tutors would indicate that this is not sufficiently the case and that fundamental aspects of ITT within physical education are not being made available to every student. It could be acknowledged that this is no different from pre-Circular 9/92 practice but, while this is true, the impact of a greater proportion of time being spent in schools coupled with the enhanced role of the mentor means that the effect on the student is now very much more significant.

A student should be entitled to expect that, within the physical education department:

- the National Curriculum is placed within a total curriculum from pre-school(4) to 19-year-olds and that planning, performing and evaluating are being interpreted fully and appropriately throughout;
- the programmes of study are progressive and continuous from KS1 to KS4 and that this is evident in the written planning of the department;
- the physical education curriculum is broad and balanced in respect of the six areas of activity and the range of single activities on offer within each of these;
- a broad range of teaching strategies and styles are used as and when appropriate;
- assessment strategies and processes are integrated within teaching and learning, and that systems are as simple and consistent as possible;
- the monitoring of 'good practice' in schools and HEIs is accepted and established;
- status, credibility and the respect of parents, governors, headteachers and colleagues, community partners and the young people themselves have been achieved and are maintained.

There is evidence to suggest that the above are not necessarily common practice in all schools. As a result, students are liable to experience discontinuity both within one school and, almost certainly, from one school to another with inevitable gaps in their development. Whereas pre-Circular 9/92 any student who experienced a school with a heavy bias towards games or gymnastics could offset this by choice of focus in university courses, this may no longer be possible. Schools, therefore, must look carefully at the breadth and balance of the programmes in their physical education curriculum.

It seems only reasonable that students should sense a common purpose and rationale underpinning schools planning for physical education, at least in a local area. Traditionally, within the subject of physical education, there has been a significant degree of freedom in what children will be expected to learn and when this should take place. Despite the introduction of the National

Curriculum this can still be the case as interpretation can be flexible. Now that teachers in training are spending much more concentrated and longer periods in schools and moving between schools there is a real danger that unless planning is consistent, alarming gaps or major overlaps in knowledge and experience will result.

Where the delivery of the curriculum does not meet the above fundamental structural criteria, the quality will inevitably be less than satisfactory for both pupils and students. A young, inexperienced teacher in training, meeting a less than acceptable curriculum structure, may well accept it as an example of good practice or if not happy to accept it, may be very uncomfortable about showing dissatisfaction. The danger of a downward spiral of standards is very likely.

Much work needs to be done with teachers and university departments together in preparing guidelines and working documents that will secure a shared philosophy about the teaching of physical education and the ways in which this can best be provided within the concept and practice of partnership. This will inevitably call for both sides of the partnership to effect some compromise of their long held well-established beliefs.

If such working plans were available, it would make it possible to introduce the idea of a learning contract for each student, which would sharpen up the student's commitment to their own development and involvement in personal profiling. Students may then enter the process of learning to teach, with some well-developed skills and competences. In preparing a learning contract, each student would estimate the relevance of previous experience in relation to the expectations of both university and school and would contract to complete or extend aspects of personal development within an agreed time. The other half of the contract is that of both schools and university agreeing to support the student's planned learning. This contract is particularly appropriate for post graduate certificate students who have to plan limited time very carefully.

All this presupposes that there is shared understanding of what the student's progressive experience will be and this should be a key aspect of quality partnership.

### Continuing Professional Development

Quality provision is very dependent on the ability and skill of the providers. A significant strength for a trainee teacher is to realize that all those who are in support are also involved in a learning and professional development process. Both physical education teachers as mentors and university tutors are in need of regular professional development activity particularly when the profession is grappling with the rapidly increasing and confusing number of partners and co-providers within physical education, sport and dance. Many universities are offering joint training where the process of the partnership and its developmental needs can be examined and the roles of the partners sharpened and integrated. University tutors have a need to become as familiar as possible with the expectations of subjects other than their own. The fact that a tutor is visiting a student whose subject area is different is a source of tension but as the concept of moderation rather than supervision is becoming established this becomes more possible. Nevertheless, the demands placed on the mentor to carry the major role as the source of subject knowledge is pointing to the need for regular updating on subject developments. It is often assumed that where such developments occur they have originated in places other than schools but there are many examples where strong subject innovation has been the result of good physical education department planning. This raises the concept of teacher peer development and the area of mentoring possibly offers the best forum for this to be established when all teachers feel more confident as they acquire new competences and a new professional focus.

The assumption that staff development for mentors and tutors would be initiated always from within universities is ready to be challenged. Schools as training establishments and teachers as mentors have as good if not better reasons for assuming more responsibility for professional development. This will require a shift in attitude from within the school which should acknowledge that there is much to be shared in good practice while at the same time there is the opportunity to establish the ethos of the school in this comparatively new role. The concept of 'the expert' is not one that has been in favour of late but as new roles are assumed, new expertise will become available and should be developed.

The concept of continuing professional development is becoming established through the co-ordination, integration and progression now established across the initial teacher training, induction and in-service training continuum. Within this context, work on developing progressive competences is well underway within the research project. This could have a profound effect on the perceptions of the student's place in the hierarchy. Traditionally the student has been regarded as a 'new' recruit with everything to learn while teachers and tutors were established and had 'arrived professionally'.

That each member of the team is involved in professional development at the respective and appropriate stage in their experience will strengthen the autonomy of the student and also enhance the student's confidence in having something significant to offer to the school. In the words of one student, reported in Hudson and Latham (1995), who was recognized as making a contribution to the mentor's learning:

> He wanted any new stuff that we got, information from the university, or any lectures that we had had that would be useful for him and the school, you know, that's the way it worked. (p. 27)

That the student can be more than a purveyor of university material and procedures but can contribute to the continuous professional development of colleagues is well illustrated in the following comment by a student about his mentor:

> He wants us to give him feedback on his lesson he'd evaluate his own lessons . . . he's always looking for new ways to develop his teaching which was brill . . . so it gave us a good view on life that teaching is progressive, even when you're experienced, you know, you're still learning. (p. 28)

## Conclusion

There is no doubt in the minds of all partners in this development that it is already having very positive outcomes in a number of ways. The learning ethos and atmosphere is good for the student in being in the real world for a significant amount of time. The consistent relationship with a mentor on a day-to-day basis is proving of value to the student. The fact that the student entitlement, in good partnership situations, is placed at the centre of the partnership is giving the student a significant role in both personal development and also in the development of the partnership as a whole and of the other partners in it. This allows the student to make a full contribution to the school and become a significant added resource.

But, despite all the undoubtedly positive educational benefits, the constraints imposed still by as yet unsolved financial situations are causing concern. The recent proposals, that finance is forthcoming from the school budget to fund the contribution of teachers to the students' training, have raised a strong protest from the headteachers associations. A fundamentally sound educational initiative based on school and HE partnership, is in danger of being submerged by inappropriate funding arrangements with the strengthening of one partner while reducing the contribution of the other. The clear intention of the government to give schools more and more responsibility for education is raising protest as heads and governors are being called upon to resist the pressure on them to take on, as a statutory obligation, initial training of teachers. While this is a completely understandable reaction there is grave danger that, while the situation is being resolved, schools may by both choice and default reduce the possibility of placements for students such that the sector is seriously undermined. It is inconceivable that the teaching profession can be put seriously at risk in the long term, but the uncertainty that could come in the wake of such radical reforms must inevitably threaten the quality of ITT and general professional development during this critical period of change.

The teaching profession is at a crossroads.

On the one hand, there is a need to provide a quality training system that recognizes and believes in a *partnership model* that combines the philosophy of education and training defined by Circulars 9/92 (DFE, 1992) and 14/93

(DFE, 1993): and on the other hand, teachers of physical education need to be well prepared through established subject knowledge, teaching and learning expertise and familiarity with relevant theory, to be able to provide for the activity needs of all children within the curriculum.

This is placed in the context of the whole school, the extended curriculum and developing links with a range of professional colleagues in the community which are all part of a co-ordinated provision for the same children.

The least that students can expect from the training institution and its partner schools is:

(i) a rigorous and high quality training system which provides under-standing of the context of physical education within the National Curriculum and how this relates to extra and extended opportun-ities between school and community;

(ii) the development of quality assurance and improvement procedures to ensure consistency across the partnership schemes;

(iii) continuing professional development for HEI tutors and school teachers linked to accountability and accreditation;

(iv) proactive communication links between partners in the form of agreed terminology, newsletters, courses and local conferences;

(v) a more imaginative and constructive approach to the development of funding and resources, particularly through initial teacher train-ing, induction and developing professional competence;

(vi) consistency of formative and summative assessment procedures continuously maintained and continually improved through the development of professional competence with a particular focus on Records of Achievement;

(vii) putting the students back at the centre of any decision-making using student entitlement, empowerment and feedback as a critical point of reference.

Partnership in action is achieved between university tutors and teachers co-operating and mutually respecting and understanding each others skills, ex-pertise and enterprise so that together they can create structural pathways of opportunity for physical education students in training.

## References

DFE (1992) *Initial Teacher Training* (Secondary Phase), (Circular 9/92), London, HMSO.

DFE (1993) *Initial Teacher Training* (Primary Phase) (Circular 14/93), London, HMSO.

HMI (1995) *Partnership Schools and Higher Education in Partnership in Secondary Initial Teacher Training*, Report from Office of Her Majesty's Chief Inspector of Schools, London, HMSO.

HUDSON, J. and LATHAM, A-M. (1995) 'PE and dance students perceptions of mentoring under the partnership scheme', *Mentoring and Tutoring*, **3**, 1, summer, pp. 23–31.

McIntyre, D. and Hagger, H. (1993) 'Teachers expertise and models of mentoring' in McIntyre, D., Hagger, H. and Wilkin, M. (Eds) *Mentoring: Perspectives on School-based Teacher Education*, London, Kogan Page, pp. 86–102.

Maynard, T. and Furlong, J. (1993) 'Learning to teach and models of mentoring' in McIntyre, D., Hagger, H. and Wilkin, M. (Eds) *Mentoring: Perspectives on School-based Teacher Education*, London, Kogan Page, pp. 69–85.

Wilkin, M. (1993) 'Initial training as a case of postmodern development: Some implications for mentoring' in McIntyre, D., Hagger, H. and Wilkin, M. (Eds) *Mentoring: Perspectives on School-based Teacher Education*, London, Kogan Page, pp. 37–53.

# 2    What is Mentoring?

*Michael Taylor and Joan Stephenson*

### Well, What is it?

Well . . . there is a problem.

It's not that we don't basically know what mentoring is; it's not that it can't be defined. There are plenty of definitions including some handy, sound-bite sized ones that range from the spiritual and almost purply poetic picture of mentors as leading

> us along the journey of our lives. We trust them because they have been there before. They embody our hopes, cast light on the way ahead, interpret arcane signs, warn us of lurking dangers, and point out unexpected delights along the way. (Daloz, 1986)

through modern pseudo-management descriptions of mentoring as

> a process increasingly used in management development whereby the skills and techniques learned on the management development pro-gramme can be put into practice through the support and help of an experienced manager back in the workplace. (Jenkins *et al*, 1991)

to the neo-brutalist school of mentoring where the mentor describes their role in people's development as

> I listen to what they say. Then I tell them what they're going to do. (anonymous police mentor).

The problem is not that there aren't definitions to be trotted out as needed but that, so far, they haven't been pulled together into one unified, all-encompass-ing version. Right across the English speaking world, from the Pacific Rim via the North American continent to our own northern European offshore islands the complaints go up that:

> there seems to be little agreement on what is meant by the term 'mentor' (Wilkin, 1992; Clutterbuck, 1991)

the concept of 'mentoring' remains imprecise and unclear (Harvard and Dunne, 1992) and depends on who is writing about it (Barlow, 1991)

trying to isolate exact or universally accepted definitions of mentoring is next to impossible (Stott and Walker, 1992)

where theoretical 'models' of mentoring exist they are partial and inadequate (Maynard and Furlong, 1993)

in mentoring research, there is little agreement on basic notions so that findings remain a crazed patchwork of separate and irreconcilable results (Jacobi, 1991)

there is a need for a more clearly defined role for mentors (Turner, 1993) — a complaint that mentors make in surveys (Powney *et al*, 1993; Taylor, 1994b and 1995a)

These lacks of agreement, precision, clarity and definition are hardly surprising given that even the language used about mentoring is more than a little confused — and confusing. Take 'coaching' for example. Some people see this as something very different from, even opposed to, 'mentoring' (Megginson, 1988; Parsloe, 1992). Others see it as an integral part of mentoring, something without which mentoring might not actually be 'mentoring' (Jacobi, 1991; Jenkins *et al*, 1991).

This confusion does not help the work of researchers into mentoring, designers of mentoring schemes or mentoring practitioners. Nor is their work helped by the 'real thing syndrome'. In places where researchers, scheme designers and practitioners gather, anywhere that the purposes and practices of the mentor are debated, at some moment or other someone is bound to say, about some mentoring scheme or other, 'Of course, that's not real mentoring!'. This is usually said definitively and with almost absolute certainty. The person saying it usually has a tight definition of mentoring, the major purpose of which seems to be to ensure that the speaker's particular set of prejudices is accepted as the 'real thing' and that everything else is excluded. Even when people are not trying to establish their prejudices as the norm there is still a feeling that nice tight definitions are the proper thing to try and achieve. People try to keep coming up with them. This urge towards crisp, clean edged definitions probably comes down to us, via the old 'classical' education and the old philosophers, from the ancient Greeks: from Socrates' endless questioning to get to the heart of things, to get to their essentials; and from Aristotle's rigid, inflexible laws of logic — which even, at one stage, became known as the 'laws of thought'. Things have moved on a little since the ancient Greeks. Nowadays there is fairly general agreement that the laws of logic are not the laws of thought — 'Logic no more explains how we think than grammar explains how we speak' (Minsky, 1988). Even the real experts in the province of neat, clear-cut definitions — the analytic philosopher of language, the researcher into categorization, the professional taxonomist and classifier, and, especially, the mathematician and logician (for example, Wittgenstein, 1968; Rosch, 1977; Sokal, 1974; Kosko, 1994) — have accepted the inevitable blurry fuzziness of everything and that things in the real world don't necessarily have nice, crisp cores of essentials that can be neatly laid out to produce classifications that have sharp, well delimited edges and boundaries. The experts have long since got round to the notion that such things may well be wills o' the wisp, flickering ghostly lights that are either pure marsh gas, or figments of the imagination. Real life is vague and untidy with endlessly blurred edges: 'We know well enough how to distinguish urban from rustic areas, games from work, and spring from summer, and are *unembarrassed by the discovery of undecidable marginal cases*' (Ryle, 1963). The real world is full of categories that have fuzzy edges and overlap.

Over the last thirty or forty years techniques and technologies have been developed that can cope with, analyze, and produce workable models of things that are blurry and vague and undefined, groups of things and activities that aren't all exactly alike but differ markedly in some respects and have strong resemblances in others, situations where there may be, at least as far as the hard edged definers see it, embarrassingly undecidable marginal cases. There are: neural networks in artificial intelligence and industry; chaos and complexity theory in maths, science, economics and even weather forecasting; fuzzy chips in washing machines and cameras. Now the world of mentoring is part of the real world and the edges between being a 'coach' and being a 'mentor' are fairly blurry and overlapping (Parsloe, 1992). It flies in the face of experience and expertise in other parts of the real world to continue trying to set up clear boundaries between such roles that mark out only the differences and then exaggerate them. It is much more in accord with what happens in the real world to look at the similarities as well as the differences, at the overlaps as well as the distinctions, and develop a view of a whole spectrum of more or less closely related activities. There's little need now for definitions that mark out boundaries and barriers, or even for large scale unified, all encompassing definitions. Instead of attempting monolithic definitions picking out the common factors in all the approved kinds of 'mentoring' — and excluding things that aren't the 'real thing' — what is needed is a proper look at them all. And 'if you look at them you will not see something that is common to *all*, but similarities, relationships, and a whole series of them . . . a complicated network of similarities overlapping and crisscrossing: sometimes overall similarities, sometimes similarities of detail . . . I can think of no better expression to characterize these similarities than "family resemblances"' (Wittgenstein, 1968). Such a look may not produce a nice sharp picture, it may only produce an indistinct one, but 'Is it even always an advantage to replace an indistinct picture by a sharp one? Isn't the indistinct one often exactly what we need?' (*ibid*) — especially when there are techniques and technologies to make better use of an indistinct one than a sharp one.

But it's odds on that at the next conference, or symposium, or workshop on mentoring there's going to be someone somewhere with a gospel light glowing in their eyes stoutly maintaining their own little separatist definition and denigrating all the others. There's bound to be someone saying with a slight air of condescension 'Of course, that's not real mentoring'.

### Well Then, You're Looking at it. So What is it?

Well . . . it depends on where you're looking.

There are probably three levels at which mentoring can be examined: firstly, as a principle or idea or concept — a former Secretary of State for Education in England, whose departure probably went largely unlamented, once said that he found 'the *concept* of the mentor teacher with a particular responsibility for a student or a group of students an attractive one' (Clark, 1992). At this level things are vague ideas in the minds of the gods — but still waiting to be put into some sort of programmatic form for actual action.

This programmatic form can be found at the next level down, where 'mentoring' is looked at from the perspective of those who set up mentoring schemes or who investigate and theorize about mentoring. At this level people don't produce sound-bite sized aphorisms, or get attracted by notional concepts. They are much more likely to produce lists of what mentors are *meant* to do, what mentors are meant to provide their protégés with, like:

    acceptance, support, encouragement
    advice, guidance
    bypassing bureaucracy, access to resources
    challenge, opportunity, 'plum assignments'
    clarification of values and goals
    coaching
    information
    protection
    role model
    social status, reflected credit
    socialization, 'host and guide'
    sponsorship, advocacy
    stimulate acquisition of knowledge
    training, instruction
    visibility, exposure              (Jacobi, 1991)

Formulations at this level may also specify what the mentor-protégé relationship should be like, what the aspects of the mentor's role should be, and even lay down how long the relationship should last, for example:

| | |
|---|---|
| the sort of relationship: | mentoring is the building of a dynamic relationship; the process is the shared and supportive elements that are based on common values; an enabling relationship in personal, organizational and professional terms; |
| the roles of the mentor: | *adviser* — support and advice, career and social; awareness of protégé's merits and abilities; aids building image and confidence;<br>*coach* — mutual setting of guidelines; advice and instruction; feedback analyzed and refined;<br>*counsellor* — psychological support; listener and sounding board;<br>*guide/networker* — guide to helpful contacts; introduction to values and customs;<br>*role model* — observable image, of skills and qualities, for emulation;<br>*sponsor* — facilitates entry to culture; provides introductions;<br>*teacher* — sharing knowledge; facilitating learning opportunities; focussing on individual needs and learning styles; |
| the relationship's duration | two to fifteen years (Morton-Cooper and Palmer, 1993). |

But at this level the 'real thing' syndrome pops up again. What has just been described is, so they say, 'true' mentoring. If the relationship doesn't last as long as prescribed, if it is not the right sort, if the mentor does not adopt all the roles prescribed, then what the mentor is doing, even if it is called 'mentoring', isn't 'true' mentoring. Whatever this so called 'mentor' does is relegated to something that isn't quite the premier division of the mentoring league. It gets called 'quasi' or 'pseudo' mentoring (Head *et al*, 1992; Morton-Cooper and Palmer, 1993). If, say, the relationship lasts less than a year then it must be 'quasi' mentoring — despite, of course, the fact that the original research on which 'true' mentoring is based pointed very clearly to significant and important mentoring relationships that in practice lasted only a very short time (Levinson *et al*, 1978). It also gets called 'quasi' or 'pseudo' because it uses mentoring approaches in 'appearance only' (Morton-Cooper and Palmer, 1993). It may look like the 'real thing' — but it is a fake.

The whisky industry in Scotland has invested millions in sophisticated equipment — a 'whisky-sniffing computer that can tell its Glenlivet from its Glemorangie' — to root out fakes and protect the industry from Bombay Bells and Taipei Teachers. In its battle with the bootleggers the electronic whisky sniffer creates an extremely complex model to analyze the fake and the real thing, and then tell them apart (Warren and Watson, 1995). In the world outside mentoring a lot of costly investigatory and analytical work goes into telling real from fake. In the world of mentoring it is apparently possible to tell the 'true' from the 'quasi' (or even 'pseudo') very quickly with just a couple of quick tests. A lot of hard work in social and psychological research and a lot of hard experiences in people's day-to-day lives seems to indicate that it's not very easy at all to tell the real thing from the appearance of the real thing when it comes to dealing with a person (probably the most complex known single object in the universe) interacting (in the incredibly complex and largely undecipherable way the people do) with another person (another one of the most complex single objects known in the universe) — which is, after all, what mentoring involves. It's difficult to put one idea — that it takes extremely complex modelling by sophisticated and very expensive computers to tell different variations of a relatively simple substance like Scotch from each other — alongside another idea — that it is very simple to tell one human relation-ship, the 'real' one, from another, the 'quasi'. If, outwith the mentoring world, empirical investigations are used to tell fake from real, then within it, it is perhaps worth asking what empirical research techniques might exist, say, for telling the 'real' coaching function of the 'true' mentor from the *appearance* of coaching provided by the 'pseudo-mentor'? How do you tell 'real' advice and support from a 'true' mentor from the *appearance* of advice and support from a 'quasi' mentor — especially if the protégé treats it as real and is actually helped by it? If the secret of success is in what mentors *do* for and with their protégés, how do you tell the appearance of someone doing something for someone from their really doing it? How, in the interaction between mentors and protégés, can the 'real' be told from the 'fake'?

It's what happens here, between mentor and protégé, that forms the third level of investigating mentoring. There is something of a debate as to whether, at this level, it's what mentors do for and with their protégés that's important, or whether it's the qualities that mentors have, the sort of person they are, that counts. Looking at what students teachers say about the experience of being mentored (Taylor, 1994a, 1994b, 1995a and 1995b) it's difficult to come down on one side or another. Student teachers praise their mentors, both for their qualities and for their actions. They also damn their mentors both for their qualities, or lack of them, and for their actions, or the lack of them. The trouble with 'qualities', whether of relationships or of people, is that they are rather nebulous things. 'Qualities' are basically interpretations people make about what people seem to be like from what they seem to do. Since qualities are inferences, 'transcendent hypotheses', they are inherently difficult to investig-ate empirically. It would therefore seem wise not to get drawn into looking at mentors' 'qualities' (Taylor, 1995d). It would be much easier to go straight to what mentors do in the first place, to get as close as possible to things that people can observe and categorize relatively directly, easily and reliably, in-stead of having to deal with the unreliable world of inferences.

This would certainly get investigation away from the sorts of frameworks at the second level. Most of them are 'top-down': they start from the 'top' with ideas and concepts and work 'down' to actual practices and activities. Being 'top-down', they are usually 'theoretical', perhaps even 'ideological'. Even where frameworks have an original empirical research base (for example, Levinson *et al*, 1978; Zey, 1984) things have usually, over the course of time, been so worked over and speculatively developed that they have lost touch with their basis in the real world of acts and activities and have become simply theoretical prescriptions (for example, Morton-Cooper and Palmer, 1993).

To really look at mentoring at this third level, accounts of mentoring are needed that are based on what actually happens at the level of mentor and protégé, accounts that are 'bottom-up': what mentors actually do for and with their protégés, what people see happening, what people report as happening, what people value and see as significant. Unfortunately there are very few of these about. One of the few is the TEAM (Teacher Education and Mentoring) model (Sampson and Yeomans, 1994a and 1994b).

From case studies, from observations of and interviews with mentors, student teachers and articled teachers an account emerged of what happens, what mentors do, in the everyday world of mentoring. The account is an everyday one of mentors advising, chatting, collaborating, confronting, discussing, encouraging, explaining, facilitating, feeding back, informing, joking, observing, persuading, praising, questioning, recording, suggesting, telling — the sorts of things that occur day-by-day in ordinary everyday human interactions; the sorts of things that people can on the whole, more or less, perhaps somewhat fuzzily, observe and categorize relatively directly, easily and reliably. These everyday activities can be combined into aspects of mentors' roles. The TEAM model's list of what teacher mentors actually do, rather than are meant to do in the top-down lists, is

> assessing
> befriending
> counselling
> educating
> hosting
> inducting
> negotiating
> organizing
> planning
> training

These ten aspects in turn group together into three main dimensions of the teacher mentor's work:

> structural support
> personal support
> professional support

These dimensions, and the role aspects that make them up, don't look very different from the top-down lists, but they have one great advantage: they are based not on theorizing but on the actual practice of mentoring as people experience it and see it everyday.

The model does, however, have one great disadvantage: it is based on what is seen and reported as happening in primary school teacher training. But then most of the models that have any sort of empirical research base suffer from similar problems. One of the great seminal studies of mentoring (Levinson *et al*, 1978), one that sets the framework for much discussion, investigation and practice of mentoring is based on the views of young, white, American businessmen — which shouldn't really be a good model at all for mentoring in contexts such as: training doctors, support for postgraduate students, the development of headteachers, nursing training, initial training of teachers, professional development of experienced teachers, industrial management and staff development, inducting new employees, helping gifted children, in distance learning, in schemes for 16–19 students from ethnic minorities, in developing creativity, and even training mentors — in almost any area that can be turned up on educational literature data bases.

Given the TEAM model's background it isn't really possible to claim it as a framework with which to look at mentoring right across the range of contexts above. That would be stretching its applicability, and its credibility, well beyond any elastic limit. It is, however, perhaps not too far to stretch it from primary teacher training into secondary teacher training — there are probably enough similarities for a transfer to be plausible. It's certainly a great deal more plausible than using, say, an imported US model. But plausibility isn't quite enough. The TEAM model's valid transfer as a framework for secondary teacher mentoring has been looked at — as a preliminary to testing it out for usefulness in other areas. It seems to work quite happily as a tool for mentors and student teachers (and researchers) to look at and analyze and judge the mentoring process (Taylor, 1994a, 1994b, 1995a and 1995b). It seems to be the sort of bottom-up, experience based model for primary and secondary teacher mentoring that 'provides a detailed and useful account of how one might conceptualise the mentoring task . . . provides useful ways of thinking about the mentoring role . . .' (Calderhead, 1994).

### Is That it Then?

Well . . . no.

The mentoring process and support for student teachers in school seems a bit more complicated than that.

Sometimes in looking at the development of the student teacher through mentoring during school experience the obvious is sometimes overlooked: the obvious being that the student teacher's school experience contains more than just the designated mentor and the classroom. It is jam-packed with other people, many of whom are likely to be sympathetic and helpful to student teachers. The TEAM model is a reminder of this. Mentors may be found advising, chatting, collaborating, discussing, encouraging, explaining, informing, joking, observing, persuading, questioning, suggesting, telling etc, But so can other people. These activities are by no means the special preserve of the mentor. Structural, personal and professional support can come from other directions. Mentors themselves say they are only part of a network of teacher support for students in schools (Powney *et al*, 1993; Taylor, 1994b, 1995a and 1995b). It is clear that there is considerable potential for the student teacher to experience a wealth of informal minor mentoring or even to be informally multi-mentored. Mentoring possibilities for the student teacher is not a clean cut world; it is a messy and fuzzy series of overlaps and blurred edges.

Even from mentors' own perspectives (Stephenson and Taylor, 1995; Taylor, 1994a), the mentoring process itself and the aspects of the mentor's role, seems to be fairly blurred. Mentors don't necessarily always have the prime responsibility for individual aspects of the mentoring role (it varies from school to school) though the vast majority of the time in the vast majority of schools it is the mentor who is, as it were, 'in charge'. Even when mentors are in charge, both they, and their students, seem to see other people as being involved in the individual aspects of the mentoring process. It is little wonder then that mentors seem to see themselves as having a managerial function, not just in respect of student teachers, but in respect of professional colleagues as well (Taylor, 1995a).

Moving from the particular world of mentoring processes and into the more general world of support for students, though still within the TEAM model's superstructure of 'personal support', 'professional support' and 'structural support', that support can come from almost anywhere. Student teachers in one study (Taylor, 1995a) reported the following people from within school and university as having had an effect (usually, but not always, a positive one) on their school experience:

| | |
|---|---|
| subject department members | 100% of student teachers |
| mentor | 97% |
| university tutors | 74% |
| other student teachers in the same school | 72% |
| staff in pastoral roles | 72% |
| other subject staff | 72% |
| deputy head | 59% |
| other, non-teaching staff | 56% |
| other student teachers not in the same school | 46% |
| headteacher | 46% |

But support was not only reported from within school and university. God, grandad and the bank also came in for mentions, presumably in the order 'personal', 'professional' (grandad is a retired teacher) and 'structural' — though one has to credit God with the ability to handle all three dimensions, and a great many more, simultaneously!

The student teacher's environment during the school experience phase contains: not only their mentor (nominally responsible for their development); but other people, within or outwith school and university, (who may be co-mentors or minor mentors or just helpful and mentor-like in some of the things they do); along with opportunities and challenges (through which the student teacher can develop — sometimes perhaps on the basis of self-mentoring). There seems to be something of a 'mentoring matrix', a matrix in which mentor, co-mentors, minor mentors and helpers and opportunities are all embedded. All of which provides the student teacher with the process for development.

Confining things to the student teacher's official public world within school, the mentoring process is unsurprisingly perceived as having to do with the mentor but the school experience as a whole is something else. The mentoring process can fail without the school experience necessarily having failed. The 'mentoring matrix' may have succeeded where the 'mentoring process' may have failed. People step in to take up burdens that aren't theirs; students find unlooked for sources of support; one element seems to have failed and other elements have taken on extra. At times, from students' reports, the mentoring matrix almost seems to be self-repairing (Stephenson and Taylor, 1995).

There may well be a temptation to draw general conclusions about the 'mentoring matrix', perhaps even a temptation to institutionalise it and so begin to manage and control it, perhaps with the best of intentions, as a safeguard against possible failure of mentoring and the mentoring process. But the school experience and the mentoring and the help that go on within it provide a complex and difficult situation to analyze. The situations may offer self-contradictions and paradoxes (Stephenson, 1994) that may only be teased out on individual bases and do not offer generalizable possibilities. For example, peers, fellow student teachers, are clearly prime candidates for embedding in the mentoring matrix, but may or may not be significant elements of the mentoring matrix in individual cases: 'It is interesting to note that of the very few students who did not cite peers as significant, one subsequently was unsuccessful and another gained a distinction' (*ibid*).

Student teachers' idiosyncratic choice of the human elements of their mentoring matrices and the consequent difficulty in making generalizations about it may lie in individual personality, biography, expectation, learning style or sensitivity. One person's meat may be another person's dead animal tissue. One person's close support may be another person's loss of autonomy. Differences can be quite marked, even with two students in the same school teaching the same age range and having the same mentor (Stephenson and Taylor, 1995).

But is everything down to individual student personality, tastes etc., all entirely individual and idiosyncratic? Or are there general factors? The mentoring matrix seems to go in for self-repair, to support the student even if individual elements of it fail. This does not always happen, but when it does it does it often seems to be connected with a general state of good organization in the school. Students' judgments of the quality of their school experience seem to be very strongly connected to their perceptions of the school's organizational state and professional climate (Taylor, 1995a). What students seem to see as valuable during their school experience seems to correlate highly with good organization, with high job competency and the trouble taken during the school experience by those involved to ensure a productive one (Stephenson, 1994). Although these factors are only reported through students' perceptions they are not necessarily related to the students' own particularities, preferences and perceptions. The self-repairing capabilities of the mentoring matrix, something quite independent of the student, can be seen in the context of the whole school, and this would seem to make the success, or failure, of initial teacher training on the mentored model a whole school issue and not something that is just down to individual mentors. Success or failure would seem to be a whole school issue, not in some philosophical or catch-phrasey and jargon sort of way, but in exactly the same way, and for exactly the same practical and pragmatic reasons, that pupil success is a whole school issue and not just down to individual teachers.

### What's all this Stuff about Mentoring 'Failure'?

Well . . . that might be a touchy subject.

The educational literature doesn't go in much for talking about it. There is the odd exception (Shaw, 1992; Stephenson and Taylor, 1995), but, on the whole, the UK educational literature doesn't admit of anything that might be a problem with mentoring. After all mentoring is meant to solve problems — problems of access to higher education, problems of dropping out of higher education, communication problems, educational problems, young people at risk problems, social isolation problems, managerial problems, emotional and behavioral problems. If there's a problem that involves people it's an almost certain bet, at least in the US, that there's a proposed solution that involves mentoring. As for 'failure', the only connection that there seems to be between mentoring and failure is that mentoring may help solve that problem too — or at least may help people cope with it. Mentoring isn't meant to have problems or be a failure; it is stereotypically seen as the solution to all problems and failures. It has even been metaphored as providing an 'emergency service' (Ganser, 1994) — which could mean that it can't afford to fail, or, to be slightly 'political', it can't afford to be seen to fail.

The UK industrial and management literature on mentoring is a little more forthcoming: its books have sections devoted to 'Problems between mentor and protégé' (Clutterbuck, 1991); it gives warnings that mentoring may even be a dangerous process because it can amplify favouritism and create cliques (Parsloe, 1992). But the management literature doesn't have quite the same degree of up-front forthrightness of the UK nursing literature which boasts titles like 'Impossible dream: why doesn't mentorship work in UK nurse education?' (Barlow, 1991), though even that looks pretty feeble against titles that US authors give their pieces — 'What to do about toxic mentors' (Darling, 1985) has to be a favourite.

Looking briefly at one evidence based account (Clutterbuck, 1991), factors associated with problems between mentors and protégés in UK industry include:

> simple mismatch between the pair, simply not feel at ease with each other or even getting into a clash of personalities;
>
> mentors having heavy workloads, over full schedules and being too pressured to make time available or let a relationship develop;
>
> mentors dominating protégés, not giving them room for their own ideas;
>
> mentors failing to respect the confidentiality of their interactions with their protégés;
>
> poor definition of mentor and protégé roles, with consequent over-, and under-, expectation on either or both sides;
>
> mentors' inability to give negative feedback constructively; over-caution on the mentor's part.

These can, singly or in combination, produce a breakdown in the relationship, which is why many industrial schemes have 'no fault' quit clauses, with either person being able to walk away without having to attach blame to the other person.

It is tempting to transfer this sort of 'faults diagnosis' straight over from industry into teacher training and education, but it is difficult to be reasonably sure that it will transfer, as the contexts, at first sight, seem so different. Can information about mentoring problems and failures in, say, an industrial mentoring scheme run by a privatized public utility really be applied to, say, mentoring a PE student teacher? There may be a strong urge to do so, and, even without proper evidence, it might be wise to, but the wholesale importing of models, systems, and analyses from different contexts needs to be treated with caution. The world may be fuzzy and blurred around the edges, but similarities and dissimilarities need charting before they are assumed.

However, there is some indication from student teachers' reports (Taylor, 1995a) on their school experiences that parallels may exist:

| | |
|---|---|
| mentor too pressured? | 'Mentor "showed willing" but with other responsibilities taking precedence students' needs were not predominant, ie meetings cancelled or postponed' |
| mentor dominating? | 'Had definite strong ideas about "teaching" which they expected me to adopt' |
| mentor overcautious? | 'At first school, mentor was not up to the task. . . . was not prepared fully for the role of mentor required by PGCE. . . . seemed somewhat insecure' |

poor negative feedback? 'Last week: unexpected criticism after chance to discuss'; '*School* — fine. *Teachers* — fine. *Mentor* — uninformed, not supportive, critical without guidelines'

But there may be more than that to it all. It is worth having a look at what each side of a mentoring pair reported about a particular school experience:

*The student teacher*: 'Not getting my interim reports until it was too late — how could I develop? Lack of observation. Lack of time and organization. Left to get on with it. I feel that having assignments marked on time is essential — for example, I have waited ten weeks for assignment 4's report!! I got a lot of support from fellow students . . .'

*The mentor*: 'This was a "real life" experience. The students were accepted and treated as teachers with the firm guidance and support of the department. We looked at their strengths on an individual basis and found ways to use this to good effect. This helped student confidence. Professional development was encouraged at every opportunity through school-based insets, departmental meetings and pastoral meetings. If a student . . . intimated that they wanted more involvement we tried to facilitate this. Mentoring is an ongoing process and cannot be limited to a time and a place — ADDITIONAL to this are discussions over coffee, on the move and as situations occur. Students were prepared to play a full part in the department and this was outlined early on so our expectations are clear for students. A really positive experience and both secured jobs!'

This mentor and student teacher clearly have very different perceptions of what went on during the school experience. Comparing mentors' and student teachers' reports of the mentoring process (Stephenson and Taylor, 1995) seems to show that:

mentors' perceptions of their mentoring and its individual aspects may be consistently rosier than their student's perceptions of it;
mentors may very rarely see that the mentoring process is in need of anything more than improving on what is already basically OK;
mentors may very rarely, if ever, see that the whole process or individual aspects of it have failed in their students' views;
mentors may well remain completely oblivious to the destructiveness that their protégés may be experiencing;
mentors may see themselves as more important overall to the students' general success than the student perception would support.

As is the way with practically all educational research nothing conclusive can be claimed about this. But it is worrying, as is a finding across three separate teacher training schemes that something like 25 per cent of student teachers saw the mentoring they got during their school experience as 'OK — but only just', *or worse*, and the majority of the rest could only rate it as 'OK — but clear room for improvement' (Taylor, 1994a, 1994b, 1995a and 1995b).

There is so little in articles and books on mentoring in initial teacher training and education (ITTE) about mentoring problems and failures, with little reference to studies of mentoring problems and failures outwith ITTE, that it might be far too easy to assume that there are no real problems with mentoring, and that both mentors and student teachers see it more or less in the same light. The world, however, even when viewed through rose tinted glasses, is probably not quite that fuzzy or blurred.

## Well is that about it then?

Well . . . no.

Since the world is blurred and fuzzy and there are no nice clear cut definitions but only degrees of resemblance and dissimilarity, then there are no nice handy clear cut prescriptions about mentoring — apart, of course, from those put forward by benighted souls clinging to Socratic essentials and Aristotelian logic who circle round seminars and conferences and symposia with their dismal cry of 'Of course, that's not real mentoring'. And there are no certainties. If there are no certainties about mentoring then every scheme, every school in every scheme and every mentor in every school in every scheme has, at least in part, to reinvent mentoring for themselves according to their own particular context (Monaghan and Lunt, 1992) — but far less in the light of top-down, prescriptive 'definitions' and far more in the light of evidence led, bottom-up, real world accounts. 'Mentor' and 'mentoring' may well be 'transcendental semantic signifiers', viewable from a variety of perspectives, open to various interpretations in different applications and settings (Morton-Cooper and Palmer, 1993). But not enough, at least from 'real evidence', is yet known about mentoring, about its similarities and differences from context to context, about what may or may not really make for successful mentoring in different contexts, about what may or may not transfer reliably from one context to another, or about what problems there may be in mentors having different perceptions of mentoring from their protégés, for anyone to say with any reliability that there is anything more than perhaps a set of vague and fuzzy guidelines. This leaves teacher mentors very much in the position of being autonomous professionals having to do the best they can for their student teachers in their own context while keeping a wary eye on what is going on elsewhere.

There really is no definitive answer to the question 'What is mentoring?' — or even to the one that is more pressing for most mentors, 'What do I have to do if I am a mentor'.

## References

BARLOW, S. (1991) 'Impossible dream: Why doesn't mentorship work in UK nurse education?', *Nursing Times*, **87**, 1, pp. 53–4.

CALDERHEAD, J. (1994) 'Learning on the job', *Times Educational Supplement*, 25 November, p. 13.

CLARK, K. (1992) Speech to the North of England Education Conference, DES.

CLUTTERBUCK, D. (1991) *Everyone Needs a Mentor: Fostering Talent at Work* (2nd edn), London, IPM.

DALOZL, A. (1986) *Effective Teaching and Mentoring*, San Francisco, CA, Jossey-Bass.

DARESH, J.C. and PLAYKO, M.A. (1992) 'Mentoring for head teachers: A review of major issues', *School Organization*, **12**, 2, pp. 145–52.

DARLING, L-A.W. (1985) 'What to do about toxic mentors', *The Journal of Nursing Administration*, **15**, 5, pp. 43–4.

GANSER, T. (1994) 'Metaphors for mentoring: An exploratory study', paper presented at the annual meeting of the American Educational Research Association, New Orleans, April.

HARVARD, G. and DUNNE, R. (1992) 'The role of the mentor in developing teacher competence', *Westminster Studies in Education*, **15**, pp. 33–44.

HEAD, F.A., REIMAN, A.J. and THIES-SPRINTHALL, L. (1992) 'The reality of mentoring: Complexity in its process and function' in BEY, T.M. and HOLMES, C.T. (Eds) *Mentoring: Contemporary Principles and Issues*, Reston, VA, Association of Teacher Educators.

JACOBI, M. (1991) 'Mentoring and undergraduate academic success: a literature review', *Review of Educational Research*, **61**, 4, pp. 505–32.

JENKINS, H., STROUD, M., DAVIES, W. and PROBERT, H. (1991) 'Managing maths by mentoring: The Gwent experience', *Management in Education*, **5**, 4, pp, 18–20.

KOSKO, B. (1994) *Fuzzy Thinking: The New Science of Fuzzy Logic*, London, Flamingo.

LEVINSON, D.J., DARROW, C.N., LEVINSON, M.H. and MCKEE, B. (1978) *The Seasons of a Man's Life*, New York, Knopf.

LYONS, W., SCROGGINS, D. and RULE, P.B. (1990) 'The mentor in graduate education', *Studies in Higher Education*, **15**, 3, pp. 277–85.

MAYNARD, T. and FURLONG, J. (1993) 'Learning to teach and models of mentoring' in MCINTYRE, D., HAGGER, H. and WILKIN, M. (Eds) *Mentoring: Perspectives on School-based Teacher Education*, London, Kogan Page, pp. 69–85.

MEGGINSON, D. (1988) 'Instructor, coach, mentor: Three ways of helping for managers', *Management Education and Development*, **19**, 1, pp. 33–46.

MINSKY, M. (1988) *The Society of Mind* (Picador edition), London, Pan Books.

MONAGHAN, J. and LUNT, N. (1992) 'Mentoring: Person, process, practice and problems', *British Journal of Educational Studies*, **XXXX**, 3, pp. 248–63.

MORTON-COOPER, A. and PALMER, A. (1993) *Mentoring and Preceptorship*, Oxford, Blackwell Science.

PARSLOE, E. (1992) *Coaching, Mentoring and Assessing: A Practical Guide to Developing Competence*, London, Kogan Page.

POWNEY, J., EDWARD, S., HOLROYD, C. and MARTIN, S. (1993) *Monitoring the Pilot: The Moray House Institute PGCE (Secondary) 1992–93*, Edinburgh, Scottish Council for Research in Education.

ROSCH, E. (1977) 'Classification of real world objects: Origins and representations in cognition' in JOHNSON-LAIRD, P.N. and WASON, P.C. (Eds) *Thinking: Readings in Cognitive Science*, Cambridge, CUP, pp. 212–22.

RYLE, G. (1963) *The Concept of Mind*, London, Penguin Books.

SAMPSON, J. and YEOMANS, R. (1994a) 'Analysing the work of mentors: The role' in YEOMANS, R. and SAMPSON, J. (Eds) *Mentorship in the Primary School*, London, Falmer Press, pp. 62–75.

SAMPSON, J. and YEOMANS, R. (1994b) 'Analysing the work of mentors: Strategies, skills and qualities' in YEOMANS, R. and SAMPSON, J. (Eds) *Mentorship in the Primary School*, London, Falmer Press, pp. 76–100.

SHAW, R. (1992) *Teacher Training in Secondary Schools*, London, Kogan Page, pp. 69–77.

SOKAL, R.R. (1974) 'Classification: Purposes, principles, progress, prospects', *Science*, **185**, pp. 115–23.

STEPHENSON, H.J. (1994) 'The changing face of teaching practice — student supervision in the change to mentoring', paper presented at the annual conference of the ATEE, Prague, September.

STEPHENSON, H.J. and TAYLOR, M.I. (1995) 'Diverse views of the mentoring process in initial teacher training', paper presented at the International Mentoring Association Conference, San Antonio.

STOTT, K. and WALKER, A. (1992) 'Developing school leaders through mentoring: A Singapore perspective', *School Organization*, **2**, pp. 153–64.

TAYLOR, M.I. (1994a) 'Mentoring and being mentored: differences in teacher mentors, and student teachers' perceptions', unpublished paper, De Montfort University, Bedford.

TAYLOR, M.I. (1994b) 'The mentors' and the students' tales: Worm's eye views of the new Bedford partnership secondary PGCE 1993–4', evaluation report, De Montfort University, Bedford.

TAYLOR, M.I. (1995a) 'More worms' eye views', evaluation report for the secondary PGCE partnership, De Montfort University, Bedford.

TAYLOR, M.I. (1995b) 'The DMUB primary PGCE 1994–5', evaluation report for the primary PGCE partnership, De Montfort University, Bedford.

TAYLOR, M.I. (1995c) 'Will the real mentor please stand up?: towards an industry standard classification of mentorings?', paper presented at SRHE Mentoring Network Research Seminar 'Illuminating Mentoring', March.

TAYLOR, M.I. (1995d) 'Mentoring: qualities are everywhere', paper given at the Department of Educational Studies, University of Hull, May.

TURNER, M. (1993) 'The role of mentors and teacher tutors in school based teacher education and induction', *British Journal of In-Service Education*, **19**, 1, pp, 36–45.

WARREN, P. and WATSON, J. (1995) 'Scotch-testing computer deployed against fakes', *Scotland on Sunday*, **371**, p. 1.

WILKIN, M. (1992) 'On the cusp: From supervision to mentoring in initial teacher training', *Cambridge Journal of Education*, **22**, 1, pp. 79–90.

WITTGENSTEIN, L. (1968) *Philosophical Investigations* (2nd ed), Oxford, Basil Blackwell.

ZEY, M.G. (1984) *The Mentor Connection*, Homewood, IL, Dow Jones-Irwin.

*Part Two*

*An Insight into the Trainee's Perspective*

# 3  Changes in Physical Education Students' Anxieties and Concerns on School Experience: A Longitudinal Study

*Susan Capel*

## Introduction

*The Importance of School Experience[1] in Initial Teacher Education Courses*

When we reflect on our own initial teacher education course many of us will identify school experience as that part of our course in which we learned most about teaching. Likewise, many of our students[2] recognize the importance of school experience in their own learning. These anecdotal accounts are supported by the results of studies over a long period of time which have identified school experience as the most important part of initial teacher education courses (Locke, 1979; Lortie, 1975; Mancini, Goss and Frye 1982; Tannehill and Zakrajsek, 1988).

The importance of school experience in the professional preparation of teachers is also highlighted by recent developments in initial teacher education in England and Wales. Department of Education and Science (DES) Circulars 3/84 and 24/89 (DES, 1984 and 1989) both emphasized the importance of practical teaching competence and led to Department for Education (DFE) Circulars 9/92 (for secondary initial teacher education) and 14/93 (for primary initial teacher education) (DFE, 1992 and 1993). These encouraged the development of school-based initial teacher education courses in which students spend a much greater proportion (and in some cases all) of their course in school and in which teachers play a greater role in the supervision of students on school experience. Whatever the political motives for these initiatives they have placed school-based experience at the centre of initial teacher education courses.

In order for these developments to succeed, and for the learning experiences of students to be maximized, it is essential that the learning needs of students are central to the planning of school-based experiences, and that all concerned with school-based initial teacher education courses understand their role in facilitating students' appreciation of the complex activity of teaching and have the skills to support this process effectively. This requires an understanding of, and empathy with, students' anxieties and concerns as these emerge during their initial teacher education course and a sound understanding of supervisory principles, skills and techniques.

## Students' Perception of School Experience

Research has found that students in general, and physical education students in particular, are anxious about school experience (Capel, 1992 and 1993; Hart, 1987). Studies have shown that students are anxious about many aspects of teaching, such as standing in front of a class, not being able to manage or control a class, not being able to motivate pupils or maintain their interest, lacking understanding of the subject matter or material to be taught, not having a range of strategies or experience on which to draw in order to cope with situations which arise in the classroom or to discipline pupils effectively, not being able to answer pupils' questions, not being accepted by pupils or other teachers, not being good enough as a teacher or not meeting the expectations of those observing the lesson, and being observed, evaluated and assessed whilst teaching.

Some studies have looked specifically at concerns of physical education students on school experience. For example, Pelletier and Martel (1994) analyzed the contents of weekly journals kept by physical education students on school experience to determine the difficulties they encountered. They found that problems identified related to the tasks of a teacher, together with those of being a student and those of a personal nature. The most frequently mentioned problems were related to teacher tasks, and especially to managing pupil behaviour. The most frequently mentioned problem of being a student was managing the workload, and the most frequently mentioned personal problems were an inability to devote adequate time and energy to the university course and part-time jobs, the quality of professional support provided by co-operating teachers, and the student's own self confidence. Behets (1990) asked ten physical education students to record their concerns in a logbook after teaching their classes. Analysis of these into categories of concern revealed five main sources of concern, which accounted for more than 60 per cent of the written concerns. These were control (22 per cent), organization (9 per cent), time (7 per cent), motivating pupils (7 per cent) and pupils' learning and enjoyment (6 per cent). Other concerns mentioned by some students included evaluation by the supervisor, their ability to demonstrate, problems with individual pupils and the intensity of the activity.

Capel (1992) administered the Student Teacher Anxiety Scale (Hart, 1987) to 132 physical education students immediately prior to starting their school experience. Results showed that these students were moderately anxious about the forthcoming school experience. The event causing most anxiety was being observed by the school experience supervisor whilst teaching, followed by other events related to being observed, evaluated and assessed by the school experience supervisor, such as assessment by the supervisor, how the supervisor may react to one or more unsuccessful lessons if they should occur and wondering how the school experience is going in the supervisor's eyes. The events causing least anxiety related to good working relationships with school staff, such as getting on or co-operation with the school staff and how helpful members of staff may be.

### *Stages of Development of Students*

Research has also suggested that students progress through different stages in their development as teachers. Leask (1995) identified three broad overlapping stages through which students can be expected to pass in order to become effective teachers: *self-image and class management; whole class learning; and individual pupil's learning.* She commented that 'many students are six or eight weeks into their school experience before they feel a level of confidence about their image and the management of their class (phase 1). They can then start to focus on whether the learning taking place is what was intended (phase 2). Once a student teacher feels reasonably competent in classroom management and in achieving global objectives, they should be able to shift their focus to the needs of individuals (phase 3)' (p. 21).

Maynard and Furlong (1993) identified five stages in the development of students:

- *early idealism* which occurs before school experience has started. At this stage students are often idealistic in their feelings towards their pupils, identifying with the perspectives of pupils rather than those of the class teacher;
- *survival* which occurs as students start their school experience. At this stage the realities of the classroom replace the earlier idealism. The major focus becomes class control, classroom management, fitting into the school and becoming established as a teacher;
- *recognizing difficulties* which occurs as students, having survived the initial adjustment to the realities of teaching, become sensitive to the different demands placed on them. They often think about being assessed on their teaching, wondering whether they will be good enough and therefore wanting to perform well. This often results in them focusing on teaching methods and materials;
- *hitting the plateau* which occurs after students have learned how to control their classes and have identified what does and does not work in the classroom. They therefore want to 'stick to' what works. At this stage they often have trouble changing the focus from themselves and the material they are teaching to focus on the needs of the pupils; and

- *moving on* which occurs when students can make this shift and therefore can focus on the needs of pupils and experiment with their teaching.

These stages can be related to research by Fuller (1969) who identified the change in concerns (defined as perceived problems or worries) of students over time. In a new situation requiring interaction with other people, an individual is initially most concerned about him/herself and the demands made on him/her by the situation. Only when these initial concerns about self have been addressed is the person ready to address other concerns and to learn about the task of teaching. Fuller and Brown (1975) refined Fuller's (1969) concerns theory by identifying three stages of concern through which teachers must pass in their development, *self-concern, task concern and impact concern*. Self-concerns are about coping and survival in the teaching environment (being able to control the class, being liked by the pupils, finding a place in the power structure of the school, understanding expectations of supervisors, principals and parents and being observed and evaluated). Task concerns are about mastering the routines and day-to-day tasks of teaching including working with too many pupils, lack of instructional materials and time pressures. Impact concerns are concerns for, and about the learning of pupils, pupils' progress and ways in which the teacher can enhance this progress (recognizing the social and emotional needs of pupils, being fair to all pupils, recognizing the effect of their teaching on individual pupils and being able to individualise teaching and tailor content to maximize intellectual and emotional growth based on pupils' learning problems, motivation etc.). These three stages are developmental and it is therefore suggested that if students are still concerned with themselves, they are not yet ready to address concerns about the task of teaching or the impact of their teaching.

### Changes in School Experience Anxiety or Concern Over Time

Some research has been conducted which has considered changes in physical education students' concerns on school experience over time. Boggess, McBride and Griffey (1985) administered the Teacher Concerns Questionnaire (George, 1978) to sixty-nine physical education students three times during a school experience semester: before the start of the school experience; at mid-semester; and the day after the school experience was completed. Results suggested that these students were mainly concerned about their ability to control and manage pupils in their classes. Overall, results showed no significant decrease in concern about self during the semester, although the pattern of change was different for different items on the questionnaire. These students became less concerned about doing well in the presence of a supervisor as the semester progressed, which may have indicated that they became more comfortable in the supervisor's presence as they established and understood their role as a teacher. However, they became increasingly concerned with 'maintaining class control'. Concern with the task of teaching increased slightly, but not significantly, during the course of the semester, the increased concern being due especially to 'working with too many students'. This may have indicated that, as students experienced teaching large classes, the realities of the situation became increasingly important. Scores on the impact scale rose, but not significantly, over the course of the semester, which suggested that despite their own insecurities and the demands of teaching, students were becoming increasingly aware of their pupils' learning. These results were not significantly different to results obtained by George (*ibid*) and in other studies using the Teacher Concerns Questionnaire (Wendt and Bain, 1989; Wendt, Bain and Jackson, 1981).

With the exception of the study by Wendt, Bain and Jackson (1981) these studies have tended to concentrate on changes in the amount and/or causes of anxiety or concern over the course of one particular school experience rather than changes as students have gained experience of teaching on successive school experiences.

The purpose of the study described in this chapter was to look at changes in the amount and causes of school experience anxiety and concern for physical education students on a four-year secondary Bachelor of Education (BEd) physical education degree course.

## The Study

### The Students

Secondary BEd physical education degree students were administered a questionnaire after their first school experience, during the academic year 1992/93, after their second school experience, during the academic year 1993/94, and after their third school experience, during the academic year 1994/95. Eighty-eight students who responded to the questionnaire after all three school experiences were included in the analysis.

### The Questionnaire

In order to measure the changes in anxiety and concern over time, the same questionnaire was administered after all three school experiences. Two scales were included in this questionnaire, the Student Teacher Anxiety Scale (STAS) (Hart, 1987), and the Teacher Concerns Questionnaire (TCQ) (George, 1978).

The STAS measures the extent to which each of twenty-six events included on the scale causes anxiety (see table 3.1). Each item is scored on a scale of 1 to 7, with 1 indicating 'no anxiety' and 7 indicating 'very anxious', therefore a high score indicates high anxiety. The TCQ was developed from

*Table 3.1: The items on the student teacher anxiety scale (Hart, 1987)*

1  How to give each child the attention he/she needs without neglecting others
2  Being observed by my teaching practice supervisor while I am teaching
3  Setting work at the right level for the children
4  Class control
5  Whether or not my performance is satisfactory from the point of view of the class teacher
6  Wondering how the teaching practice is going in my supervisor's eyes
7  How helpful members of the school staff may be
8  Whether or not my schemes of work are adequate
9  Problems within the class of individual disruptive children
10  Completing lesson plans in the required form
11  Getting on with the school staff
12  Wondering what my teaching practice supervisor expects
13  Incidents of misbehaviour in class
14  How the teaching practice supervisor may react to one or more unsuccessful lessons if they should occur
15  Whether or not I am covering the material adequately
16  Wondering whether the head of department at the school is happy with my work
17  Controlling the noise level in class
18  How a member of the school staff may react to one or more unsuccessful lessons if they should occur
19  Selecting suitable lesson content
20  Maintaining a 'buoyant' enough approach
21  Co-operation with the school staff
22  How to handle defiance from a child
23  Maintaining a good enough standard of preparation
24  Assessment by the teaching practice supervisor
25  Getting all the paperwork done in time
26  What lessons the teaching practice supervisor comes in to see

the developmental theory of concerns of Fuller (1969). It contains fifteen items which assess self, task and impact concerns (see table 3.2). The self-scale comprises items 3, 7, 9, 13 and 15, the task scale comprises items 1, 2, 5, 10 and 14 and the impact scale comprises items 4, 6, 8, 11 and 12. Each item is scored on a scale of 1 to 5, with 1 indicating 'not concerned' and 5 indicating 'extremely concerned', therefore a high score indicates high concern. Both of these scales have been found to be valid and reliable.

### The Analysis of Data

Mean scores were calculated for each scale as a whole. The mean score and rank order were calculated for each individual item on the two scales included in the questionnaire. Correlation analysis was conducted to determine whether there was any relationship between the scores obtained on each of the two scales after the three school experiences. Factor analysis was also conducted on the data in order to confirm or otherwise the factor structure of the two scales for secondary physical education students in England. The results of the factor analysis are not reported in this study. For further detail about this please refer to Capel (1992, 1994, 1995a, 1995b and 1996).

*Table 3.2: The items on the teacher concerns questionnaire (George, 1978)*

| | |
|---|---|
| 1 | Lack of instructional materials |
| 2 | Feeling under pressure much of the time |
| 3 | Doing well when a supervisor is present |
| 4 | Meeting the needs of different kinds of students |
| 5 | Too many instructional duties |
| 6 | Diagnosing student learning problems |
| 7 | Feeling more adequate as a teacher |
| 8 | Challenging unmotivated students |
| 9 | Being accepted and respected by professional persons |
| 10 | Working with too many students each day |
| 11 | Guiding students toward intellectual and emotional growth |
| 12 | Whether each student is getting what he/she needs |
| 13 | Getting a favourable evaluation of my teaching |
| 14 | The routine and inflexibility of the teaching situation |
| 15 | Maintaining the appropriate degree of class control |

## Results

### *Mean Scores and Rank Order of Items*

The mean score and rank order of items on the STAS after each school experience are shown in table 3.3. The event causing most anxiety after the first school experience was 'being observed by my teaching practice supervisor while I am teaching' (ranked third and fifth after the second and third school experiences, respectively). After the second and third school experiences the event causing most anxiety was 'how the teaching practice supervisor may react to one or more unsuccessful lessons if they should occur' (ranked second after the first school experience). The other events causing most anxiety after the three school experiences were 'wondering how the teaching practice is going in my supervisor's eyes', 'assessment by the teaching practice supervisor' and 'wondering what my teaching practice supervisor expects'. After all three school experiences those events causing most anxiety were therefore related to being observed, evaluated and assessed by the school experience supervisor.

As table 3.3 shows, the event causing least anxiety on the STAS after the first school experience was 'getting on with the school staff', after the second school experience was 'co-operation with the school staff' and after the third school experience was 'completing lesson plans in the required form'. The other events causing least anxiety after the three school experiences were 'controlling the noise level in class' and 'class control'.

The mean score and rank order of items on the TCQ after each school experience are shown in table 3.4. The two events causing most concern were the same after all three school experiences. These were 'doing well when a supervisor is present' and 'getting a favourable evaluation of my teaching'. This was followed by 'challenging unmotivated students' after the first and third school experiences and 'meeting the needs of different kinds of students' after the second school experience, with the fourth item after the first and

*Table 3.3: Student teacher anxiety scale (STAS): Means and standard deviations for the total anxiety score and each individual question (in rank order)*

| First administration of the questionnaire | | | | Second administration of the questionnaire | | | | Third administration of the questionnaire | | | |
|---|---|---|---|---|---|---|---|---|---|---|---|
| Rank | Item number | Mean | SD | Rank | Item number | Mean | SD | Rank | Item number | Mean | SD |
| | Total anxiety score | 3.87 | 0.76 | | Total anxiety score | 3.88 | 0.76 | | Total anxiety score | 3.64 | 0.83 |
| 1 | 2 | 4.73 | 1.66 | 1 | 14 | 5.40 | 1.12 | 1 | 14 | 5.11 | 1.48 |
| 2 | 14 | 4.60 | 1.30 | 2 | 24 | 5.17 | 1.26 | 2 | 24 | 5.04 | 1.59 |
| 3 | 6 | 4.52 | 1.31 | 3 | 2 | 4.88 | 1.48 | 3 | 6 | 4.96 | 1.66 |
| 4 | 24 | 4.52 | 1.49 | 4 | 6 | 4.83 | 1.30 | 4 | 12 | 4.54 | 1.63 |
| 5 | 5 | 4.49 | 1.26 | 5 | 26 | 4.48 | 1.71 | 5 | 2 | 4.42 | 1.53 |
| 6 | 26 | 4.37 | 1.55 | 6 | 18 | 4.40 | 1.39 | 6 | 26 | 4.19 | 1.60 |
| 7 | 22 | 4.14 | 1.39 | 7 | 12 | 4.38 | 1.19 | 7 | 5 | 4.08 | 1.23 |
| 8 | 12 | 4.09 | 1.17 | 8 | 5 | 4.33 | 1.20 | 8 | 18 | 3.85 | 1.40 |
| 9 | 9 | 4.02 | 1.29 | 9 | 16 | 4.28 | 1.32 | 9 | 16 | 3.81 | 1.23 |
| 10 | 15 | 4.02 | 1.09 | 10 | 15 | 4.15 | 1.15 | 10 | 7 | 3.73 | 1.66 |
| 11 | 25 | 4.01 | 1.64 | 11 | 9 | 3.98 | 1.45 | 11 | 25 | 3.65 | 1.85 |
| 12 | 16 | 3.91 | 1.27 | 12= | 22 | 3.95 | 1.38 | 12= | 3 | 3.61 | 1.17 |
| 13 | 3 | 3.87 | 1.02 | 12= | 25 | 3.95 | 1.73 | 12= | 9 | 3.61 | 1.27 |
| 14 | 8 | 3.83 | 1.27 | 14 | 3 | 3.85 | 1.26 | 12= | 8 | 3.61 | 1.47 |
| 15 | 18 | 3.75 | 1.27 | 15 | 8 | 3.77 | 1.25 | 15 | 15 | 3.58 | 1.06 |
| 16 | 4 | 3.71 | 1.49 | 16 | 19 | 3.72 | 1.50 | 16 | 22 | 3.50 | 1.45 |
| 17 | 13 | 3.68 | 1.32 | 17 | 13 | 3.57 | 1.29 | 17 | 1 | 3.46 | 1.30 |
| 18 | 19 | 3.63 | 1.14 | 18 | 1 | 3.52 | 1.19 | 18 | 13 | 3.35 | 1.20 |
| 19 | 7 | 3.49 | 1.46 | 19 | 7 | 3.35 | 1.41 | 19 | 19 | 3.15 | 1.22 |
| 20 | 23 | 3.46 | 1.37 | 20= | 20 | 3.28 | 1.34 | 20 | 23 | 3.08 | 1.41 |
| 21 | 1 | 3.39 | 1.12 | 20= | 23 | 3.28 | 1.45 | 21 | 20 | 2.96 | 1.34 |
| 22 | 20 | 3.37 | 1.17 | 22 | 4 | 3.15 | 1.59 | 22= | 21 | 2.88 | 1.70 |
| 23 | 17 | 3.27 | 1.31 | 23 | 17 | 2.97 | 1.30 | 22= | 11 | 2.88 | 1.77 |
| 24 | 10 | 3.02 | 1.38 | 24 | 11 | 2.83 | 1.54 | 24= | 4 | 2.54 | 1.03 |
| 25 | 21 | 3.00 | 1.24 | 25 | 10 | 2.75 | 1.43 | 24= | 17 | 2.54 | 1.03 |
| 26 | 11 | 2.99 | 1.39 | 26 | 21 | 2.62 | 1.21 | 26 | 10 | 2.46 | 1.58 |

second school experiences being 'whether each student is getting what he/she needs'. Thus, the two events causing most concern were self-concerns, with the next two events being impact concerns.

As table 3.4 shows, the event causing least concern on the TCQ after the three school experiences was 'working with too many students each day'. This was followed by other task concerns such as 'too many instructional duties',

Table 3.4: *The teacher concerns questionnaire (TCQ): Means and standard deviations for the total concern score and each individual question (in rank order)*

| First administration of the questionnaire | | | | Second administration of the questionnaire | | | | Third administration of the questionnaire | | | |
|------|------|------|------|------|------|------|------|------|------|------|------|
| Rank | Item number | Mean | SD | Rank | Item number | Mean | SD | Rank | Item number | Mean | SD |
| | Total concern score | 3.25 | 0.49 | | Total concern score | 3.16 | 0.60 | | Total concern score | 3.06 | 0.48 |
| 1 | 3 | 3.97 | 0.89 | 1 | 3 | 4.30 | 0.77 | 1 | 3 | 4.15 | 0.83 |
| 2 | 13 | 3.85 | 0.95 | 2 | 13 | 4.02 | 0.91 | 2 | 13 | 3.85 | 0.88 |
| 3 | 8 | 3.70 | 0.86 | 3 | 4 | 3.48 | 0.95 | 3 | 8 | 3.65 | 0.89 |
| 4 | 12 | 3.68 | 0.91 | 4= | 12 | 3.45 | 0.91 | 4 | 4 | 3.54 | 0.99 |
| 5 | 15 | 3.57 | 1.00 | 4= | 9 | 3.45 | 1.27 | 5 | 12 | 3.38 | 0.94 |
| 6 | 9 | 3.46 | 1.05 | 6 | 8 | 3.40 | 1.01 | 6= | 6 | 3.15 | 0.83 |
| 7 | 7 | 3.40 | 0.88 | 7 | 6 | 3.17 | 0.89 | 6= | 11 | 3.15 | 1.05 |
| 8 | 4 | 3.52 | 0.77 | 8 | 11 | 3.15 | 1.20 | 8 | 2 | 3.04 | 1.18 |
| 9 | 11 | 3.25 | 0.86 | 9 | 7 | 3.10 | 1.39 | 9 | 9 | 2.96 | 1.18 |
| 10 | 6 | 3.24 | 0.94 | 10 | 15 | 2.97 | 1.27 | 10 | 7 | 2.92 | 1.05 |
| 11 | 1 | 2.92 | 0.84 | 11 | 2 | 2.92 | 0.98 | 11 | 1 | 2.65 | 1.44 |
| 12 | 2 | 2.77 | 1.00 | 12 | 1 | 2.85 | 0.84 | 12 | 14 | 2.65 | 1.09 |
| 13 | 14 | 2.70 | 0.90 | 13 | 5 | 2.60 | 1.20 | 13 | 5 | 2.50 | 0.81 |
| 14 | 5 | 2.65 | 0.80 | 14 | 14 | 2.52 | 1.08 | 14 | 15 | 2.50 | 1.10 |
| 15 | 10 | 2.07 | 1.02 | 15 | 10 | 2.07 | 1.41 | 15 | 10 | 1.77 | 0.71 |

'the routine and inflexibility of the teaching situation', then 'feeling under pressure much of the time', 'lack of instructional materials' and 'maintaining the appropriate degree of class control'. These are all task concerns.

### Correlation Analysis

There were significant correlations of .3860, p. < .0001, .5355, p < .0001 and .4206, p < .002 between scores on the STAS and .5199, p.006, .4477, p.001 and .4519, p.001 between scores on the TCQ after the first and second, first and third and second and third school experiences, respectively.

## What do these Results Mean for Initial Teacher Education?

### Experience of Anxiety and Concern on School Experience

The results of this study showed that the physical education students in this sample experienced moderate levels of anxiety or concern on the three school experiences and this supports the findings of other studies which have shown school experience to be a cause of anxiety and concern for students (Capel, 1992; Hart, 1987).

Results showed a significant relationship between the level of anxiety or concern after the three school experiences. Thus, students experienced roughly the same amount of anxiety or concern on all three school experiences. This is probably due largely to being observed, evaluated and assessed being the cause of the anxiety or concern (see below).

## Implications of experiencing anxiety on school experience

The experience of anxiety affects a student personally. A student's anxiety is also communicated to pupils directly and/or indirectly, mainly through its negative effects on teaching performance (for example, it reduces flexibility, inventiveness and resourcefulness, impairs decision-making ability resulting in confused thinking and actions, hesitant, tentative or hurried instructions or ineffective use of teaching and management strategies). Thus, when anxious, students are less able to meet the demands of the teaching situation.

## Learning to cope with anxiety

It is therefore important that supervisors and co-operating teachers/mentors[3] recognize and take seriously students' anxiety and concerns about school experience. Students should be prepared beforehand for the anxiety and concerns they experience on school experience, especially in light of the potentially damaging effects of anxiety (and stress which may result from the anxiety and concern) to both themselves and to pupils being taught, both in the short term and over a longer period of time. Time spent helping students to recognize anxiety, the causes of anxiety, how it affects them and various coping methods which can be used, is time well spent. Some teacher educators might perceive that this time could be better spent on specific aspects of teaching or classroom management and might therefore need to be persuaded of the importance of incorporating anxiety/stress management into the initial teacher education course.

Techniques that can be employed to reduce the anxiety and concern generated about specific aspects of teaching include: developing routines to reduce the number of aspects of a lesson which have to be thought about each time; planning a lesson extra thoroughly to reduce the likelihood of confusion; or practising giving instructions and visualizing teaching particularly difficult parts of the lesson. Additional techniques can be employed to reduce anxiety and concern about teaching generally. These might include: talking to other students about teaching; developing a support group to discuss aspects of teaching found to produce anxiety, such as planning lessons in aspects of the subject which are less familiar or dealing with disruptive pupils. Further, students should be allowed opportunities to reflect on, and ask questions about, each school experience after they have completed it. Boggess, McBride and Griffey (1985) suggested that if anxieties and concerns at the end of school experience are not addressed, it may lead to students questioning teaching as a career.

Students might also be introduced to more general techniques for managing anxiety and stress, such as taking exercise, developing a hobby and leaving time for themselves and not allowing the school experience to take over their whole life. Developing time management techniques is important as management of workload has been identified as a problem for students (Pelletier and Martel, 1994) and ineffective management of time can be stressful (see Capel, 1995c). Although students can develop techniques to manage their workload better, Pelletier and Martel indicated that teacher educators must also consider whether the demands of the initial teacher education course are such that students cannot hope to manage the workload successfully. There may be inherent weaknesses in the design of the course in general or of school experience in particular which need to be addressed if students are to learn effectively.

Anxieties and concerns do not stop when students gain qualified teacher status (QTS). Although the responsibilities of teacher educators cease when students gain QTS, one of the aims of initial teacher education is to prepare students for the anxieties, concerns and stresses of teaching itself. Students should therefore be helped to develop a positive yet realistic picture of a teacher's life and be equipped with skills and techniques to enable them to reflect on their teaching and management in order to assess their current practice and learn from this to develop further as teachers. Research has shown (Blix, Cruise, Mitchell and Blix, 1994) that the ideal work situation is one where there is a good match between an individual's needs and motivational style and the rewards available from the job. If such a match exists, the individual is then more likely to cope with the situation, and the resulting enhanced self-worth and self-esteem may help to prevent stress before it happens. Therefore, near the end of their initial teacher education course students might be encouraged to identify the types of school in which they would be happy to teach and to consider carefully to which schools they apply for their first post (see Capel, 1995d).

### Causes of Anxiety and Concern for Physical Education Students

Results of the study described in this chapter seem to suggest that there are a number of specific causes of anxiety and concern for physical education students on school experience. Most anxiety and concern was about self, particularly about being observed, evaluated and assessed by the school experience supervisor and/or school staff. Results also showed that least anxiety or concern was caused by events related to the task of teaching and (on the STAS) working relationships with school staff.

*Susan Capel*

## Being observed, evaluated and assessed on school experience

Anxiety and concern caused by being observed, evaluated and assessed must be recognized and taken seriously as these are important elements of school experience and teacher appraisal throughout a teacher's career, and therefore cannot be eliminated entirely. Students must be prepared for being observed, evaluated and assessed on their school experience, and hence throughout their teaching career, as well as being prepared for the task of teaching.

Those observing students on school experience must also be aware of the impact of their presence in the classroom, gymnasium or playing field on students' anxiety and, possibly, on their teaching performance. As indicated previously, anxiety negatively affects teaching performance, therefore it is likely that while being observed, evaluated and assessed, students will not perform to the best of their ability in the classroom. Observation, evaluation and assessment must therefore be undertaken in a positive and sensitive manner in order for supervision of students on school experience to be effective in effecting change in students' teaching performance.

## Changes in Students' Perspectives of Teaching Over Time

Results of this study showed that the events causing most anxiety and concern on both the STAS and the TCQ were the same after the three school experiences. These results supported findings by Fuller (1969) who identified very little change in the concerns of students over time, with continuing concern about self, particularly about being observed, evaluated and assessed. However, results also suggested an increase in anxiety about being assessed as a result of being observed.

## Assessment of students' teaching performance

It is important that teacher educators recognize the growing importance of assessment to students. However, assessment must not be allowed to become the major focus of the school experience for students. Steps must therefore be taken to alleviate anxiety and concern about being assessed on teaching performance. This can best be done by providing regular, consistent evaluation of teaching performance throughout the school experience rather than relying on 'one-off' formal assessments of students so that students know where they stand at all times and the school experience grade does not come as a surprise. If this assessment is linked directly to students' professional development profile, to which students contribute fully, and hence also to their developing skills of reflection, the effectiveness of this can be enhanced as students can be helped to recognize that assessment of their teaching is part of an ongoing, career long process extending well beyond their initial teacher education course. Thus, students may be less preoccupied with, and hence, less anxious about, being assessed, therefore they can concentrate on enhancing their teaching skills. If such steps are not taken, it is likely that students will remain in the 'recognizing difficulties' or 'hitting the plateau' phases identified by Maynard and Furlong (1993) rather than 'moving on' to recognize the needs of pupils and experiment with their teaching, or remain in the 'self-image and class management' phase identified by Leask (1995), rather than moving onto the 'whole class learning' and 'individual pupil's learning' phases.

It should also be recognized that there is potential for students' anxiety and concern about being assessed on school experience to be exacerbated in the school-based model of initial teacher education. It is important that the advantages of school staff undertaking a greater role in initial teacher education are not outweighed by the dangers of a model in which the same person is acting as guide, tutor, counsellor, friend and assessor. There is potential for the role of the mentor in assessing the students' teaching performance to detract from the role of the mentor in facilitating the students' learning. In such a situation, students may feel inhibited on school experience from talking freely and openly to their mentor about anxieties or concerns or from seeking advice because of the mentor's role in the assessment of their teaching performance, as identified by Pateman (1994). This dual function of the mentor does not, there-fore, take account of and may, in fact, detract from the role school staff have traditionally undertaken in addressing the students' needs for guidance, tutoring, counselling and friendship. If students are unable to talk freely to a mentor who is also assessing them, ways of providing this support have to be found.

## Other concerns of students

Although the events causing most concern on the TCQ were related to self, they also included those concerned with the impact of teaching on individual pupils, such as 'challenging unmotivated students' and 'meeting the needs of different kinds of students'. This suggested that although impact concerns were not as important as self-concerns these students were concerned about the impact of their teaching.

Results of research in this area are contradictory. For example, Behets (1990) found impact concerns to be the greatest concern for physical educa-tion students on school experience whereas other studies (Arrighi and Young, 1987; Schempp, 1986) have indicated that students concerns about pupils have reduced over the duration of a school experience, with students becoming less humanistic and more custodial in their attitudes. Pettigrew (1988) found a sig-nificant decrease in physical education students sense of responsibility for pupils learning during school experience, with a corresponding increase in a teacher centred process of instruction. Results of the various studies therefore indicate that mentors should not worry unduly if students cannot take on board fully the needs of pupils as individuals whilst in initial teacher educa-tion, although they should be concerned if students concerns for pupils are decreasing or their attitudes to the pupils become more custodial.

*Susan Capel*

*Helping students move through the phases of development*

Appropriate interventions are needed to help students develop as teachers and move through the different phases of development. Such interventions should not be based on intuition by teacher educators but should be developed from research findings which provide knowledge and understanding of the anxieties and concerns of students on school experience. Reflection on research results allows teacher educators to develop realistic expectations of students at different phases in their development as teachers and to develop initial teacher education courses based on what students are ready to learn at these different phases, in order to maximize students learning experiences. The structure and focus of the course, the order and timing of delivery of the content and the teaching strategies adopted should therefore be relevant to students' needs at a specific time which should help them through the phases of development as teachers. Further, if students' anxieties and concerns are addressed at the appropriate time they can be alleviated (or even prevented).

For example, before undertaking any school experience students anticipate what school experience and teaching will be like from their experience as pupils or what other people have told them. They are therefore apprehensive but do not know exactly what to be concerned about and express vague concerns rather than specific concerns about teaching. At the beginning of their school experiences students are concerned about their relationship with the teacher who usually teaches the class, what the teacher expects of them in relation to the class, whether the teacher allows them to be in charge of the class, how much freedom the teacher gives them to experiment and try things out and how much support the teacher gives. However, these concerns are often not expressed overtly, perhaps because students perceive that this is not acceptable. Instead, students may express overtly concerns about being able to cope in the classroom, such as controlling the class and disciplining pupils, having adequate understanding of the subject matter they are teaching, and being able to answer questions and responding to changing classroom situations.

In order to alleviate concern about discipline and classroom management initial teacher education courses have traditionally included a range of situations including observation, micro-teaching and small group teaching situations before students are expected eventually to teach a full class and take overall responsibility for that class. The theory is that this enables teaching skills to be practised in relatively contained situations before being tried out in the classroom. However, it has been suggested that students have had difficultly in generalizing their learning from such experiences into a full class situation. McIntyre and Hagger (1993) suggest that collaborative teaching, in which the mentor and student take joint responsibility for a lesson, planning it together, then each playing a different part in the teaching, with the parts played by the student being selected to provide focused learning experiences, provides a situation in which the student can practice the necessary skills in a safe environment, but without the problems of being unable to transfer the learning to a full class situation. Further, joint planning of lessons is an advantage because lesson planning has been perceived to be a problem for students. For example, Boggess, McBride and Griffey (1985) suggested that concern by supervisors about unit and lesson plans early in their school experience produces anxiety for students, especially when considered in relation to concern for evaluation. This is because early in their school experiences students are not familiar with the situation for which they are planning therefore may be able to plan 'what', but are less able to plan 'how' the lesson plans will be implemented. They suggested that this anxiety can be alleviated by supporting increasing sophistication of lesson planning rather than grading students on their early attempts at lesson planning. Burn (1992) suggests that collaborative teaching can also help to make the complexity and sophistication of lesson planning more accessible to students and therefore facilitate their professional development in this aspect of their teaching.

Likewise, strategies should be devised to help students through the later phases of their development as teachers.

### Conclusion

Learning to teach is a complex, multi-dimensional activity unique to each student. In order to maximize students' potential for development it is important that teacher educators have knowledge and understanding about how students learn and develop as teachers in order to provide appropriate learning opportunities and experiences. This requires knowledge and understanding about phases of development and students' changing anxieties and concerns over time. The basis for this development should be research rather than intuition. The results of this study add to our knowledge about students' anxieties and concerns during school experience. However, results of research findings should not be accepted without question. Some contradictions in the findings of research have been highlighted in this chapter or are apparent in other research on the issues considered. For example, other phases of development for students have been identified in studies by Calderhead (1988) and Pigge and Marso (1987) and the emphasis on discrete, sequential development at each phase in development has been criticized as it has been suggested that development of students does not follow such a pattern. For example, Guillaume and Rudney (1993) found that as well as thinking about different things as they developed, students also thought about the same things differently. Furthermore, the changing situation in initial teacher education may reduce or negate the relevance of findings of research in different contexts. For example, in a study by Hardy (1995) very few concerns were expressed by students about control and discipline. There could be many reasons for this, one of which could be that these students actually were not concerned about control and discipline. However, Hardy suggested that this was due to these students perceiving that this was not an acceptable concern to express, 'perhaps because students felt that any admission of control and discipline problems to subject mentors suggested that they were failing, whereas, with their limited backgrounds, any concerns about subject knowledge would be expected of them' (p. 7). Therefore, the findings of this study and other studies serve to further develop our understanding of the development of students but must be interpreted cautiously in order for initial teacher education courses to meet the unique needs of each individual student.

To conclude, the political debate has been, and continues to be, mainly about the model of initial teacher education and within that the models of school experience adopted. No doubt the political debate will continue about appropriate models for initial teacher education courses but whatever the outcome of that debate, teacher educators in higher education institutions and schools should develop effective partnerships to design and develop courses with the students' perspectives placed firmly at the centre of the course.

## Notes

1   Studies variously refer to teaching practice, teaching experience and school experience. For consistency in this chapter any experience which students undertake in schools as part of their initial teacher education course is called school experience.
2   The word student is used to refer to student teachers.
3   Although the term mentor is used to describe a certain role of school staff in relation to students in school-based initial teacher education courses, a great deal of research with physical education students in initial teacher education in USA (and in the UK prior to the introduction of school-based initial teacher education courses) has been conducted with co-operating teachers.

## References

ARRIGHI, M.A. and YOUNG, J.C. (1987) 'Teacher perception about effective and successful teaching', *Journal of Teaching in Physical Education,* **6**, pp. 122–35.
BEHETS, D. (1990) 'Concerns of preservice physical education teachers', *Journal of Teaching in Physical Education,* **10**, 1, pp. 66–75.
BLIX, A.G., CRUISE, R.J., MITCHELL, B.M. and BLIX, G.G. (1994) 'Occupational stress among university teachers', *Educational Research,* **36**, 2, pp. 157–69.
BOGGESS, T.E., MCBRIDE, R.E. and GRIFFEY, D.C. (1985) 'The concerns of physical education student teachers: A developmental view', *Journal of Teaching in Physical Education,* **4**, pp. 202–11.
BURN, K. (1992) 'Collaborative teaching' in WILKIN, M. (Ed) *Mentoring in Schools,* London, Kogan Page, pp. 133–43.
CALDERHEAD, J. (1988) 'The development of knowledge structures in learning to teach' in CALDERHEAD, J. (Ed) *Teachers' Professional Learning,* London, Falmer Press, pp. 51–64.
CAPEL, S.A. (1992) 'Causes of teaching practice anxiety for student physical educators', unpublished paper.

Capel, S.A. (1993) 'Students anxieties on their first teaching practice' in Proceedings of the 36th International Council for Health, Physical Education and Recreation (ICHPER) World Congress: Creating Active Lifestyles: Health, Physical Education and Recreation in Lifelong Learning, Yokohama, Japan, pp. 481–6.

Capel, S.A. (1994) 'Help — its teaching practice again!', paper presented at the 10th Commonwealth and International Scientific Congress, Victoria, BC, August.

Capel, S.A. (1995a) 'Changes in students' anxieties after their first and second teaching practices', unpublished paper.

Capel, S.A. (1995b) 'A longitudinal study of anxiety on teaching practice', paper presented at the European Conference on Educational Research, Bath, September.

Capel, S.A. (1995c) 'Managing your time and preventing stress' in Capel, S., Leask, M. and Turner, T. *Learning to Teach in the Secondary School: A Companion to School Experience*, London, Routledge, pp. 28–35.

Capel, S.A. (1995d) 'Getting your first post' in Capel, S., Leask, M. and Turner, T. *Learning to Teach in the Secondary School: A Companion to School Experience*, London, Routledge, pp. 356–71.

Capel, S.A. (1996) 'Anxieties of physical education students on first teaching practice', *European Physical Education Review*, **2**, 1, spring.

Department for Education (1992) *Initial Teacher Training* (Secondary phase) (Circular 9/92), London, HMSO.

Department for Education (1993) *The Initial Training of Primary School Teachers: New Criteria for Courses* (Circular 14/93), London, HMSO.

Department of Education and Science (1984) *Initial Teacher Training: Approval of Courses* (Circular 3/84), London, HMSO.

Department of Education and Science (1989) *Initial Teacher Training: Approval of Courses* (Circular 24/89), London, HMSO.

Fuller, F.F. (1969) 'Concerns of teachers: A developmental conceptualization', *American Educational Research Journal*, **6**, 2, pp. 207–26.

Fuller, F.F. and Brown, O.H. (1975) 'Becoming a teacher' in Rehage, K.J. (Ed) *Teacher Education*, NSSE 74th Yearbook, part II, Chicago, University of Chicago Press.

George, A.A. (1978) *Measuring Self, Task; and Impact Concerns: A Manual for Use of the Teacher Concerns Questionnaire*, Austin, TX, University of Texas, Research and Development Center for Teacher Education.

Guillaume, A.M. and Rudney, G.C. (1993) 'Student teachers' growth toward independence: An analysis of their changing concerns', *Teaching and Teacher Education*, **9**, 1, pp. 65–80.

Hardy, C. (1995) 'Perceptions of mentoring in physical education classes: The subject mentor's view', paper presented at the European Conference on Educational Research, Bath, September.

Hart, N.I. (1987) 'Student teachers' anxieties: Four measured factors and their relationships to pupil disruption in class', *Educational Research*, **29**, 1, pp. 12–18.

Leask, M. (1995) 'The student teacher's roles and responsibilities' in Capel, S., Leask, M. and Turner, T. *Learning to Teach in the Secondary School: A Companion to School Experience*, London, Routledge, pp. 17–27.

Locke, L.F. (1979) 'Supervision, schools and student teaching: Why things stay the same', *The Academy Papers*, **13**, pp. 65–74.

Lortie, D.C. (1975) *School Teacher: A Sociological Study*, Chicago, University of Chicago Press.

McIntyre, D. and Hagger, H. (1993) 'Teachers' expertise and models of mentoring' in

McINTYRE, D., HAGGER, H. and WILKIN, M. (Eds) *Mentoring: Perspectives on School-based Teacher Education*, London, Kogan Page, pp. 86–102.

MANCINI, V.H., GOSS, J. and FRYE, P. (1982) 'Relationships of interaction behavior patterns of student teachers and their co-operating teachers', *Abstracts of Research Papers: American Alliance for Health, Physical Education, Recreation and Dance (AAHPERD) Convention — Houston*, Reston, VA, AAHPERD, p. 116.

MAYNARD, T. and FURLONG, J. (1993) 'Learning to teach and models of mentoring' in McINTYRE, D., HAGGER, H. and WILKIN, M. (Eds) *Mentoring: Perspectives on School-based Teacher Education*, London, Kogan Page, pp. 69–85.

PATEMAN, T. (1994) 'Crisis, what identity crisis?' *First Appointments Supplement, Times Educational Supplement*, 14 January, pp. 28–9.

PELLETIER, J. and MARTEL, D. (1994) 'Problems physical education student teachers encountered during initial teaching experiences', paper presented at the International Association for Physical Education in Higher Education (AIESEP) Conference, Berlin, June.

PETTIGREW, F. (1988) 'The effect of student teaching on instructional styles of preservice physical education majors', paper presented at Midwest District AAHPERD Conference, Dearborn, MI.

PIGGE, F.L. and MARSO, R.N. (1987) 'Relationships between student characteristics and changes in attitudes, concerns, anxieties and confidence about teaching during teacher preparation', *Journal of Educational Research*, **81**, pp. 109–115.

SCHEMPP, P.G. (1986) 'Physical Education student teachers' beliefs in their control over student learning', *Journal of Teaching in Physical Education*, **5**, 3, pp. 198–203.

TANNEHILL, D. and ZAKRAJSEK, D. (1988) 'What's happening in supervision of student teachers in secondary physical education', *Journal of Teaching in Physical Education*, **8**, 1, pp. 1–12.

WENDT, J.C. and BAIN, L.L. (1989) 'Concerns of preservice and inservice physical educators', *Journal of Teaching in Physical Education*, **8**, pp. 177–80.

WENDT, J.C., BAIN, L.L. and JACKSON, A.S. (1981) 'Fuller's concerns theory as tested on prospective physical educators', *Journal of Teaching in Physical Education, Introductory Issue*, pp. 66–70.

# 4 Trainees' Concerns, Experiences and Needs: Implications for Mentoring in Physical Education

*Colin Hardy*

## Development of Trainees

A pre-teaching phase, an early teaching phase and a late teaching phase were posited by Fuller (1969) as a three-phase developmental conceptualization of teachers' concerns. With the pre-teaching phase, trainees expressed concerns based mainly on hearsay, and many of them did not know what to be concerned about. In general, 'they thought of teaching in terms of their own experiences as pupils and as college students' (p. 219). The early teaching phase concerns focused on such areas as class control, content adequacy and supervisor evaluation, and it was suggested that 'all are assessments of the teacher's adequacy, by the class and by the supervisor' (p. 221). Although Fuller was more tentative about the concerns of experienced teachers, it was noted that concerns seemed 'to focus on pupil gain and self-evaluation as opposed to personal gain and evaluations by others' (p. 221). Later, Fuller and Bown (1975) proposed a three-stage trainees' developmental model suggesting that there was a progression from 'survival concerns' to 'task concerns' to 'impact concerns'. However, Guillaume and Rudney (1993), in their identification of six broad areas of concerns reported by trainees, noted that these concerns were held simultaneously by the trainees throughout their school-based experiences although the nature of these concerns shifted as the trainees moved towards independence and took more responsibility as teachers. The six broad categories identified by the authors were lesson planning and evaluation, discipline, working with pupils, working with co-operating teachers and adjusting to their classrooms, working with others in the profession and 'transitions from trainee to professional teacher'. Furlong and Maynard (1995), whilst adopting the notion of stages as characterizing trainees' development, indicated that the progress of trainees is far from linear. They suggest that 'development from "novice" to "professional educator" is dependent on the interaction between individual students, their teacher education programme, and the school context in which they undertake their practical experience' (p. 70). Consequently, Furlong and Maynard regard trainees' learning to teach as 'complex, erratic and in one sense unique to them as an individual' (p. 70). From their research they identified five broad stages in trainees' development while on their school experience, and these were characterized as early idealism, personal survival, dealing with difficulties, hitting a plateau and moving on. It is suggested that at the start of their teacher education, trainees are idealistic in how they feel towards the pupils and the image they hold of themselves as teachers. This idealism appears to fade in the light of school experience and trainees focus on personally surviving. According to the authors, this means 'detecting and "fitting in" with the teacher's routines and expectations, being "seen" as a teacher and, in particular, achieving some form of classroom control' (p. 76).

Gradually, this survival stage gives way to the stage where trainees start to identify some of the difficulties that have to be addressed. The 'hitting the plateau stage' tended to take place towards the end of a first teaching experience when trainees felt more confident and competent in managing and organizing pupils and resources. It appears that at this stage trainees are inclined to relax a little and that their detailed planning and evaluations and experimentation with new strategies are substituted by a more limited preparatory phase and a reliance on strategies that they felt worked for them. With the 'moving on' stage the authors felt that the trainees had to be challenged and it was necessary 'to become much more "interventionist" when working with the students' (pp. 92 and 93).

From such studies it would appear that discrete stages of trainees' development in learning to teach can be identified but that they should only be regarded as broad guidelines. As trainees' progress is very much dependent on existing factors encountered during their school experiences the path taken can be irregular and individual.

In physical education, several authors have used the model formulated by Fuller and Bown (1975) as a basis for their research and they have noted that trainees do not significantly decrease concerns about self or increase feelings towards task or impact concerns (Boggess, McBride and Griffey, 1985; Wendt, Bain and Jackson, 1981). Behets (1990) administered the fifteen-item Teacher Concerns Questionnaire (TCQ; George, 1978), revised from the fifty-item questionnaire developed by Fuller and Borich (1974), on three occasions to 100 trainees during their early field experience and reported that the only significant difference over time was an increase in the value of the impact category. However, a comparison of the TCQ results with a content analysis of the logbook entries of ten of the trainees, revealed contradictory findings; with the logbook entries concerns about pupil control and organization were more frequently cited than those related to impact. It was suggested by the author that TCQ results may reflect the idealistic concerns of trainees whereas the daily reporting in a logbook in each lesson could reflect their realistic concerns. Fung (1993), in finding no significant difference between the concerns of trainees and in-service physical education teachers based on TCQ data, questioned the sensitivity of the instrument with regard to measuring concerns among these groups. Hardy (1994) administered the TCQ to two cohorts of one-year postgraduate trainees (n = 119) on two occasions in successive years and reported that Fuller and Bown's progressive stages of concerns, in which the immediate concerns for survival gradually shifted to task and then to impact concerns, were not borne out. He suggested that the idea that concerns about the self make way for task concerns and finally impact concerns is a logical one, but it is possible that shift in concerns moves in both directions and are specific to the trainees being measured. Trainees' perceptions of self, task and impact concerns, their relationship with significant others and their socialization into schools all have a bearing on the strength of their responses at a particular time. In addition, Hardy questioned the validity of the instrument in assessing the complex area of trainees' concerns. Pelletier and Martel (1994) investigated trainees' concerns by analyzing the weekly reports of thirty-two trainees during a fifteen-week placement and then classifying the data according to the concerns model formulated by Fuller (1969). Of the personal difficulties, the most often reported were the trainees' inability to devote adequate time and energy towards university courses and part-time jobs, the quality of professional support provided by the co-operating teachers and their own self-confidence. The most frequently identified difficulties were those related to 'teacher task' and, of these concerns, managing pupil behaviour and managing their own workload were cited the most. Difficulties related to 'impact concerns' were only mentioned on five occasions during the fifteen-week experience. In contrast, Sebren (1995), in her close examination of three trainees during a field-based methods course, reported that they transformed their orientation from teaching as control to teaching for learning. At the beginning of the semester the trainees had an orientation towards teaching as a problem of control 'characterized by an expressed need for a sense of self safety, an expressed lack of confidence or sense of self as authority, and a tendency to blame the children' (p. A-69). By the end of the semester their orientation towards teaching had shifted to a focus on teaching for learning 'characterized by an understanding of the relationship between management and learning, a greater ability to identify what they wanted to teach and what they were looking for in the children's movement, and an ability to vary task structure in relation to an instructional goal' (p. A-69). However, the constant attention that would have been afforded to the three trainees within the context of the methods course may not be representative of trainees' difficulties during a fifteen-week placement, but it may indicate that orientations can change with adequate support networks.

A recent investigation by Hardy (1995a) of twenty-three postgraduate trainees who had just completed their predominantly school-based initial teacher training year within the context of a school-university partnership scheme found that their concerns were predominantly teacher-centred with the occasional focus on the impact of the lesson material on pupils' learning.

Teacher-centred problems that focused on the task were in the areas of content knowledge, general lesson structure, choosing and organizing material and how to make the best use of facilities and equipment, and when they focused on the pupil the areas were managing and organizing pupils and controlling them. When the emphasis was on themselves they approached staff concerning their professional skills and development. Although the results are not too different from those noted by Pelletier and Martel (1994), the general concern of trainees about their lack of knowledge in the activity areas of the physical education curriculum perhaps reflects a problem specific to mainly school-based schemes. If trainees are going to spend less time in higher education institutions building up a content pedagogical base, in-service provision must become an integral part of the new teacher education policy.

It would appear from the investigations carried out on trainees' concerns in physical education settings that reported concerns are not only complex and varied but may also reflect the trainees' teacher education programme and the methodologies used by researchers. However, as the intention of any teacher education programme is to help trainees learn to teach, the interventionist techniques used by significant persons in schools and universities must be towards this end. Therefore, if trainees are to progress, perhaps erratically, deliberate strategies to challenge trainees (Furlong and Maynard, 1995) to help them go beyond 'fitting in' and 'passing the test' to 'exploring' (Calderhead, 1987) must be organized and supported by permanent structures.

## Trainees' Concerns and Mentoring

The implication of DFE Circular 9/92 (DFE, 1992) is that the more experiences trainees accumulate the more effective teachers they will become. However, Booth (1993) suggests that 'simply placing students in schools without adequate mentoring support would give students little chance to develop their classroom and subject teaching skills and understanding' (p. 194), and Kennedy (1991) refines this point by emphasizing that for trainees to 'learn a series of specific teaching techniques without understanding their rationale and without help in adapting them to particular students and classroom situations, they will be unable to make lasting changes in their practice' (p. 17). Thus, mentoring of trainees is more than just seeing them through their experiences, it is about deliberate strategies to help them understand what it means to become a teacher and how to learn to teach. Within the new predominantly school-based teacher education schemes the subject mentor will be at the centre of the trainees' development. Therefore, the training and the selection of subject mentors is crucial to any partnership arrangement between a higher education institution and schools, as the availability of subject mentors does not guarantee that trainees will learn to teach if the mentors do not have the ability to translate their knowledge into classroom curricular events in a way that considers the trainees' concerns and stage of development.

## The Research Study

The focus of the study was on the concerns of postgraduate physical education trainees during a five week and an eleven week block practice. The teacher education course was a university-school partnership scheme based on DFE Circular No. 9/92. During the year 1993/94, fifty-three trainees completed and returned a report each week on 'your concerns about teaching at the moment', and, altogether, 1510 concerns were reported on the 848 forms. A content analysis (Holsti, 1969) of the concerns revealed four broad categories of concern, and these were labelled as:

(i)    coming to terms with being a teacher;
(ii)   learning to teach and work with pupils;
(iii)  coping with the demands of the course;
(iv)   dealing with school and university personnel and the school's working arrangements.

Of these concerns 321 (21.26 per cent) were recorded under category (i); 673 (44.57 per cent) under category (ii); 135 (8.94 per cent) under category (iii); and 381 (25.23 per cent) under category (iv). Inter-coder and intra-coder reliabilities were checked using Scott's Pi Coefficient of Reliability (Darst, Zakrajsek and Mancini, 1989) and values of 0.88 and 0.91 respectively were computed. Differences were examined and resolved by the two coders. The range of concerns for each trainee varied from no concerns to four.

From the results it appears that concerns about themselves as teachers can arise just as easily at the end of a practice as at the start, and that the impact of their work on pupils can be cited early in the training year as well as later. For example, in the first week of the first block experience, one female trainee commented: 'I haven't experienced taking lessons yet — so apprehension of the unknown is my biggest concern. Although I have taught/coached before, it has always been with fairly small groups and to people who want to be there.' Another female trainee in the ninth week of her final block experience was still having doubts about her ability as a teacher: 'Still very little (if any) feedback. One teacher told me what I'd been doing "wrong" this week — and that he'd written this on my record of achievement — why he hadn't told me this weeks ago, I'll never know. It makes me very angry to think perhaps I've been wasting my time in his lessons. Suddenly, very disillusioned, my confidence level is low. Two weeks left to raise it to normal.' With regard to the impact area, in the second week of the first block experience, one female trainee noted about the pupils: 'Are they learning anything, and if so, are they remembering it?' In a similar vein, a male trainee in the ninth week of his second and final block experience said: 'Sometimes I become frustrated when practices don't produce the results I wish, or retention is weak when tested in later lessons.'

### *Coming to Terms with Being a Teacher*

Within this area of concern the trainees focused on their adequacy as a teacher, their knowledge of activity areas and school procedures and policies, and the realities of the profession.

Trainees' adequacy as a teacher centred around their confidence in physical education settings and how they perceived or felt others perceived their teaching performances. For example, one male trainee said, 'I still have not taught a decent PE lesson. Possibly I am expecting too much of myself at this stage and I am very critical of lessons, often dwelling upon negative factors as opposed to looking at the many positive factors that arise', and a female trainee noted, 'The mentor expressed concern that I appear flustered in lessons, even if they were working well. I do still sometimes feel uncomfortable in teaching if another teacher is watching even if everything is running smoothly.'

Trainees' knowledge of activity areas was a constant concern throughout the teacher education year. However, with less time being spent on practical activities in both undergraduate and postgraduate certificate of education partnership schemes, it is not surprising that trainees feel vulnerable when planning for the range of National Curriculum activities. In addition, teaching in a school involves not only understanding school procedures and policies but how school staff interpret those procedures and policies. With regard to subject knowledge some trainees were concerned that they had little knowledge about an activity and others were concerned about the application of that knowledge to the lesson. One male trainee said, 'I have found myself teaching sports such as rounders and softball with which I am not greatly familiar but the school has a strong tradition in such sports', and a female trainee reported, 'I am continually learning and it is always about content for example, the breaking down of a tennis stroke. I do it automatically but what makes pupils' shots go so wrong? It is the mechanics of the movement that I am beginning to learn so I can teach.' Some trainees find the school procedures and policies are a concern as they realise that this is part of 'fitting in' to the school environment. One male trainee noted how he did not understand the policy when he said, 'What is assertive discipline? Something to do with five warnings and vanilla slips?' and a female trainee was concerned about the teachers' way of dealing with pupils when she noted, 'There is a very laid back joking atmosphere between teachers and pupils which I find quite difficult to fit in with sometimes because often the pupils don't know when they are over-stepping the mark. Pupils don't realise when I'm being serious and I even have to say, "I'm not joking".'

As the trainees became more familiar with the school climate, some of them started to become more aware of the 'downsides' of teaching. For example, one female trainee noted the problems of implementing the National Curriculum when she said, 'At school this week we have been looking at NC in PE and geography. In theory a good idea but in practice a nightmare. Teachers just don't seem to have the time to set it up, assess pupils, do the paper work etc. It just causes a lot of worry and stress amongst teachers.' Another trainee focused on the administrative aspect of the teaching role when she commented, 'Attended a staff meeting on Wednesday, and it worries me the amount of paperwork etc. teachers are now being expected to complete. No extra time is provided. It's as though classroom teaching is becoming the easy side of the job, compared to the administration.'

With many of these concerns trainees were sometimes reluctant to approach their subject mentors as they felt it would appear that they were not coming to terms with the teaching role. However, even if a trainee did approach a subject mentor, the trainee had to feel that the relationship with the mentor was a comfortable one. The importance of this relationship is highlighted by one student who had different experiences of subject mentors in the two phases of the partnership programme. Of the first phase school mentor, she said, 'I did actually feel very intimidated by him because he gave little positive feedback and I found that I could not give my point of view', and of the second phase school mentor, 'Oh, he was much better, he was more approachable basically, I got on a lot better and I felt that I could discuss problems with him.' In addition, students often perceived teachers whom they could approach as the ones who had an awareness of how they felt; for example, 'He kept asking me about my lessons and whether I was happy with the classes, and he said that he understood my worries.'

## Mentoring implications

It would appear that if subject mentors are to help trainees with these types of concerns it is important that they are approachable and available, they listen and that they are sympathetic to, and empathize with, the trainees' concerns. Such 'emotional support' is an ongoing strategy irrespective of the trainees' stage of development and it should become an integral part of both formal and informal discussions. In addition, as trainees tend to build up their own network of contacts a team mentoring structure within, and even across subjects, may have to be considered (Hardy, in press).

The trainees' perceptions of the pressures placed on school staff is also more of a general issue and one that schools may find difficult not to portray. However, it may be necessary for subject mentors, as well as other staff, to examine the advantages and disadvantages of the teaching profession in order that trainees can make balanced and independent decisions about their future careers.

## Learning to Teach and Work with Pupils

The concerns cited by trainees in this area were related to the planning of lessons, the act of teaching, pupil characteristics, controlling pupils and pupil learning outcomes.

It appears that lesson planning worries trainees on two fronts; firstly, that the material is appropriate for the group of pupils and secondly, the time it takes to prepare lessons. For instance, one male trainee was concerned about, 'Finding appropriate content for pupils in certain areas because of wide differences in abilities and wide range of activities the school offers', and one female trainee noted, 'Having to do lesson plans and evaluations which take up so much time so that nothing else can be done in the evenings.'

Trainees' concerns about the act of teaching tended to focus on either the lesson that didn't quite develop as planned, a teaching skill that needed working on or a particular incident during the lesson, and, as with all concerns related to teaching, managing and organizing pupils was a constant worry for the trainees. One male trainee said, 'I find it frustrating when I plan a unit of work and then take the first lesson only to find that the targets are not suitable', and one female trainee noted, 'I speak so fast sometimes so pupils miss some key instructions. I must focus on just brief concise instructions so my intentions are properly understood'. Sometimes when a particular incident happened during their teaching trainees found it difficult to adjust. For example, one female trainee reported, 'Teacher kept interfering in my lesson so I forgot what I was going to say.' With regard to managing and organizing pupils trainees reported concerns about the activity taught and the number of pupils involved in the lesson. One male trainee was concerned with, 'Balancing safety with activity level in athletics — I'm finding it hard doing discus and javelin because of the concerns about safety. Pupils are getting minimal experience', and a female trainee was worried about, 'Having to deal with the organizations of fifty-five children in one sports hall — same activity, other staff present but I'm leading.'

Lack of interest and disruptive behaviour were the pupil characteristics that appeared to demand the attention of the trainees. In most cases the trainees felt that they had been 'landed' with groups of difficult pupils and that there was little that they could do other than occupy them. Such a response is not uncommon and it is well documented in literature (Lortie, 1975). One male trainee said, 'Having problems dealing with children who show a lack of interest. What is the best way to get them involved in the lesson? Still find myself feeling impatient with bored, uninterested children', and a female trainee said, 'I am concerned about how to keep a very wild rugby group occupied. They want to run before they can walk, they are totally undisciplined and don't want to listen or co-operate. Some boys have no respect for female teachers in particular.' Another female trainee said, 'In my year 9 hockey lesson (mixed), I've got one boy who consistently disrupts those working around him, he doesn't seem to care if I tell him off. I have tried to have a "quiet chat" to him, which also didn't work. What else can I do other than send him in to get changed?' As pupil control is perceived by beginning teachers as the most serious problem area (Veenman, 1984), it is not surprising that it features prominently in the trainees' concerns.

Concerns involving pupil learning outcomes were seldom reported by the trainees, and it could either be that the trainees didn't see this as an area of concern or that other concerns were always more pressing. However, considering other authors (Pellatier and Martel, 1994) have reported similar results, the latter argument is probably more viable. Nevertheless, a male trainee showed an awareness of the problem when he noted, 'We are advised to use task cards which simply have challenges on them. Hence lessons are active but are the children learning? For example, sprint challenges are fine but shouldn't we be talking about elements of technique to use or look for?'

*Mentoring implications*

As planning in a variety of activities with a range of pupil abilities can be a difficult task for trainees, subject mentors could consider collaborative teaching as part of the training experience. A lesson could be jointly planned and jointly taught by a trainee and a subject mentor or by a trainee and another physical education teacher. However, the lesson must be planned to ensure that the trainee has a clearly defined responsibility within it. Collaborative lessons between two trainees are another possibility although there is evidence to suggest that a mismatching of trainees can cause other problems (McIntyre, Hagger and Burn, 1994). In addition, if trainees are to prepare in detail they will need to have time put aside during the school day to plan as, with the 'long day', tiredness starts to influence the thoroughness of lesson plans. Such comments as the one uttered by a female trainee were not uncommon during the present study, 'I'm just exhausted! How will I cope for the full year?!' Another suggestion is that trainees should be given less preparations in the early stages with more opportunity to reflect upon the same content (Livingston and Borko, 1989).

Helping trainees learn to teach should involve deliberate strategies on the part of subject mentors. Trainees should be encouraged to set goals and to use their school experience in a systematic way to achieve the goals. It is also important that the trainees see themselves as playing an active role in orchestrating their experiences in order that they begin to 'see' classrooms in conceptual terms (Copeland, 1981). If subject mentors are to help trainees to develop an awareness of the significance of events or behaviours, physical education lessons must be seen as laboratory situations rather than material to be taught.

Expert teachers, with their '. . . larger better-integrated stores of facts, principles and experiences' (Livingston and Borko, 1989, pp. 36–7) are able to deal better with the many characteristics and backgrounds that pupils bring with them to classes than trainees, but simply telling the latter about classes will not produce expertise. Therefore, it is important that subject mentors explain the organization of their thinking in detail to trainees in order that the rationale behind decisions is understood. Telling trainees what to do may produce short-term solutions but this does not help to provide a firm base for learning to teach.

Many physical education texts present guidelines for controlling pupils in physical education settings (Graham, 1992; Rink, 1993), and, although such techniques can be successfully implemented by trainees, it is the reasons for making decisions that trainees need. As a knowledge of pupils is paramount in effectively controlling pupils, subject mentors will need to give trainees the opportunity to try out the various techniques with a range of classes. In addition, the trainees' effectiveness in using the techniques and the pupils' responses will need to be examined if trainees are going to understand the implications of their decisions.

If trainees are to focus on pupils' learning outcomes as well as themselves as teachers, subject mentors will need to structure their mentoring, taking into consideration the trainees' stage of development. Accepting that trainees' concerns about the self and task do take priority, subject mentors should still try and assist trainees to see pupils' learning outcomes as central to the complex and multi-faceted task of learning to teach. However, it is important that any assessment of such outcomes in trainees' lessons takes into consideration what can realistically be expected of trainees with their many other concerns.

### Coping with the Demands of the Course

This area of concern focused on trainees' own assignment demands, and the mental and physical stresses of the experiences. The former was related to actual course deadlines and the trainees' perceived value of the work within the context of the school experience, and the latter to the debilitating effect of the total experience.

For many trainees the time to hand in assignments was never the right time. One male trainee said, 'I'm worried about my "learning" essay to be handed in next week. I've still got lots of it to do on top of lesson planning', and a female trainee noted, 'Still the lack of hours in the day. Life is school at the moment with assignment dates getting nearer and nearer. There just seems a never ending pile of things to be done.' With regard to the usefulness of assignments, one male trainee openly challenged their value when he said, 'I find the assignments (2000–3000 words) that we are required to do, pointless. I don't see how writing a long essay is going to improve our teaching. I want more hands-on experience and more time devoted to planning, evaluation and resource-gathering.'

The tiredness expressed by trainees was a common concern throughout the year, and it was often an accumulation of the pressures of the 'long day' involving travelling, preparation, teaching, course demands, applying for posts and, sometimes, health problems. One female trainee noted, 'Getting up to travel on the 06.33 train is not conducive to an enjoyable teaching practice. Neither is my attitude towards lesson planning when I arrive home twelve hours later. I feel like a PGCE robot', and a male trainee said, 'Filling out applications forms is taking ages and it is proving very difficult to keep up with planning and evaluation. I'm shattered.' At times, more specific health problems were noted such as the male trainee who reported, 'I spent the majority of this week ill in bed. This bothered me more than normal due to my report being written this week. I feel like they might think I am on the skive.'

*Mentoring implications*

The concerns related to assignments are perhaps wider than the remit of subject mentors. Assignments are set for general educational issues as well as specifically for the subjects and, therefore, the preparation and presentation of assignments need to be co-ordinated for the training year in order that the demands are well-spread. In addition, if data can be collected from actual school experiences, the relationship with theory can be examined in a more realistic way.

Although the mental and physical stresses of the experience will vary from trainee to trainee and according to their own situation, subject mentors will need to monitor the trainees and help them to pace themselves over a strenuous period.

### Dealing with the School and University Personnel and the School's Working Arrangements

Many trainees noted their concern when conflicts arose between themselves and either subject mentors, other school staff, university tutors or peers, and when subject mentors and university staff did not fulfil their obligations. A further worry was when they perceived a conflict between the demands of the school and those of the university.

Conflicts that arose between trainees and persons in authority were particularly worrying for trainees as they were always very aware that such persons would be involved in the compilation of their final report and decisions on their competence as teachers. One male trainee was, 'Very dismayed at mentor's attitude. This week has confirmed my concern of last week in that he put down his personal feelings against me as a bias on my ROA', and one female trainee, commenting on another physical education teacher, said,

> The female PE teacher (not my mentor) has made it quite obvious that she doesn't like students and has made life extremely difficult. At the start of a tennis lesson, when I asked her whether I would be taking the inside or outside group, she replied in a bitchy, nasty tone that I should know exactly what I was doing and should buck up my ****ing ideas. She ignored me for the following few days. Other staff told me later that she had cursed me behind closed doors.

On another occasion a female trainee reported, 'I had an unpleasant episode with my tutor. I disagreed with what he was saying, and it all got out of control.'

With peer conflicts the main concern was that trainees did not feel that they could work with their partners' methods. For instance, one female trainee, discussing her male partner, said, 'Me and my partner cannot work together. We clash to say the least. We get on socially but team teaching of a lesson does not work for us', and a male trainee commenting on his male partner said, 'Not very keen on team-teaching — get on well personally but our teaching methods differ. I feel like I'm treading on his toes and I like to do things my way.'

Failure of subject mentors and university tutors to carry out their expected duties was a frequent concern among trainees. For example, one female trainee said, 'Concerned about support from my mentor, has only observed for one lesson in four weeks. Little time to discuss problems', and a male trainee noted, 'My tutor came in for the second time this week — the last week of the practice — what is the point in coming now, it seems pointless to me.'

Sometimes trainees felt that they were in a vulnerable position when there was a clash between the expectations of school and university staff. At times trainees felt that school staff were not giving them the opportunities to follow ideas presented to them by university staff and that they were being expected to follow the rather rigid guidelines of the school system. For example, one male trainee noted, 'I have made my lessons in gymnastics progressive, for example, in vaulting — doing landings, take-offs, using mats and benches, then, when they are happy, trying to help them become accustomed to the box — vaulting around box etc. Comments/feedback have been to get them on the box vaulting and practising as soon as possible. Totally against what I've been advised!' and another male trainee said, 'Keeping mentor and his idea of lesson content and the university's idea of what to include (i.e. strict NC) together is difficult.'

## Mentoring implications

Trainees perceive conflicts as threatening to their development as teachers. Therefore, it is important that subject mentors, with the help of other staff, ensure that such clashes are preempted or they are dealt with in ways that do not inhibit trainees' progress. Although it is almost inevitable that both personal and work conflicts arise, the onus must be on the person in authority to ensure that such conflicts do not overshadow the focus on learning to teach. Whether such conflicts are dealt with on a personal basis or whether a third party is brought in to defuse the situation, it is unlikely that the trainees will feel confident enough or in a position to initiate such discussions. It is more likely that trainees will keep quiet about their feelings and comply reluctantly in order to 'pass' their teaching.

## Summary

Trainees' concerns are many, and subject mentors must be aware that such concerns go beyond those immediately surrounding the teaching event. Therefore, subject mentors will need to allay these wider concerns while at the same time focusing their attention on how trainees learn to teach.

Learning to teach is not something that is passed on by building up a 'bank' of experiences, it is about deliberately helping trainees understand the rationale behind decisions made in physical education settings. For this to happen, structured opportunities will have to be offered to trainees and time will have to be made available to reflect upon the outcomes of such experiences.

If mentors are going to have an impact on the trainees' development they will not only need an understanding of trainees' concerns, but they will need time during the school day to deal with those concerns. The future of partnership schemes may depend upon the effectiveness of the school mentors and, therefore, more thought must be given to their training and the school support structures.

## References

BEHETS, D. (1990) 'Concerns of pre-service physical education teachers', *Journal of Teaching in Physical Education*, **10**, 1, pp. 66–75.

BOGGESS, T.E., McBRIDE, R., and GRIFFEY, D.C. (1985) 'The concerns of physical education student teachers: A developmental view', *Journal of Teaching in Physical Education*, **4**, 3, pp. 202–11.

BOOTH, M. (1993) 'The effectiveness and role of the mentor in school: The students' view', *Cambridge Journal of Education*, **23**, 2, pp. 185–97.

CALDERHEAD, J. (1987) 'The quality of reflection in student teachers' professional learning', *European Journal of Teacher Education*, **10**, 3, pp. 269–78.

COPELAND, W.D., (1981) 'Clinical experiences in the education of teachers', *Journal of Education for Teaching*, **7**, 1, pp. 3–16.

DARST, P.W., ZAKRAJSEK, D.B. and MANCINI, V.H. (1989) *Analyzing Physical Education and Sport Instruction*, Champaign, IL, Human Kinetics.

DEPARTMENT FOR EDUCATION (1992) *Initial Teacher Training (Secondary Phase)* (Circular 9/92), London, DFE.

FULLER, F. (1969) 'Concerns of teachers: A developmental conceptualization', *American Educational Research Journal*, **6**, 2, pp. 207–26.

FULLER, F. and BORICH, G. (1974) *Teacher Concerns Checklist: An Instrument for Measuring Concerns for Self, Task and Impact*, Austin, TX, University of Texas, R and D Center for Teacher Education.

FULLER, F.F. and BOWN, O.H. (1975) 'Becoming a teacher' in RYAN K. (Ed) *Teacher Education: The Seventy-fourth Yearbook of the National Society for the Study of Education*, Chicago, IL, University of Chicago.

FUNG, L. (1993) 'Concerns among pre- and in-service physical educators', *Physical Education Review*, **16**, 1, pp. 27–30.

FURLONG, J. and MAYNARD, T. (1995) *Mentoring Student Teachers*, London, Routledge.

Colin Hardy

GEORGE, A.A. (1978) *Measuring Self, Task and Impact Concerns: A Manual for Use of the Teacher Concerns Questionnaire*, Austin, TX, University of Texas, R and D Center for Teacher Education.

GRAHAM, G. (1992) *Teaching Children Physical Education: Becoming a Master Teacher*, Champaign, IL, Human Kinetics.

GUILLAUME, A. and RUDNEY, G. (1993) 'Student teachers' growth towards independence: An analysis of their changing concerns', *Teaching and Teacher Education*, **9**, 1, pp. 65–80.

HARDY, C.A. (1994) 'The concerns of two groups of physical education pre-service teachers during their teacher education year', *Bulletin of Physical Education*, **30**, 1, pp. 55–61.

HARDY, C.A. (1995) 'Types of teaching problems experienced by pre-service teachers during their predominantly school-based teaching year', *British Journal of Physical Education*, **26**, 4, pp. 21–4.

HARDY, C.A. (in press) 'Pre-service physical education teachers' help-seeking strategies', *Journal of Teacher Development*.

HOLSTI, O.R. (1969) *Content Analysis for the Social Sciences and Humanities*, London, Addison-Wesley.

KENNEDY, M.M. (1991) 'Some surprising findings on how teachers learn to teach', *Educational Leadership*, **49**, 3, pp. 14–17.

LIVINGSTON, C. and BORKO, H. (1989) 'Expert-novice differences in teaching: A cognitive analysis and implications for teacher education', *Journal of Teacher Education*, **40**, 4, pp. 36–42.

LORTIE, D.C. (1975) *Schoolteachers: A Sociological Study*, Chicago, IL, University of Chicago Press.

MCINTYRE, D., HAGGER, H. and BURN, K. (1994) *The Management of Student Teachers' Learning*, London, Kogan Page.

PELLETIER, J. and MARTEL, D. (1994) 'Problems PE student teachers encountered during initial teaching experiences', paper presented at the AIESEP World Congress, Berlin.

RINK, J. (1993) *Teaching physical education for learning* (2nd ed) St Louis, MO, Times Mirror/Mosby College.

SEBREN, A. (1995) 'Preservice teacher's orientations toward teaching: The transformation from teaching as control to teaching for learning', *Research Quarterly for Exercise and Sport*, **66**, March Supplement, A-68–A-69.

VEENMAN, S. (1984) 'Perceived problems of beginning teachers', *Review of Educational Research*, **54**, pp. 143–78.

WENDT, J.C., BAIN, L.L. and JACKSON, A.S. (1981) 'Fuller's concerns theory as tested on prospective physical educators', *Journal of Teaching in Physical Education, Introductory Issue*, pp. 66–70.

# 5  An Account of Laura's First Term on a School-based PGCE Course

*Emma Tait*

## First Encounters

During the first year of my research I attended the interviews of prospective candidates for a PGCE PE (Secondary) course with a view to choosing four that I could work with for the year. I wanted four postgraduates who would be willing and open enough to talk to and share with me, their experiences on the course. From my first encounter with Laura[1] I thought she would be ideal. When she had arrived for the interview she got out of the car with a man and a young child. I assumed she was married and had a child and was therefore not a 'typical' candidate straight from university. During the group interview Laura had demonstrated a willingness to speak her mind and I gained the impression that she was a confident, independent individual.

In September 1994 the PGCE course began and I had to approach those postgraduates that I wanted to work with. Laura had been offered and accepted a place on the course, and was prepared to participate in my research.

## The Course

The PGCE Secondary course that Laura embarked on came into existence in 1993. The course was developed in response to the Department for Education (DFE) Circular 9/92 (DFE, 1992) and was one of the first created in response to this Circular. It was planned jointly as a partnership programme by a college of higher education and a county association of headteachers, with the transfer of more responsibility to schools for the preparation and assessment of postgraduates.

Each postgraduate spends a period of twenty-five weeks out of thirty-six, in school. When they are not on a school placement they attend professional preparation and main subject lectures in college. During the first term they spend ten weeks in their 'parent school'. During the second term the postgraduate is in what is termed their 'twin school', for seven weeks. For the final term they return to their parent school for eight weeks. While they are on placement they attend a main or subsidiary subject lecture on a Thursday afternoon in college.

The course structure identifies a number of 'key' people that the post-graduates will work closely with throughout the year: the training manager (a senior member of school staff) takes responsibility for the postgraduate when they are in their school, and acts as a co-ordinator of professional development activities, provider of tutorial support and as an assessor of competencies; the subject mentor (a member of the subject department) is the person whom the postgraduate has the most contact with in school on a day-to-day basis, and is described in the college handbook as playing a key role in helping the postgraduate's progress; the subject co-ordinator (a college lecturer or teacher) takes responsibility for providing tutorial support and delivering the main subject pathway modules in the college and has no formal role within the schools.

## The Research Project

The aim of my project is to research the experiences of four PE postgraduates (two male and two female) and how they 'become' a PE teacher on this PGCE school-based course. In particular I want to gain an insight into the nature of their experiences, how they make sense of them in the situations they find themselves in, and the changes that they undergo in this process of 'becoming' a teacher. One way of gaining an insight into the postgraduate's perspectives is to adopt a phenomenological approach. Such a perspective perceives that the everyday experiences of individuals are a valid and fruitful source of knowledge (Husserl, 1952). Such was Husserl's conviction that he called for researchers to 'go back to things themselves'. Van Den Berg (1961) reinforcing the value of an individual's experiences, talks about life in terms of a 'layer' as opposed to 'layers', and it is in this one layer, that the 'depth' of life is found.

Phenomenologists therefore study phenomena, that is things or events, in the everyday lifeworld of the individual. It is argued that the best way to study and seek to understand the everyday events of the individual is to do so from the viewpoint of the experiencing person, thereby obtaining the insider perspective.

Having embraced this perspective my methodology took the form of working very closely with each of the postgraduates throughout the year, trying to walk in their world with them. I did as Becker (1992) advocates:

> The phenomenologically oriented researcher asks the expert of their
> life events, the people doing and experiencing them, to describe
> experiences from daily life. (p. 8)

I conducted regular in-depth, informal interviews with the postgraduates throughout the year, visiting them once a week in school to observe, read their files and diaries (if they kept one) and attended their PE lectures. Other key people involved in their professional development, such as training managers, subject co-ordinator and subject mentors, were also interviewed.

Having now spent a year working with the four postgraduates I have got to know them very well, acquiring what I refer to as a 'data mountain'. The data is vast, very rich and in-depth, enabling me to gain a privileged and enlightening insight into their experiences on the course and how they made sense of them. Such is the nature and extent of the data that it is only possible to share with you the experiences of one postgraduate, Laura, during her first term on the course. Despite only sharing her first term's experiences, it is hoped that the reader will gain an insight into the initial processes of Laura's 'becoming' and the role that her mentor played in this. As the researcher and author of this text I do not regret only being able to share such a small part of my research with you. Indeed the richness of the data is an asset that confirms the view of White (1975) that:

> Lives cannot be adequately understood unless they are described at considerable length. (p. 6)

This is not to say that what follows is purely a description of what happened or indeed even an exact representation of her experiences and how she perceived them. (It is arguable whether it is possible to present an exact representation of somebody else's experiences (Riessman, 1993)). Alternatively, the account is presented as a 'configurative narrative' (a term used by Polkington (1995)), whereby data elements are configured into a coherent developmental account. Just as individuals tell stories of their experiences that represent their interpretations and how they have made sense of reality, so I, as a researcher, having analyzed the data attempted to identify relationships within it, have sought to construct and compose a narrative, a story with a plot.

The use of such a rhetorical style does not present an 'author evacuated text', or reflect an 'interpretative omnipotent researcher'. The text is not a 'realist tale', that seeks to objectively represent what occurred (Vann Mannen, 1988; Sparkes, 1995). This configurative narrative is constructed and told by myself as the researcher who has been in the position of interviewing and observing Laura and the significant people that played a part in her experiences.

## First Encounters are not always What they Seem

It is now October 1995 and I have just spent a year with Laura seeking to explore her experiences on the PGCE PE course. Over the year I became what felt like a sheep, following Laura around where ever she went and was always there to see and hear what was going on. But it was more than a detached objective sensation that I experienced. I became Laura's shadow, I say shadow because during the course of the year we became friends and she played a significant part in my life. Indeed she was my life along with the three other postgraduates that I worked with for the year. It was a friendship that was reciprocated as Laura shared many sensitive feelings and emotions with me that only her family and close friends had access to.

As I look back over the year and consider Laura's experiences (and attempt to portray them from her perspective) in her process of 'becoming' a teacher, I realize that my first encounter and impressions of Laura created an image of her that is in stark contrast to the person that I came to know.

## Becoming

The epitome of Laura's 'becoming' is based not upon a young Welsh post-graduate parent who is confident, independent and sure of herself. Laura is in actual fact not married, has no children, although she does, however, have a boyfriend. The process of her 'becoming' is dominated by the desire to 'belong' and the never ending quest to find the answer to the personal question of 'what am I, am I really a teacher?'

## Belonging

The importance of belonging was apparent from the first time I spoke with Laura and asked her to share with me her life story. She began by telling me that she was one of eight children of a Welsh family, seven girls and one boy and that she had always lived with or near them in Wales until embarking on the PGCE course. Early on in the record I began to have a glimpse of the 'real' Laura as she perceived herself to be. As Laura recounted her life story, the foundations of her desire to belong were made apparent as she described friendships. Whether Laura was talking about school, the clerical job with the DVLC, college, or her work in an electronics factory, friends and the need to make them, were always a prominent feature.

During the year this necessity to make friends as a form of belonging, continued. However it began to take on a new dimension when she started the course. Making friends became an indication of being accepted by teachers and pupils and therefore gave her a sense of belonging to the school, and specifically to the department. I became intrigued with Laura's unfaltering desire to place such a strong emphasis on friends and asked her why they were so evidently important to her. Her reply represented the rationale for her past needs and also for their continuing fulfilment:

> Just nice to have them, someone to talk and rely on. I think my friends and family are like that. They are so important, otherwise you could become so lonely and so detached and in this inner world. That, I wouldn't like that. I've got to have people I can relate to. . . . I think it is just nice to talk to somebody, you can say things maybe that you

wouldn't to somebody else who wasn't your friend, you can be honest can't you.

Friends were a means of being accepted and gaining a sense of belonging. The friends that Laura made were those in the PE departments where she worked during the year, particularly those in her parent school. Who these people were and what they represented in the PE department was significant to Laura, for they were the teachers who would initiate her into the culture of teaching and, specifically the PE culture.

### What am I? Am I a Teacher?

Such means of belonging carried for Laura the status of being 'a teacher'. The search for such a status and its achievement was fundamental to her process of 'becoming'. When she began the course Laura described to me the teacher she wanted to be (her 'self as teacher') and this was based upon her own experiences at school and informed further by her experiences at college. Laura explained how she perceived her own experiences of PE at school to be dominated by a lack of opportunity to develop according to her individual needs, she experienced lessons devoid of enjoyment, and was always told what to do, without the how and why being taken into consideration. Thus her image of 'self as teacher' was based upon a contrast with what she perceived her school PE teacher to be like, one whom she described as 'a bad one':

> I want to be a good one. I know it sounds stupid but that's what I want to be. I used to know a bad PE teacher and I want to do more for people than she did for me . . . I want to give them the opportunity to develop out of school . . . Skills and making them enjoy it, making lessons fun. Give them the opportunity of enjoyment, but they enjoy my lessons and they are learning something from them, . . . They remember something and the next week when they come they can remember what we did the week before because they were interested the week before.

When Laura began the course she had created in her own mind an ideal image of the 'good PE teacher', and she was then faced with the daunting prospect of living up to that image. She described how she felt when faced with this situation:

> I felt as if I had to be someone in order to go there (school), it was like all questions, what do you do, like an interrogation and thinking can I really do this? I always had it on my mind, am I good enough to do this? I suppose it's just lack of confidence . . . It's the thought I

know I want to do it, but it's a case of not just wanting to do it, I want
to do it well.

This was how Laura felt when she began her PGCE course. The quest had
begun to achieve her ideal reality and become a 'good teacher'. But this process became a very turbulent and unsettling one which Laura struggled pain-
fully with for the whole year. The overriding issue to Laura was: 'what am I?
Am I a teacher?' From my first encounter with Laura once she began the
course, to the last time we spoke at the end, this preoccupation featured
regularly in our conversation, as the following example shows:

> *L:* Like I was saying to my mum last night: 'only another three weeks
> left and then it is another seven weeks teaching' and then my
> boyfriend said: 'yes and then she's a teacher' and I said: 'am I, am
> I really?' I thought I don't know, I said: 'I teach, but I don't know
> if I am a teacher . . . I don't know.' It is a frightening thought to
> think right you are going to do this and you are a teacher, then
> you are going to go out there and going to teach. I just think oh.
> *E:* What do you see yourself as then?
> *L:* I don't know.
> *E:* (we laugh) We have this conversation every time you know, what
> are you?
> *L:* I don't know, I think I am a teacher, but I don't know if I have
> got the confidence enough to say to myself, yes I am a teacher
> now and this is what I am going to teach.

Laura could be described in terms of being in what Turner (1974) suggests is
a 'liminal state'. That is:

> A period of ambiguity and paradox, a confusion of all the customary
> categories . . . betwixt and between. (p. 7)

Laura was in a liminal state, she was 'betwixt and between' leaving work at the
electronics factory because she wanted to be a teacher, and actually 'becoming' a teacher. Between these two points she did not know what she was.

These two images of Laura's 'becoming' took on different forms and new
dimensions throughout the year depending on her needs and the nature of the
process as she experienced it.

I will now illustrate this with an account of her first term on the course.
Particular attention is given to the subject mentor and the role she played
for Laura. The mentor's role in the process cannot be perceived as a pre-
determined, objective one. Rather it was defined through an interactive process (Blumer, 1969). Laura looked to the mentor to fulfil her needs and the
mentor created a role for herself that she perceived to be appropriate given
the situation.

## Term 1

My reading of Laura's data record gives an impression of her efforts to settle in and belong in the PE department in her parent school, the Coastal School. In an early entry in her diary she wrote:

> I immediately experienced a feeling of welcome. They totally accepted me as part of the group I felt, offering me coffee, chatting about previous students and also general information about the PE department itself. From the very beginning they expressed that they would like me to spend as much time as possible with them, as part of the department, even when I am not timetabled to do so.

The welcoming impression that the members of the department created and the desire they expressed that Laura become part of the department, instantly signalled to her that she was in an environment where her need to belong might be fulfilled.

The department that Laura wanted to belong to is part of a large, rural, coeducational, comprehensive school. The PE department is located in a separate building, apart from the main school site. The department consists of four full-time members of staff, two male and two female. Pete and Simon have been teaching for over fifteen years as has Jessica who is the head of the department and the designated subject mentor. Clare is a relatively young teacher in comparison, in her third year of teaching. The department has what can be described as a very traditional games-centred PE curriculum.

During the first three weeks of her placement in the Coastal School, Laura was supposed to concentrate on observing pupils in their lessons and thinking about how children learn. Laura worked on this task but always in the context of her own lifeworld (Schutz and Luckmann, 1974). Rather than concentrating on the pupils, Laura focussed on the process of belonging to the department and being identified as a teacher both by the other members of the department and by the pupils.

Initially this search for belonging took the form of drinking coffee and chatting with Jessica (her subject mentor) and Clare in the office, accepting the acknowledgment from them that they were there to help her.

During this period the sense of belonging came to have more depth and meaning as the teachers she interacted with began to involve her in the activities of teaching, and referred to her as 'a teacher' and 'member of staff', to the pupils. Laura recounted to me in detail the first time she was involved in actually working with a group of pupils and the impact it had on her. The episode referred to occurred during a year 7 netball lesson her mentor was taking when she herself was observing:

> It was at this point that I really felt like a teacher and that's what the children also perceived me as and this really gave my confidence a boost, being accepted by the children as a member of staff.

This feeling of being like a teacher, was increased when the other teachers, particularly Jessica, shared with her their department routines and expressed a desire that she should replicate them. Examples included: registering the pupils, bringing them into the changing rooms, collecting valuables, being available for extra curricular activities:

> All of these are important aspects of departmental policies which need to be followed, so that all rules are carried out by all members of staff, especially for myself coming into the department as a new member of staff.

Such tasks illustrate elements of the process by which Laura came to belong to the department as a person and as a teacher, a status that was created by herself, other teachers and the pupils.

Jessica arranged Laura's timetable and said that she and Laura would meet together each week to discuss lesson observations, lessons she had been involved in, and her lesson planning.

It was during this time that Laura began to expand her definition and redefine her 'self as teacher'. Although she visualised an ideal image that she had created by the time she began the course, she did acknowledge openly that it was not a rigid one. Rather, it was an image that was based upon her 'present-past', that is, the past as it appeared within the present moment and is influenced by it (*ibid*, p. 38) and was flexible and therefore likely to develop and change when she went into school and worked with other PE teachers:

> I want to be as good as I can but hopefully I want to learn from the teacher who is there as well, stand me in good stead really, observe and see what I can do with them.

During the period of observation Laura observed the four members of the department. Although Laura had said that she wanted to learn from them, they did not become role models whom she would copy. As stated, Laura already had a conception of the teacher she wanted to be and it was this that she used as a reference point, a 'lens' (Knowles, 1992) through which to interpret her observations. However, Laura did share with me elements of the observations of the other teachers, that were significant to her and helped her to continually redefine and develop elements of her conception. With regard to Jessica as a teacher Laura noted:

> She is so lively, a lively teacher. It is good to see a lively teacher . . . she has so much knowledge.

After observing a hockey lesson Clare had taught, Laura commented about the way the teacher had involved the pupils for demonstrating:

I found that a good way of doing it, I had never thought of doing anything like that, I thought I had to do it all myself.

Laura noted the teaching style both Jessica and Pete adopted in their lessons. She noted that there was a lot of interaction between the teacher and pupil, that the teachers evaluated the pupils knowledge, consolidating and building on it during the lessons. Laura commented on the various methods of differentiation that Pete and Simon used in their swimming lessons.

On a number of occasions Laura wrote in her diary after observing lessons:

Would I do it this way if I were teaching?

I found this a good point to start the lesson on and was impressed by it, it stood out in my mind clearly and thought that I would myself use such an approach when I start teaching if it is entirely possible.

Laura explained to me the means by which she made sense of the situations she was in:

By looking at other teachers and if you like their style, maybe that is the way I want to teach, so I'll take something from there . . . pick up something else from there, or like the way they do . . . I mean you don't like everything they do but, you know it does give you ideas on what you do believe.

Laura explained that during the period she was observing lessons, the teacher would take the time (either before or after the lesson) to point out particular aspects of the lesson. For example, Laura wrote in her diary that Jessica had told her about the structure[2] that each lesson should have:

Warm up, skills and progressions, small practices and a game at the end using the skills learned, if that was entirely possible.

Laura recalled how Clare had told her:

Encourage pupils, sit them down, tell them what you want them to do, don't be afraid to repeat your instructions because some of them may not have got a grasp of it the first time.

On another occasion Jessica shared with Laura how the mood of the teacher could affect the pupils and that if possible the teacher should not 'take it out on the pupils' if they were having a bad day.

As well as the teachers explaining to Laura what they were doing, Laura also took the opportunity to discuss some of her observations with her mentor on an informal basis. On one particular occasion Laura told me how she had discussed the apparent contrast in teaching style between Pete and Simon. Jessica replied that it had been a conscious decision on her behalf to ensure that she observed both of them teaching:

> I thought you would notice the difference. I mean you would notice it, that was one reason why I put you in with them . . . I wasn't going to tell you, but I was hoping you would come back.

The discoveries that Laura was making about teaching were consistent with her view of how she thought she was going to learn on the course:

> You only learn from experience. You don't learn from sitting down in a classroom and people telling you 'well this is the way you teach, like this'. Observing different teachers, as they have all got different styles, but I think it is much better.

After half-term in her first term, Laura began teaching on her own but arrangements for this were occasionally confusing. Jessica once asked Laura to prepare a warm up for a lesson, which she eagerly did. However, some days later when the time arrived for the lesson to take place, Jessica taught the whole lesson herself and Laura only observed. Laura, making no mention of this incident arranged with her to take the warm up for a lesson the following day. Jessica consented and the event passed as planned. At the same time Laura took the initiative and arranged with other teachers when she would teach their lessons.

Laura talked about how she looked forward to teaching lessons, but at the same time how time consuming she found the planning to be. She frequently found herself working very late at night. When I enquired why it took her so long, two reasons were given: that the department had no comprehensive schemes of work[3] which she could refer to and therefore she had to work out the structure and progressions of lesson content for herself; and secondly, that her subject knowledge was such that she had to work hard to remedy her deficiencies.[4]

Laura taught a number of lessons as planned. After the lesson she always received some form of verbal feedback. This usually occurred at the end of the lesson as Laura and the teacher walked back to the PE office, at break or lunchtime. One exception was when Jessica wrote a sheet out after a lesson and gave it to her. The weekly sessions that Jessica said they would have did not take place. Despite this Laura spoke of the value of even just being observed and offered any kind of feedback:

> There are important things you wouldn't think of yourself if there wasn't somebody watching and I think that is nice to know . . . She always says something, which is good.

I was keen to hear more from Laura about the nature of the feedback that she received and enquired further. She informed me that it was usually concerned with her use of voice and the need to project it, showing more confidence, giving feedback, giving clear instructions and using pupils for demonstrations.

The peak of Laura's experiences, particularly in relation to the very personal issue of her belonging, occurred one Friday lunchtime towards the end of the first term, when she was in the pub with all the members of the department. The next week in her PE lecture, the first words Laura literally blurted out in a frenzied moment of excitement were:

> Jessica said 'I was born to be a teacher, nothing to worry about. I don't think you have got any problem with being a teacher, you have got all the potential, now we just need to work on the content, you are doing really well.

By this point in time, Laura felt she belonged, she had become part of the department and had developed an affiliation with the school. The extent of this feeling is illustrated when she talked about her leaving:

> I was gutted when I left, really, really gutted. I just enjoyed myself so much there. I had become friends with the department . . . you build things up with the kids and you go.

The use of the phrase 'I had become friends with the department' characterizes this particular emphasis in Laura's self-perception. Their relationship was dominated by Laura's need to belong and Jessica enabled this to occur. Laura stated:

> We became friendlier more than anything, it was more on a friendship bases, although she told me exactly what she thought and she was very straight, but friendly and that was nice because I could talk to her more . . . like her family and I found out everything about her family and she found out everything about mine and going shopping and things like that. And I think that is really nice, because you can relate to somebody then, it is not just on a professional level, it is like a friendly level.

From Laura's perspective, as well as being a friend, Jessica also became a critical friend:

> They can still tell me if I am doing something wrong and that won't bother me and it used to really bother me, upset me in the beginning . . . but in the end you have got to be told to enable you to do something about it. But I find that quite difficult, being told I have done something wrong, I suppose everybody does.

Having Jessica as her critical friend was significant to Laura in her 'becoming' a teacher, as it gave her a sense of security. The fact that someone in the department was actually designated her mentor was important:

> It's nice to think there is someone there who can help you if you need it definitely, and relieve the pressure.

Laura's overwhelming sense of belonging to the department and school, was unmistakably apparent when I spoke to her at the very end of the first term. However, despite her newly acquired status of being 'a teacher', the following conversation still occurred:

> *E:* Do you feel like a teacher?
> *L:* (pause) I do yes, sometimes.
> *E:* Only sometimes?
> *L:* Yeah.
> *E:* What are you when you are not a teacher?
> *L:* They always introduce me as a teacher, but I often think am I really a teacher and do I really teach, you know?

It appears now that being 'a teacher' to Laura involves more than belonging, acceptance and initiation. Laura disclosed that in order for her to actually be a teacher she must teach the pupils something:

> Just looking back you know, just asking yourself all the time, did you really teach them anything.

The dilemma facing Laura was the fact that yes, she had been the pupils' teacher for PE lessons and had acted as all the other teachers did, but she did not know whether she was actually teaching them anything or not. Laura attributed this uncertainty to what she felt to be her lack of subject knowledge. She sought to obtain the knowledge she needed from various sources including books, lesson observations and the PE lectures on a Thursday evening at college. But even though Laura had obtained some knowledge, she was frustrated further because she was unsure of how to 'break it down' and how much she 'should expect and assume pupils should know'. Laura explained how she tested her knowledge and the appropriateness of it in the lessons she taught, by 'trial and error'. Even though she received technical feedback from her mentor and others in the department, often to the effect that 'yes that was fine', Laura was still left with this feeling of uncertainty.

The complexity of Laura's reasoning became increasingly apparent to me. As she talked she classified some of the sources of knowledge about PE into different types. She did this by comparing the school and college as sources and the different types of knowledge she perceived, were apparent in each:

School . . . well they just give me information as to what I should be teaching. Whereas Thomas gives you ideas on how to teach you know.

Being in school signified for Laura as the place where she would learn to teach and as already stated that she could only 'learn by doing'. Despite the unfaltering maintenance of this view throughout the year, Laura talked about the Thursday evening PE lectures (which sought to contextualize their experiences by considering conceptual issues underpinning PE) in a way that demonstrated the significant part they played in her experiences. The lectures were perceived as valuable and represented a part in the course when she felt she learnt a lot:

I think they are very important, I wish they could be all day Thursday though. I do think it needs to be on all day sessions because we don't get enough of it anyway.

I asked Laura why she said the lectures were so important. She replied:

Gets you thinking of what you think an effective teacher might be. He gives you ideas really, to be able to think about your teaching, a basis to work from.

As the conversation continued it became clear that the lectures were deemed important and valuable because they gave access to knowledge and a type of knowledge that wasn't the same as that given at school. I asked Laura whether the things they talked about in lectures were talked about at school. I was interested to hear from Laura what she thought about the situation and how she would verbalize her thoughts. She replied:

Sometimes he talks about things and you think Thomas, you are not in the real world, because it is not happening where I am and where any one else is. So I think that is a difficulty. But in some respects it is reinforcing what you do in school, at least it gives you an idea of what you should be doing in school.

Laura's response shows an awareness of the intense nature of teachers' work, that is, the day-to-day running of the department, teaching lesson after lesson, arranging extra curricular activities, and teaching GCSE PE. The teachers that she had been working with did not necessarily have the time to consider in depth, the conceptual issues that Thomas discussed with the postgraduates in the PE lectures.

After revealing the complexity of her reasoning Laura ended her first term with the following thought about herself:

I wouldn't describe myself as a teacher. I often said, like I was saying to Clare, I can't believe it, I have got a week to go and I will have done my first term of teaching, am I really becoming a teacher you know. You stand back and look and think am I really?

## Conclusion

The aim of this chapter has been to give an insight into the lifeworld of Laura during the first term of a PGCE school-based course. The initial processes described illustrate that 'becoming' a PE teacher is an individual, unique experience, with biography, course content and school context all playing a significant part.

Within the course structure the subject mentor is identified as a key person with whom the postgraduate has the most day-to-day contact whilst in school. Clearly, in Laura's experiences it was a very significant relationship. Despite the importance of the mentoring role within the partnership scheme, it is what can be described as a 'neglected' role when looking through the course handbook description of roles. The training manager and subject co-ordinator are all identified and their roles and responsibilities clearly outlined. The subject mentor is described as 'playing a key role in helping the postgraduates' progress', but what this exactly means, is not made apparent. Subject mentor meetings were held once a term throughout the year which took the form of a forum for discussion of issues and concerns. Jessica attended one of these but liaised very little with the training manager in the school.[5] Consequently, the role that Jessica adopted was the one that she defined herself, and that she had developed through her interactions with Laura.

Despite the radical change in the course structure of the PGCE compared to the four-year BEd, the mentoring role that Jessica had adopted as a friend and a critical friend, was not very different from the way she had supported other student teachers on the BEd course in previous years. Her perceived role as mentor illustrates the taken for granted nature of teachers' thinking, that is, teaching utilizing a set of implicit assumptions about how to teach which are contained in their stock of recipe knowledge which they have accumulated over their years of being a teacher. This is demonstrated in the way that Jessica and the other teachers shared their teaching routines and approaches to interacting with pupils, with Laura. Their routines took the form of 'recipes' (Schutz and Luckmann, 1974) of teaching that they have tried and tested and therefore know them to be reliable methods of teaching. Recipes have become automated and standardized. Schutz and Luckmann (*ibid*) suggest that the determining characteristic of a routine is that:

It can be performed without it coming to one's attention . . . Routine is continually ready to be grasped without coming into the distinct grasp of consciousness. (p. 109)

Because their teaching and talk about teaching was manifested in the form of 'recipes', Laura only had access to this level and the reasoning and understanding underpinning it was not made explicit.

The nature of the feedback that Laura received from the teachers in the PE department can also be explained in the above terms. The technical orientation of the feedback she received reflected the taken for granted, 'recipe' nature of their work that is dominated by the pragmatic, the here and now. Such a scenario is exacerbated by the intensity of the teachers' day to day work in school of timetabled lessons, extra curricular activities, creating and maintaining status as a department and responding to government reforms, to name but a few. Such was the nature of teachers' work at the Coastal School that they did not talk about the conceptual issues that Laura considered and reflected upon at college.

Having provided an insight into the experiences of one postgraduate, it is hoped that a number of the issues raised may have implications for the training of mentors in physical education. It is clear that although fulfilling the postgraduate's immediate needs is important, mentors need to look beyond these and gain an understanding of how individuals learn to teach (Furlong and Maynard, 1995). This research has highlighted the significant role that biography, school context and course content play in the postgraduates' 'becoming' PE teachers. Having gained a greater understanding of the process of learning to teach, mentors can more effectively facilitate learning. This will involve mentors challenging experiences, developing ideas, transforming knowledge, encouraging critical reflection with regards to pedagogy and conceptual issues, to name but a few of necessary mentoring skills.

Initial teacher education is undergoing a period of great change and roles and responsibilities are being redefined. In particular the role of the teacher as a mentor, is changing. In order for mentoring to be effective roles must be clearly defined rather than being left to chance. Mentors on school-based courses are being asked to perform a very different role to that which they may have done previously. At the same time as redefining roles through training and understanding, it is fundamentally important that those planning school-based training courses in physical education take into consideration the context and time consuming nature of teachers' work in schools.

### Notes

1  All the names used in this account are pseudonyms.
2  During the course of the year Laura began to challenge this structure and tried out alternatives in her lessons.
3  Laura was told by the head of the department that the schemes of work were being rewritten.
4  This was despite the fact that she had completed a Human Movement Studies degree. This situation demonstrates the need as Nutt (1995) suggests, for undergraduate

programmes to be sensitive to the 'professional needs of intending PE teachers' (p. 6).

5 In a mentors' meeting held in the summer of 1995, the issue of roles and responsibilities was discussed in great detail. Thus the emphasis on the need to train mentors has been recognized and they are now working collaboratively with other key people in the partnership scheme.

## References

BECKER, C.S. (1992) *Living and Rethinking: An Introduction to Phenomenology*, London, Sage.

BLUMER, H. (1969) *Symbolic Interactionism: Perspectives and Method*, Englewood Cliffs, NJ, Prentice Hall Inc.

DEF (1992) *Initial Teacher Training* (Secondary Phase) (Circular 9/92) London, HMSO.

DODDS, P. (1989) 'Trainees, field experience, and socialisation into teaching', in TEMPLIN, T.J. and SCHEMPP, P.G. (Eds) *Socialisation into Physical Education: Learning to Teach*, Indianapolis, Benchmark Press, pp. 81–101.

FURLONG, J. and MAYNARD, T. (1995) *Mentoring Student Teachers*, London, Routledge.

HUSSERL, E. (1952) *Phanomenologische Untersuchungen Zur Kanstitution*, The Hague, Nijhoff.

KNOWLES, G. (1992) 'Models for understanding preservice and beginning teachers' biographies: Illustrations from case studies', in GOODSON, I. (Ed) *Studying Teachers' Lives*, London, Routledge, pp. 99–152.

NUTT, G. (1995) 'Physical Education at a Crossroads?: Weighing Up the Way Forwards'. Paper Presented at Cheltenham and Gloucester College of Higher Education.

POLKINGTON, D. (1995) 'Narrative configuration in qualitative analysis', in HATCH, J. AMOS and WISNIEWSKI, R. (Eds) *Life history and Narrative*, London, Falmer Press, pp. 5–23.

RIESSMAN, C.K. (1993) *Narrative Analysis*, London, Sage Publications.

SCHUTZ, A. and LUCKMANN, T. (1974) *The Structures of the Lifeworld*, London, Heinmann Educational Books Ltd.

SPARKES, A. (1995) 'Writing people: Reflections of the dual crises of representation and legitimation in qualitative inquiry', *Quest*, **47**, 2, pp. 158–195.

TURNER, V.J. (1974) *Dramas, Fields and Metaphors*, London, Cornell University Press.

VAN DE BURG, J.H. (1961) *The Changing Nature of Man*, New York, Norton.

VANN MANNEN, J. (1988) *Tales of the Field: On Writing Ethnography*, London, Routledge.

WHITE, R.W. (1975) *Lives in Progress*, New York, Holt, Rinehart & Winston Inc.

# 6 Learning to Teach Physical Education in the Primary School

*Mick Mawer*

## Introduction

Both Maynard and Furlong and Booth have put forward the view that before one can begin to plan the school-based experience of trainee teachers, and consider the role of mentors within that process, then one ought to:

> . . . begin with the trainees' perpective. . . . (Maynard and Furlong, 1993, p. 71)

— and:

> . . . reconsider ITT in the light of the experiences students receive in schools. (Booth, 1993, p. 193)

This chapter attempts to provide an insight into the school-based experiences of primary trainees as far as the teaching of physical education (PE) is concerned, with a view to raising a number of issues that might enable both 'partners' in the teacher training process (school and higher education institution) to develop initial training courses in PE that will provide the primary generalist trainee teacher with the knowledge, experiences and support to enable them to feel confident about the teaching of PE as a newly-qualified teacher (NQT).

Little is known about the school-based experiences of primary trainee teachers in the UK as far as the teaching of PE is concerned, nor have primary trainees or NQTs been asked their opinions concerning their training needs, or their views of the quality of the training and support they have received in preparing them to teach PE. In order to remedy this situation in some way, this chapter draws upon the results of a preliminary small-scale study of primary generalist trainees during their PGCE (Postgraduate Certificate in Education) year in one higher education institution (HEI).

*Mick Mawer*

### The Study

The study was conducted in three phases. In the first phase the complete cohort of fifty primary generalist trainees from one HEI completed questionnaires at the end of their first period of school placement.

The second phase of the study entailed a sample of twenty trainees being asked to complete a 'log' of their experiences during the second and final period of school placement, and at the end of this period the same twenty trainees were interviewed about their experiences using a semi-structured interview schedule.

The third phase involved the same twenty trainees being sent a short questionnaire towards the end of their first term of teaching as NQTs.

The sample of twenty trainees interviewed included fifteen females and five males, eleven of them being between 21 and 29 years of age and nine between the ages of 30–48. Six were on final school placement in a rural school, nine in an inner city school, and five in a suburban school.

The study attempted to investigate the following aspects of learning to teach PE in the primary school:

- trainees' background and pre-practice concerns;
- the training context;
- opportunities to learn to teach PE;
- influences on trainees' planning and practical teaching;
- difficulties experienced and training needs;
- trainees' experiences and views of the mentoring process;
- trainees' confidence to teach PE;
- experiences, difficulties and support received as NQTs.

### Trainees' Background and Pre-practice Concerns

When asked, 'What were your feelings about having to teach PE when you started the PGCE course?', half of the twenty trainees interviewed stated that they were 'looking forward to it'. The majority were active participants in some form of physical activity themselves, or had been so until recently, and they either enjoyed sport and physical activity or appreciated the importance of the subject for the overall development of the child. Typical of such comments included:

> I enjoy sport — children need to do something different that they enjoy — they need exercise.

> It is an important area of the curriculum for health reasons and for the whole development of the child.

However, seven of the trainees were 'apprehensive' about teaching PE, and the remainder simply saw teaching PE as 'part of the job'. This half of the sample were less enthusiastic about teaching PE because of a lack of knowledge, lack of experience, lack of sporting prowess, or were worried about control, safety, and the organization and management of groups. As two trainees mentioned:

> I was never really enthusiastic about it (PE) at school — and knew very little about it.

> I lack knowledge and understanding of PE so don't feel particularly well qualified to teach it. I wasn't particularly enthusiastic about it at school.

The full cohort of fifty trainees were asked whether they had any concerns about teaching PE prior to starting their first period of school placement. The most frequently mentioned issues related to (with percentage of trainees mentioning the issue in brackets):

- safety — particularly with large apparatus (50 per cent);
- organization and management of pupils and equipment (46 per cent);
- lack of knowledge — particularly in dance and gymnastics (36.5 per cent);
- control and discipline (23 per cent).

Other less frequently mentioned issues of concern related to planning lessons, teaching skills (for example, ability to demonstrate, voice projection), and assessment.

When the fifty trainees were asked 'in what way were these concerns different to your more general concerns about starting to teach?', a number of interesting points were made by the group:

> Organization of bodies in an open space is very different to a normal classroom environment and presents new problems.

> This is an area in which mistakes cannot be made in schools.

> The nature of PE makes the management of movement, noise, safety, very difficult.

> Childrens' attitudes change when faced with a PE lesson — there is a high level of excitement which is very different to the situation in the classroom.

A number of trainees was noticeably apprehensive about working with the children in a larger, less confined space, and in several cases were worried that the children 'might run away', and they would have difficulty controlling them.

Trainees concerns didn't seem to change a great deal prior to the second period of school placement. Of the twenty trainees interviewed twelve were still concerned about issues related to the organization and management of pupils and equipment, ten had concerns about their lack of knowledge, eight still had safety concerns, and five were worried about control and discipline. However, three-quarters of the group felt that they had alleviated these concerns by the end of the second period of placement, although four of these trainees stated that this had been done by their own initiative and efforts.

As so many trainees had been concerned about safety issues prior to both periods of placement it is a pity that only six of them (30 per cent) had been informed by the school of safety issues concerning PE, and only half of them had been given a 'tour' of the school PE facilities and equipment.

## The Training Context

The school in which trainees are placed may be considered to be the 'context' in which they learn to teach. Stephenson and Sampson (1994) have suggested that there may be 'a range of conditions that affect the effectiveness of mentorship' (p. 187) within a primary school, including the interest and involvement of the headteacher, and the culture of collaboration and professional debate amongst the staff. Similarly, there may be a variety of issues and conditions existing within the placement school that might help or hinder the trainee's professional training to teach PE, and influence their perceptions of the importance of PE within the school curriculum. The twenty trainees interviewed were asked what they thought of the teaching of PE at their placement school, whether they thought the head and staff had a positive attitude towards PE, whether they had been encouraged to teach PE or get involved with extra-curricular PE activities, and what qualities they felt a school should have to make the PE teaching experience of trainees successful.

The most frequently mentioned qualities that trainees would look for in a school related to the staff of the school. The majority (70 per cent) wanted staff to be 'enthusiastic and positive about the teaching of PE', and the head to be 'keen on PE and sport'. Most trainees (80 per cent) in fact thought that their school headteacher was keen on PE and sport. However, in most cases this perception had arisen from such observations as: 'she presented sporting certificates in assembly', or 'he took the school rugby team'. Also, over half (65 per cent) of the trainees thought that 'most' or 'all' of the staff in their school were positive about the teaching of PE, but most of the remainder (30 per cent) felt that 'not many' of the staff were positive about the subject.

Other qualities of a good school for learning to teach PE that were mentioned included that the school would 'see PE and sport as a high priority', it would have a 'good extra-curricular programme' with 'staff willing to be involved', and such a school might have a 'whole school approach to health and fitness'. However, trainees' impressions of the teaching of PE at their placement school varied considerably. These included such 'negative' impressions as:

... a lot of teachers didn't know what they were doing.

Teachers avoided teaching PE.

PE not seen as a priority in the school — hall was given up frequently for other things.

Boring — same old thing, staff would get out of it if they could.

— and positive impressions such as:

Good — the school did stick to a programme and the four-year scheme for PE was seen as important.

Good Curriculum Leader for PE — PE was excellent.

Also, for 70 per cent of the classes taught by trainees, PE was only taught twice a week, with games being by far the most popular activity.

Seven of the group (35 per cent) also felt it was important for schools to have PE schemes of work for trainees to see, and four mentioned the importance of there being a school policy for PE. Several trainees felt that being introduced to the Curriculum Co-ordinator for PE (CCPE), and being shown the school PE equipment and facilities, were essential issues to consider when introducing a trainee to the teaching of PE at a school. Yet three-quarters of the twenty trainees were not shown a scheme of work for PE, and half were not given a 'tour' of the PE facilities and equipment.

Student teachers wanted to feel 'part of the school', and see teachers 'working as a team to support each other'. Such a situation was described by one trainee:

Staff were always supporting each other with ideas for PE — I always felt part of the staff — there was a good ethos.

This issue was also mentioned by Stephenson (1995):

Where teachers are able to talk and debate current educational issues amongst themselves then this is likely to create an atmosphere in which the student can learn (p. 6)

Therefore, a positive context for learning to teach PE can be very important for a student teacher's professional development, but it can also influence a trainee's attitude towards teaching the subject. However, a positive context must also entail encouraging the trainee to practise teaching PE, and providing the opportunities for that practice to take place.

## Opportunities to Learn to Teach PE

Over three-quarters (80 per cent) of the twenty trainees interviewed in this study were 'encouraged' to teach PE when on school placement, but only four of them were encouraged to get involved with extra-curricular PE activities.

In terms of having the opportunity to practise the teaching of PE to full classes the experiences of the full sample of fifty trainees on their first placement varied considerably. Three of them had no opportunity to teach PE at all, twenty-one (42 per cent) did not teach games, twenty-five (50 per cent) did not teach gymnastics, and twenty (40 per cent) did not teach dance. The bulk of the university PE method course prior to the first period of school placement had been spent on these activities, yet many trainees did not have the immediate opportunity to practise teaching them. Just over half of the trainees (52 per cent) did have the opportunity to teach PE on six or more occasions, which is about one lesson or more a week, and the remainder taught five lessons or less during the teaching practice. Of the twenty trainees interviewed after their final school placement, half of them taught over thirteen lessons during the six full weeks of practice, and 25 per cent taught less than nine lessons. Of particular concern was the fact that six of the twenty trainees had not taught a dance lesson, and five had not taught a gymnastic lesson during the whole of the PGCE year. Over half (55 per cent) of them had taught two lessons or less of gym and dance during the year, in fact, the majority of the lessons taught by trainees had been games. Also, when one examines trainees' experiences of being involved in all aspects of the school PE curriculum, only two trainees had experienced a school residential, only six had experience of teaching outdoor and adventurous activities, and only five had the opportunity to observe the school procedures for taking the children swimming. In one case the opportunity to teach all aspects of PE were limited because the class teacher wanted to keep the teaching of a particular activity to himself. In other cases trainees 'lost' their PE lessons because the school hall was 'commandeered' by staff for other activities. One trainee had planned six dance lessons but she lost three of them because:

. . . the headteacher went in the hall when I was supposed to be there!

Another trainee commented that her main difficulty with the teaching of PE was that:

... little importance was placed on the twice weekly PE sessions, which were frequently missed in order for other sessions to take place.

Trainees themselves are often to blame for their lack of width of experience of teaching PE. If their mentor asks them whether they 'would like to do some PE?', and if so, 'what aspect would you like to teach?', some trainees are tempted to avoid an area of activity that they are concerned about:

I chose dance as my PE activity as I would have been concerned about teaching apparatus work for safety reasons.

Therefore, the opportunities for trainees to practise teaching all aspects of the school PE curriculum may vary considerably, and they may consequently begin their teaching career with a level of confidence about the teaching of the certain aspects of the PE curriculum that reflects the opportunities they had to teach the activity during their PGCE year. When the twenty trainees interviewed were asked how confident they felt about teaching the different aspects of PE to their new classes in September, over half of the group (60 per cent) felt 'not very confident' about teaching gymnastics, and about a quarter of the group felt the same way about teaching dance (30 per cent) and athletics (25 per cent). Most of the remainder felt 'confident' about teaching the different aspects of PE with a vote of 'very confident' being expressed by one trainee for gymnastics, seven for dance, seven for games, four for athletics and two for outdoor and adventurous activities.

Noticeably, when asked 'what should be added to the school experience phase of the PGCE course that would have improved your confidence to teach the different aspects of PE?', sixteen of the twenty trainees (80 per cent) mentioned that having the opportunity 'to teach the full range of PE activities' would have improved their level of confidence.

## Influences on Trainees' Planning and Practical Teaching

As McNamara (1993) has pointed out, previous studies of mentoring in initial teacher training:

... have paid too little attention to considering whether and to what extent the information, advice and support which it is assumed mentors and tutors provide actually informs student teachers' preparation for practice and subsequent teaching. (p. 3)

Part of McNamara's study of primary PGCE students investigated the resources and information that trainees drew upon in their practical teaching of the three

National Curriculum core subjects of English, maths and science, and how the contributions of their university tutors and school mentors informed and shaped their classroom practice. The aim was not to necessarily identify the information itself, but concentrate on who provided the information. In this study of twenty trainees and their planning to teach PE similar questions to that posed in the McNamara study were used: 'What advice and information did you find particularly useful during the planning and teaching of PE lessons?', and 'Who was the source of that information?'

As table 6.1 below shows, the most frequently mentioned information that trainees used in the planning of PE lessons was from the university course and the handouts provided by the course tutor. Half of the trainees (50 per cent) mentioned this as their sole source of information, while the remaining half mentioned the university course in combination with other information such as schemes of work from the school CCPE, information from the class teacher, and other teachers or fellow trainees.

Table 6.1: *Sources of information mentioned by trainees*

| Source | Number of times mentioned (N = 20) |
| --- | --- |
| University course | 10 |
| University course and class teacher/ mentor | 4 |
| University course and CCPE | 3 |
| University course and other teacher | 1 |
| University course/CCPE/fellow trainee | 1 |
| Class teacher/mentor | 1 |

When asked about the resources that they found particularly useful when planning and teaching PE, once again the university course handouts were mentioned by seventeen (85 per cent) of the trainees, the university recommended text by eleven of them and school-based resources such as schemes of work, and the class teacher's printed 'teaching ideas' and handouts by six trainees.

Therefore, whereas both school mentors and university tutors were considered to be equally important sources of information when planning lessons across the three National Curriculum core subjects in the McNamara study (*ibid*), in this study trainees tended to rely more upon the university as a source of information when planning PE lessons. In fact, 60 per cent of the trainees interviewed were 'never' given help with the planning of PE lessons while on school placement.

But, as with the McNamara study (*ibid*), another group existed that trainees drew upon for help and advice in the planning and teaching of PE lessons in addition to their school classteacher/mentor, and it included members of their social network. A quarter of the twenty trainees mentioned 'fellow students' having been useful for discussing lesson plans and sharing ideas, and one trainee had a lot of help with the teaching of dance from her sister who was a dance teacher. NQT's were of particular help to one trainee:

They would just pop in and say 'If you need any equipment or you need any help or anything, just ask', they would be quite open with advice — about equipment use or ideas.

The variety of different people involved in supporting the trainee during their periods of school placement in primary schools has been described as a 'mentoring matrix' by Stephenson and Taylor (1995), and refers to a situation whereby all of these 'co-mentors', 'minor mentors' and 'helpers' are:

> . . . embedded, the totality of which provides the student teacher with the process of development. (p. 5)

However, Stephenson and Taylor (*ibid*) do make a distinction between the mentoring 'matrix' of 'official' advice (for example, other teachers), and the part played by other 'significant others' (for example, friends, sisters) who are involved 'unofficially' in the mentoring process in a more personal than professional supporting capacity.

As far as the matrix of 'official' mentoring support is concerned a number of trainees in this study did mention that they received a combination of useful advice and support on the teaching of PE from a combination of headteacher, CCPE, their classteacher, and other teachers. In fact, when the twenty trainees were specifically asked who they felt was the best person in the school for the job of mentoring a trainee in the teaching of PE, a quarter of the trainees considered that the school CCPE would be the best person, four felt that the job should be shared by the CCPE and the classteacher, and two thought the CCPE would be the best person unless the classteacher was really 'up to date about PE'. Several trainees felt that the classteacher, while having a good knowledge of the children in the class, tended to lack the expertise and knowledge of teaching PE that the CCPE might have. In this respect the trainees in this study were probably looking for a mini-matrix of support and guidance with the teaching of PE, not necessarily because they felt that the classteacher lacked the credibility that Stephenson and Sampson (1994) suggests may occur with mentors in the primary school, but because they felt they would gain more from a matrix of mentoring support.

### Trainees' Teaching Difficulties and Training Needs

The full cohort of fifty trainees were asked about the difficulties they had with the teaching of PE during their first period of school placement and the most frequently mentioned issues were as follows (percentage of trainees mentioning the issue in brackets):

- lack of opportunity to teach PE (30 per cent);
- class control in the PE setting (22 per cent);

- planning lessons (14 per cent);
- organization of pupils and equipment in the PE setting (12 per cent);
- knowledge of how to use the PE equipment and facilities in the school (12 per cent).

Several trainees had difficulties caused by a lack of skill or knowledge, but 'lack of knowledge of certain activities' became more of a problem for 30 per cent of the group during the second school placement, when 'class and equipment organization' (35 per cent), 'safety' (25 per cent), 'control' (25 per cent) were also continuing to cause problems. There was also the occasional mention of having difficulty with a lack of continuity for their lessons, with either their teaching group changing every week, regular withdrawals of children from lessons for other activities, or the hall being taken over by other staff at the last minute. This caused planning problems, as one trainee pointed out:

> For games lessons the three year 5 classes combined, and divided into four groups which rotated about mini games (hockey, football, rounders, netball). Sometimes I wasn't sure about which game I would be teaching, and about the levels of ability of the pupils. Also, gymnastic lessons were often cancelled because the hall was being used, for play rehearsals, etc.

Over half (51 per cent) of the full cohort of trainees did not receive help with their difficulties, and 20 per cent of the trainees interviewed had to solve their problems themselves.

The trainee difficulties mentioned in this section, along with the trainee pre-practice 'concerns' mentioned earlier, may be considered to be some of the training 'needs' of the student teacher. In order to plan the training programme of a trainee, mentors need to be aware of the training needs of their mentee. Yet when mentors were asked in a later study (see chapter 9) what they considered to be the training needs or their mentee, very few were able to accurately identify a 'need' that matched the trainee's stated concerns and difficulties.

## Trainees' Experiences and Views of the Mentoring Process

The twenty trainees interviewed were asked a number of questions about their mentors, and the mentoring process as far as the teaching of PE was concerned. When asked who had been their main mentor/support for the teaching of PE, only half of the trainees named their class teacher. The school CCPE, the headteacher, other teachers, various combinations of classteacher and CCPE, were all identified by individual trainees as being their main source of support with the teaching of PE. This might have been because the classteacher lacked credibility as a source of advice in a subject that they felt underconfident about teaching themselves, (see chapter 9), or because they were quite happy to just let the trainee 'do their own thing' with very little support. In fact, three of the twenty trainees actually stated that their main mentor or source of support for PE was 'themselves'. Consequently, a number of trainees used their initiative and sought the advice of someone they felt might be more knowledgeable about the subject. Having said that, half of the trainees whose main source of support was their classteacher were full of praise for the support they received. However, it was noticeable that three of these class teachers had been PE specialists.

When asked what they felt about the effectiveness of the mentoring they had received in the teaching of PE, as table 6.2 below shows, about 40 per cent of the trainees interviewed considered that their mentoring support had been 'effective', or 'very effective' and 45 per cent considered it to have been 'not effective' or 'non-existent'.

Table 6.2: *Trainee's views of the effectiveness of the mentoring they received with the teaching of PE (N = 20)*

| | | |
|---|---|---|
| Very effective | — | 4 |
| Effective | — | 4 |
| OK | — | 3 |
| Not effective | — | 4 |
| Non-existent | — | 5 |

When asked about the kind of help and assistance they thought a trainee should receive from their mentor, the majority of issues mentioned by the trainees related to the need for background information and advice for the planning of PE lessons. For example, twelve of the twenty (60 per cent) trainees believed that they should be shown or given the school schemes of work for PE, and four would have liked to have seen the school policy for PE. Other aspects of help with planning that were mentioned included 'example lesson plans', advice on 'setting up equipment' and 'use of facilities', or simply 'ideas' for planning. As mentioned previously, fifteen (75 per cent) of the trainees had not been shown schemes of work, twelve (60 per cent) had 'never' received help from their mentor with the planning of lessons, and a further seven (35 per cent) 'never' had lesson plans discussed with them prior to lessons whilst on school placement. According to McIntyre and Hagger (1993), what they term 'minimal mentoring' should entail:

> . . . ensuring that learner teachers are helped to do planning skills as well as the skills of classroom practice. (p. 91)

The majority of trainees (65 per cent) also felt that mentors should provide a student teacher with the opportunity to observe lessons taken by the mentor, and several trainees requested 'demonstration lessons' that illustrate 'how to work in a small school hall', or 'how to use the school's large apparatus'. Giving demonstration lessons is seen by Anderson and Shannon (1988) as one of the essential mentoring activities, and Hurst and Wilkin (1992) believe that trainees should be:

> . . . given opportunities to observe other teachers who have a range of teaching styles. (p. 53)

Five trainees (25 per cent) felt that the opportunity to work initially alongside the mentor in the planning and teaching of parts of a lesson would be a valuable exercise in the early stages of learning to teach. In this respect trainees are possibly advocating a form of 'collaborative teaching' similar to that recommended by Burn (1992) and Tomlinson (1995), and discussed in chapter 9.

Two thirds of the trainees (65 per cent) considered that mentors should give advice on the management and organisation of classes and equipment, over a half (55 per cent) thought mentors should advise on safety issues, six (30 per cent) felt information should be given on the use of facilities and equipment, and several (three) wanted the mentor to provide background information on the childrens' experience and ability levels. However, the most frequently mentioned (65 per cent) individual item was the importance of receiving written and oral feedback from the mentor following lessons they had taught. In this study 33 per cent of the full cohort of trainees who taught PE in their first school placement received feedback after 'every lesson', and a further 23 per cent after 'most lessons'. However, 21 per cent of the group 'never' received any feedback after taking PE lessons on their first school placement:

> I got no help or advice at all from my teacher who sat in with me. It would have been nice to have been given some sort of feedback on how my lessons went. As it was, the children enjoyed themselves so I carried on doing the same sort of lessons.

Of those twenty trainees interviewed after their final placement, three 'always' had a post-lesson discussion with their mentors, but five (25 per cent) 'never' had the opportunity to talk about their teaching after a PE lesson. For the remainder, post-lesson discussions occurred 'occasionally'. The nature of the feedback received from mentors varied considerably from the trainee who received advice from her mentor (who was also a CCPE) about:

> 'My organization and use of voice — the advice given was really constructive'.

— to the trainee that received:

> Very little advice — just a passing comment. I felt like a spare part!

The importance of giving trainee teachers meaningful specific feedback after lessons as an essential feature of good mentoring practice is mentioned frequently in the literature. Shaw (1992) refers to the importance of 'giving and receiving positive and negative feedback' and 'debriefing'; Watkins (1992) mentions the 'giving of constructive feedback' as a part of the mentor's supervisory skills, and Anderson and Shannon (1988) refer to observation and feedback as 'essential mentoring activities'.

When trainees were also asked what they thought should be the qualities of a teacher acting as a mentor for the teaching of PE, they elaborated further on the feedback role of the mentor. They felt that mentors should be positive with their feedback, to praise trainees when they had done well, to be constructive with any criticism offered and provide clear explanations of the criticism as well offer suggestions on how to improve. In addition, trainees wanted mentors to:

... be ready to volunteer help rather than have to be asked.

... be willing to share their experiences and ideas.

... be prepared to learn from the student.

... encourage the student to try out their own ideas.

show an interest in the student and their development.

Also, three-quarters of the trainees interviewed wanted mentors to be 'enthusiastic about PE', over half (55 per cent) wanted them to be 'knowledgeable about PE', and a further 40 per cent wished to have mentors who were 'approachable'. Up to a quarter of them wanted their mentor to be 'supportive', a 'good role model', 'patient' and 'confident', while others mentioned such qualities as able to 'show understanding', have 'empathy for being a student', be 'open' and 'friendly', 'helpful', 'sympathetic', 'encouraging', 'organised', and have a 'sense of humour'.

## Starting to Teach: The First Term

Of the fourteen trainees who replied to the short questionnaire sent towards the end of their first term of teaching, eight of them had no difficulties with the teaching of PE at all, but the remaining six were experiencing a variety of problems. These included: 'lack of time for lessons', 'teaching in a small hall with a large number of children', 'limited equipment for PE', 'setting out large apparatus for gymnastics', and needing ideas for teaching games that they were less familiar with. There appeared to be a general lack of confidence about the teaching of gymnastics, particularly apparatus work, with six of them needing help with this aspect of PE. In fact, three of the NQTs had become less confident about teaching gymnastics and four less confident about teaching dance since completing the PGCE course. The NQTs would also like to have the opportunity to observe other staff teaching PE and to be observed by someone who might comment on their teaching, each being aspects of their training they had lacked during their PGCE year.

Of the fourteen NQTs eleven had a general school mentor supporting them and three did not. None of the NQTs had received any information from their Local Education Authority (LEA) about support for NQTs with the teaching of PE.

When the teachers were asked what should have been added to the PGCE year to make them feel more confident about teaching the various aspects of PE, four teachers mentioned that they should have had more opportunity during their school experience to observe and teach the full range of National Curriculum PE activities. Typical of such replies included:

> I feel it would have been useful to have observed more teaching of PE — I don't feel that I observed *any* well organized lessons with children during my time on the PGCE — it is very 'hit and miss' depending on which schools you are placed in on teaching practice.

> . . . opportunity to see more of a range of PE lessons during school experience. Mostly the only lessons you see are your own.

> I think I should have had experience in teaching at least one lesson of each area of PE.

## Implications

Although this preliminary small-scale study may not be representative of the total population of primary PGCE trainees and NQTs, the results may offer an albeit limited insight into the experiences of generalist student teachers and NQTs as they learn to teach PE in the primary school. As a result, certain issues may be raised that those planning the professional training programmes and support of trainees and NQTs in schools might take into account when designing pre-service and in-service training programmes.

### *The School Context*

As far as pre-service teachers are concerned the school context appears to be of particular importance if trainees are to receive a meaningful and progressive series of learning experiences, and at the same time develop a positive attitude towards the teaching of PE. In schools where the headteacher and staff were enthusiastic and positive about PE and sport and aware of the health benefits of physical activity for pupils; where the PE curriculum was seen as important, the full range of National Curriculum activities taught and PE lessons were not 'lost' because of last minute commandeering of the hall; where a sound PE policy and scheme of work for PE was available for consultation by all staff; and where there was a 'culture of collaboration' with all staff being prepared to share ideas about the teaching of PE — then it appeared more likely that trainees would feel positive about teaching the subject themselves.

### The Trainee's School-based Professional Training Programme

In order for the trainee to have a planned, systematic, structured and progressive professional training (which may be considered to be their basic entitlement as trainee professionals) the university and school need to work in close liaison in the planning of the trainee's learning experiences. Because of the limited time available for university primary PE courses, it is essential that those planning the school-based element of training to teach PE are aware of the need to not only provide the trainee with an opportunity to observe the full range of PE National Curriculum activities being taught, and have the chance to practise teaching these activities during the training year, but that the school also plans to 'top up' or extend the trainee's knowledge of teaching the various PE National Curriculum activities. Those trainees who had a limited experience of observing and teaching certain PE activities felt underconfident about teaching them on completion of the training year and, in most cases, remained underconfident in the first term of teaching. NQTs themselves commented upon the importance of being able to observe and teach all aspects of PE during the training year, particularly as far as gymnastics and dance is concerned. The creation of a formative professional development profile that provides a record of the trainee's experiences during the training year may well be an answer, and this is discussed further in chapter 9. Such a profile would help the school to identify the 'gaps' in a trainees knowledge and experience of teaching PE as well as to attempt to cater for their individual training needs.

### The Selection of Mentors

The selection of a teacher to take on the role of mentor for a student teacher is quite an important decision for a school. As far as the trainees in this study were concerned they wanted a mentor to support them with the teaching of PE who had credibility and was knowledgeable and enthusiastic about the subject. The majority of the trainees would therefore prefer to have the school PE co-ordinator as the person who was specifically responsible for supporting them with the teaching of PE, preferably in liaison with the classteacher who had a greater knowledge of the children.

In addition to the need for mentors to have professional credibility, the personal qualities of mentors has been shown to have an important influence on their relationship with the trainee (Yeomans, 1994). Trainees in this study preferred their mentors to have certain personal qualities that included being 'approachable', 'supportive', 'open', 'show understanding', 'patient' 'sympathetic', 'encouraging', have 'empathy' for the trainee, be ready to 'volunteer help rather than be asked', encourage them to 'try out new ideas', 'share ideas' with them, be prepared 'to learn from the trainee', and above all, to 'show an interest in the student and their development'. Although certain authors are of the opinion that it is what mentors 'do' (their mentoring behaviours) that makes for effective mentoring and not their personal qualities or traits (Taylor, 1995), many of the personal qualities of mentors preferred by trainees in this study have also been identified by other studies examining the qualities of 'effective' mentors (Corbett and Wright, 1993, Yeomans, 1994). But trainees also have opinions concerning what their mentors should 'do'.

### *Trainees' Views of the Role of Mentors in their School-based Training*

The student teachers in this study wanted their mentors to offer help and assistance in the following ways:

- provision of background information for planning (for example, schemes of work);
- advice and help with lesson planning;
- the opportunity to observe demonstration lessons;
- the opportunity to work collaboratively with their mentor;
- advice on the management and organization of classes and equipment;
- advice on safety issues;
- to observe their lessons and give oral and written positive and constructive feedback, and offer solutions and suggestions (or targets) concerning how to improve;
- to share their experiences and ideas;
- to encourage them to try out their own ideas.

Those classteachers who had been 'effective' mentors to the trainees had also appeared to be aware of their student teacher's 'training needs' and teaching 'difficulties', in other words they had shown an interest in the trainee's professional development and not left them to solve their own problems. However, even those who appeared to be effective mentors were still aware of the importance of the trainee having access to the wealth of knowledge and expertise that the school might be able to offer regarding the teaching of PE. Some trainees do appear to 'tap into' a sort of professional mentoring 'matrix' that can include the school PE co-ordinator and other teachers in addition to their class teacher. But although half of the trainees interviewed in this study did use this professional 'matrix' of support as their source of information for planning their teaching, the other half of students were left to rely solely on their university course as their main source of information for planning. This may have been because their classteacher felt 'underconfident' about the teaching of PE, or they expected trainees to arrive in the school fully prepared for teaching PE to their classes. For the 'partnership' concept of initial teacher training to really work, primary schools and their mentors will have to be prepared to take on part of the task of providing the knowledge base for the teaching of PE for their trainees, because university tutors cannot do the whole job with their present time allocation for PE courses. In their report assessing how HEI's and secondary schools had responded to the partnership system the Office for Standards in Education (OFSTED, 1995) noted that one of the characteristics of successful partnerships was that:

> The schools, with HEI guidance and exemplars, provide a programme of training . . . which builds on and supports other aspects of the student's training. (p. 12)

However, as McNamara's (1993) study noted, some primary schools are reluctant to take on more responsibility for initial training, but want the university to provide the basic content with the school's role being 'to give help with putting these ideas and suggestions into practice in the context of the classroom and with actual children' (p. 20).

Also, the question of the school being able to 'build on' and extend the trainee's knowledge of the subject may be problematic. A lot depends on the level of expertise in the school, and particularly the background of the school CCPE. Many PE co-ordinators are in post because they have 'an interest in sport'. But to be able to 'build upon' a trainee's knowledge base in PE may necessitate the presence of a PE 'specialist' in the primary school, and the Teacher Training Agency's (TTA) recent advice to the Secretary of State for Education and Employment (TTA, 1995) for 'specialist teaching in the primary phase focusing on subject co-ordinators' may well lead to the provision of that 'PE specialist' to act in the capacity of PE mentor for trainees, and to plan their school-based professional training programme. Such 'specialist' support linked to the trainee's classteacher's knowledge of the children in her class may result in the quality of school-based training and mentor support that trainees appear to request. Without this specialist mentoring in PE in the primary school, there is a danger that the next generation of primary teachers will feel as underconfident about teaching PE to their classes as many of their predecessors — and their mentors (see chapter 9).

But, for mentors to be effective in their role they will need to have protected time for the task, a commodity that at least one trainee saw as essential for her to describe the mentoring she received as effective:

> It was OK, in that I learned quite a lot from watching what she was doing but I wouldn't say she mentored me as such, it wasn't effective

because I didn't have the time to speak to her about the things I would really like to.

— but which might be particularly difficult for primary schools to provide.

### Support for Newly Qualified Teachers with the Teaching of PE

Some NQTs do appear to continue to have difficulties and feel underconfident about teaching certain aspects of PE (for example, gymnastics and dance) during their first term of teaching. In some cases this may have been caused by the shortcomings of the training year, particularly the lack of opportunity to 'practise' the teaching of these activities under the guidance of their mentor. Many local education authorities are committed to the support of NQTs in their first year of teaching (Sheraton *et al*, 1995; Bines and Boydell, 1995) and specific INSET support in the teaching of PE has been provided by LEA PE advisers. However, with the recent demise of the advisory service in some LEAs and the tendency for their support role in schools to be curtailed because of OFSTED inspection duties, the mentoring/staff development role of the primary school 'PE specialist' within a 'mentoring school' ethos (Campbell, 1995) may become even more important.

For the generalist primary teacher, becoming a confident and effective teacher of PE may well depend not only upon the knowledge and experiences provided by the 'partners' involved in planning and supporting them in their initial training, but also the continued specialist level of support they receive in their first year of teaching and beyond. As it appears unlikely that the time allocation for initial training courses in universities and colleges is to improve, for PE to be taught effectively in the nation's primary schools, the Teacher Training Agency's plan (TTA, 1995) to:

make more explicit the links between initial teacher training, induction and in-service training (Annex, p. 7)

— may become even more essential.

### References

ANDERSON, E.M. and SHANNON, A.L. (1988) 'Toward a conceptualisation of mentoring', *Journal of Teacher Education*, **39**, 1, pp. 38–42.

BINES, H. and BOYDELL, D. (1995) 'Managing support for newly qualified teachers in primary schools', *Mentoring and Tutoring*, **3**, 1, pp. 57–62.

BOOTH, M. (1993) 'The effectiveness and role of the mentor in school: The students' view', *Cambridge Journal of Education*, **23**, 2, pp. 185–97.

BURN, K. (1992) 'Collaborative teaching' in WILKIN, M. (Ed) *Mentoring in Schools*, London, Kogan Page, pp. 133–43.

CAMPBELL, A. (1995) 'The mentoring school: Tensions and dilemmas for primary schools', *Mentoring and Tutoring*, **2**, 3, pp. 6–13.

CORBETT, P. and WRIGHT, D. (1993) 'Issues in the selection and training of mentors for school-based primary initial teacher training' in MCINTYRE, D., HAGGER, H. and WILKIN, M. (Eds) *Mentoring: Perspectives on School-based Teacher Education*, London, Kogan Page, pp. 220–33.

HINES, H. and BOYDELL, D. (1995) 'Managing support for newly qualified teachers in primary schools', *Mentoring and Tutoring*, **3**, 1, pp. 57–63.

HURST, B. and WILKIN, M. (1992) 'Guidelines for mentors' in WILKIN, M. (Ed) *Mentoring in Schools*, London, Kogan Page, pp. 43–57.

MCNAMARA, D. (1993) *Student Teachers' Classroom Practice: The Influence of their Tutors and Mentors*, Report of a Mentor Teacher Training Project, The University of Hull.

MAYNARD, T. and FURLONG, J. (1993) 'Learning to teach and models of mentoring' in MCINTYRE, D., HAGGER, H. and WILKIN, M. (Eds) *Mentoring: Perspectives on School-based Teacher Education*, London, Kogan Page, pp. 69–85.

MCINTYRE, D. and HAGGER, H. (1993) 'Teachers' expertise and models of mentoring' in MCINTYRE, D., HAGGER, H. and WILKIN, M. (Eds) *Mentoring: Perspectives on School-based Teacher Education*, London, Kogan Page, pp. 86–102.

OFFICE FOR STANDARDS IN EDUCATION (OFSTED) (1995) *Partnership: Schools and Higher Education in Partnership in Secondary Initial Teacher Training*, London, OFSTED.

SHAW, R. (1992) 'Can mentoring raise achievement in schools?' in WILKIN, M. (Ed) *Mentoring in Schools*, London, Kogan Page, pp. 82–96.

SHERATON, K., CLINTON, B. and TERRELL, I. (1995) 'Learning about mentoring: The Enfield experience', *Mentoring and Tutoring*, **2**, 3, pp. 42–7.

STEPHENSON, J. (1995) 'What makes a setting effective for successful mentoring? Some thoughts on the primary context', paper presented to SRHE Mentoring Network Seminar, 'Illuminating Mentoring', London, March.

STEPHENSON, J. and SAMPSON, J. (1994) 'Conditions for effective mentorship within the school' in YEOMANS, R. and SAMPSON, J. (Eds) *Mentorship in the Primary School*, London, Falmer Press, pp. 174–88.

STEPHENSON, H.J. and TAYLOR, M.I. (1995) 'Diverse views of the mentoring process in initial teacher training', paper presented at the International Mentoring Association Annual Conference, San Antonio, April.

TAYLOR, M. (1995) 'Mentoring: Ubique sunt qualia', paper presented at the University of Hull.

TEACHER TRAINING AGENCY (TTA) (1995) 'The Continuing Professional Development of Teachers'. Advice to Secretary of State for Education and Employment, July.

TOMLINSON, P. (1995) *Understanding Mentoring*, Buckingham, Open University Press.

WATKINS, C. (1992) 'An experiment in mentor training' in WILKIN, M. (Ed) *Mentoring in Schools*, London, Kogan Page, pp. 97–115.

YEOMANS, R. (1994) 'Relationships: Mentors and students' in YEOMANS, R. and SAMPSON, J. (Eds) *Mentorship in the Primary School*, London, Falmer Press, pp. 101–21.

# 7 Trainees' Views of Mentoring in Physical Education

*Chai Kim Yau*

Preceding the recent teacher training Government reforms included within Circular 9/92 (DFE, 1992) the structure of both postgraduate and undergraduate courses in initial teacher education largely placed schools in a supportive yet subsidiary role, with higher education institutions (HEIs) such as universities and colleges overseeing the overall professional development of the student-teacher during the school experience (Miles, Everton and Bonnett, 1994). Although both the school and HEI were frequently in negotiation, the partnership arrangements put forward under the Government Circular 24/89 (DES, 1989) did not legally specify that 'schools should play a much larger part in initial teacher training as full partners of HEIs' with 'a leading responsibility for training' (p. 4). It was the responsibility of the university to initially select students, to plan and manage the course of training, and to monitor and assess trainees throughout their degree course. The school was largely concerned with the supervision of the student's school experience. Circular 9/92 (DFE, 1992) changed the emphasis and weighting of responsibilities and it is now the school and university's dual role to not only deliver, but recruit, prepare, evaluate and review courses under the new partnership schemes.

This significant shift in the ideology of teacher training has led to the teacher supervisor undertaking the complex role of mentor. As Edith (1995) suggests, the task of mentorship can carry a variety of responsibilities including not only that of pupil educator — but student-teacher educator, counsellor, assessor, appraiser and supporter.

This chapter aims to investigate physical education (PE) trainees' views of the mentoring they receive in school. Data is derived from part of a three year joint research project set up in 1993 between Liverpool John Moores University (LJMU), the University of Brighton and partner secondary schools to monitor the impact and development of school based initial teacher training. The chapter centres specifically upon the postgraduate certificate in education (PGCE) PE course based at LJMU and is a qualitative longitudinal case study of fifteen student-teachers during the academic year of 1993/94.

The mentoring process is examined using ethnographic research methods with a specific focus placed upon the trainee's views of that process. The research methods employed include semi-structured interviews, questionnaires and diary keeping. For reasons of confidentiality all students involved in the study are portrayed under pseudonyms to protect their identities. The students' interpretation, understanding and attitude towards mentoring is examined with the focus upon student perceptions of what they consider to be effective mentoring.

To summarize, the whole issue of mentoring will be discussed in relation to the wider considerations of partnerships between schools and HEIs in the initial training of physical education teachers.

## Student-Teacher Interpretations of the Concept of Partnerships within Teacher Training

'Morecambe and Wise', 'Shearer and Sutton' — a combination that works together to achieve a definite goal' was one analogy used by a student-teacher to describe the notion of partnership. Although both humorous and simplistic, it captures the underlying concept and sums up the image that most students had of partnerships. Student interpretations of the concept included the notion of partners working and communicating in co-operation with each other. They described partnership as the link between the teacher training institution and the school and viewed the relationship as a two-way process. The creation of an effective relationship was considered by the students to be dependent upon mutual trust and understanding between the two partners. It was also thought the links and relationships developed should be built upon agreement and operate in unison. One philosophy for the central notion of partnership is based around the whole concept of networking. Partnership seen in this light may be described as a web — each element of the structure individually functioning yet interrelating and amalgamating to create the whole partnership model. These views coincide with Watkin's (1992) analogy,

> If you pull one part of the web, you will change the rest, because the web is part of the system. (p. A20)

Within the teacher training context this notion implies the development of sound working relationships between school and university, staff and students. In compliance with Government legislation (DFE, 1992) the LJMU partnership scheme supports the notion of an equal sharing of responsibilities. The PGCE PE students interviewed considered the partnership model as an effective method for teacher training if based on an efficient communication between institutions, consistent assessment procedures and well trained mentors within the schools. However, if any element of the partnership structure failed, this was seen by the students to have a direct effect upon their school-based experience and consequent professional development.

The success or otherwise of the 'partnership' model of teacher training was largely based on the students' interpretation of the evolving mentoring process. The mentor dyad (i.e., the relationship between the mentor and mentee) was seen to be a critical component in the development of the student teacher. With students spending twenty-four professional weeks of a thirty-six week course within the school context the student-mentor relationship was identified by the trainees as playing a crucial role throughout the course with the mentor often being seen as the first point of reference and as a key 'significant other' (i.e., one perceived to be important and pertinent to the student and his/her situation) during their progress. Providing that the subject mentor and the school itself were recognized by the student as being effective in both their training and teaching roles, the partnership scheme was considered an efficient system for training. It is apparent from the case study material that follows that the students' experiences of teaching within the partnership model significantly relied upon the quality of the selected school, its departments and its staff. One student was particularly appreciative of the mentor support she had received, yet recognized variations in the teaching practice experience of her peers.

> Perhaps if I had bad mentors my opinions would be completely different!

### Trainees' Views of the Mentoring Process in Physical Education

Students favoured the supportive mentor who was flexible in giving their time to explain and give feedback whether that be in the form of arranged regular meetings or more casual discussions and interactions if and when the trainee felt necessary. Students responded positively to pre-lesson guidance as they felt reassured by this before 'facing' the class. Following the teaching episode student teachers preferred constructive and positive critiques of lessons from subject mentors as this gave students confidence in their teaching, yet also allowed them to develop and build on their knowledge and experience. Students also liked mentors to refer to specific areas or aspects of the teaching situation as these were easy for students to relate to and understand. If the mentor was able to draw upon evidence to support his statements or critique of a lesson students were more likely to understand the points raised and absorb the information to change or reinforce their teaching behaviour at a later stage. These points are also supported by Brawdy and Byra (1995):

> ... the success of a preservice teacher during an early field teaching experience is dependent upon sound post lesson conferencing. (p. 147)

The strategy of shared post-lesson dialogue and analysis was recognized by the trainees as a positive form of evaluation of their teaching performance. Students also preferred a consistent and developmental approach to assessment of teaching. 'Target' or 'goal setting' by mentors was seen as both a tangible and specific form of guidance for students in their lesson planning and delivery. Students wanted and valued feedback relating to individual National Curriculum areas of activity and required feedback based on generic skills such as classroom management, organization and control, and approaches to teaching as well interpersonal skills. They also preferred a mentor who they felt recognized and related to them as an individual. Thus, both professional and personal qualities were sought in the mentor role. For instance, Colin described his mentor to be 'on his wavelength' and commented,

> When I am teaching he seems to know what I am trying to do and he understands if something goes wrong and he seems more clued into me.

Another student considered her mentor

> ... good at reading situations ... after being there a few weeks, situations that I'd felt awkward about she could pick up on in the lesson.

Those students who perceived themselves as an integral and significant part of the learning process appeared to draw greater meaning from the mentoring dyad. Tina needed to be accepted as a member of staff and not referred to as 'the student' all the time. Robin also appreciated the importance (particularly in front of pupils) attached to having 'teacher status'. The empowerment of the student is an important role for the mentor in the dyadic relationship and the professional development of the teacher trainer themselves. The approachable, friendly and fair mentor was seen as promoting a two way process in the mentor/mentee relationship. Students thought 'partnerships' of this nature allowed a shared role in the development of student-teacher learning and gave students flexibility as 'active' learners with the mentor acting as facilitator. This point is also raised by Putman and colleagues (1993) when they state that,

> ... effective mentoring should involve negotiation between mentors and mentees rather than the imposition of a 'top-down' model of knowledge transfer. (p. 9)

Students in this study favoured a degree of independence in their role as teacher and enjoyed acting as a 'key determinant' (*ibid*) in the mentoring process. Taking responsibility for their own learning, by seeking help from their significant others when they felt necessary, was seen by students as an important part of the learning process and they preferred mentors who were 'willing to listen' as well as offer advice and guidance. Though the majority of students largely welcomed 'team teaching' with their mentor/teachers during various stages of their school experience, in individual or solo teaching situations at the 'chalk face' they liked to feel 'in control' and disliked a vast amount of input (both in content and delivery) from the mentor as they perceived this to undermine their authority. Although, Leanne had developed a positive relationship with her mentor and found her very helpful and easy to approach, she sensed a lack of flexibility and freedom on the part of the mentor and was aware she had 'fixed ideas' about teaching styles in physical education and believed it would be hard to change her way of thinking. The trainee admitted that in some ways she therefore felt disinclined to experiment with 'new' ideas for fear of not producing what she believed the mentor to expect. However, it is important to recognize idiosyncratic and individuality of style and approach — even in the trainee. Although it is the responsibility of the mentor to eliminate bad or unsafe practice in the classroom, it is equally important that they acknowledge and allow the trainee's own styles of teaching to develop. In this respect Colin received a more sympathetic response from his mentor.

> (My mentor) doesn't force any of his opinions on me . . . he maybe
> criticizes and suggests I do it in a different way, but he recognises that
> I teach in a different way to him.

Mentors need to allow trainees a degree of freedom to try out different approaches and not look to create a carbon copy of their own teaching style. As Jacques (1992) reinforced,

> Mentoring is not about imitating. (p. 45)

Yet students did appreciate that they were also in danger of feeling isolated if offered too much freedom. At least two of the students who were given 'space' were reluctant to approach the mentor with their problems because they felt that they were infringing upon the teacher's time and perceived their mentor to be too busy to 'interrupt' or 'bother' believing their problem to be of less importance than the teacher's schedule. Patrick also experienced feelings of isolation as he recognized a clear division of responsibility in his department and was faced with two heads of department shunning accountability — neither wished to take on the position of mentor. He commented on his view of the mentoring process in his school:

> The department did their job in relation to actually showing us things
> to do in relation to sport but once the lesson had finished they had
> washed their hands of us.

Students indicated that they needed both personal and professional help.

> To be a mentor of a student involves you not only in the professional
> growth of your student, but also with your student as a person.
> (Cameron-Jones, 1993, p. 6)

It is critical that the mentor strikes the balance between giving students support and empowering students with responsibility. The whole notion of the dyadic relationship promotes the mentor as the primary source and support mechanism for the student whilst in the school. Student-teachers need to be integrated into the whole school process in order that they may understand and fulfil their roles and responsibilities as teachers, and to feel an integral part of the department in which they are working. Although there may be 'real' reasons as to why the mentor can only offer a limited amount of support to the student-teacher, he/she needs to recognize that they often play a key role in the trainee's professional life. However, some students said they also communicated, confided and turned to other teachers with whom they had built up a rapport for support. Students said that they sought support and advice from different sources depending upon the issue with which they were faced. For example, they relied mostly upon their subject specific department for guidance in physical education matters. For information on more generic issues they sometimes referred to those they saw as the older, more experienced members of staff who had 'been there and done it' who they perceived to be friendly and approachable. Also, students did say that for moral support they might turn to their peers, other student-teachers, people in similar predicaments, or close friends. For the majority of students, however, the mentor was still seen as playing an influential and important role during the early stages of their teaching career.

In terms of their progress as physical education teachers, those students who respected their mentors wanted to perform well and prove to them that they were 'good' teachers. Graber (1995) also noted that the teacher educator was seen as a powerful significant other and 'be more important in shaping student beliefs than an entire programme of courses and experiences' (p. 157). Even in situations where the student did not respond to the mentor and relied on other teachers with whom he/she had contact for support, the subject mentor still acted as a key role model. As one student-teacher pointed out:

> I have had a great deal of support at school both informally and formally. Most importantly, I have a mentor to talk to.

A less positive role model, however, was experienced by Tina (another student from the study). For the following reasons she was not impressed with the example set by her mentor.

> She's doing her make-up and hair while I'm taking the register, telling the kids to spit out chewing gum whilst she's there walking through with a cup of coffee and an apple.

Similarly, Monica was disappointed with her teacher role model and felt unprofessionally treated by those in her department by their outwardly public comments.

I thought it was unprofessional as they would give us feedback while the kids were there. So I'm coming back from a lesson and my mentor would be coming out with 'I'm not surprised they were bored with that as they were really static for twenty minutes' . . . I thought how on earth can I have credibility when I have teachers like that.

Students responded positively to those mentors who demonstrated knowledge and competency in their field of work. Although the ability to teach well was not singled out as a necessary skill for the mentor to possess, the mentor's ability to demonstrate, discipline and organize pupils, their knowledge of different teacher strategies/approaches and their interpersonal and social skills were all noticed by students. Trainees also noticed the dedication of the mentors and their commitment and enthusiasm for the job. Such qualities created a respect for the mentor and a greater willingness to accept and act upon their advice and suggestions. Students also identified the skill of communication as essential to the role of being a mentor. They preferred their mentors to be humorous in nature, honest and encouraging. Students valued integrity in their mentor in order that they might have a realistic assessment of their progress and be able to build upon the strengths and weaknesses in their teaching. Above all, students wanted to be praised, but only when credit was due. If students received a 'pat on the back' for something they knew themselves was poor in effort, delivery, content or quality it diminished the value of any positive feedback they received for areas of teaching they believed they had done well. Contradictory statements made by mentors led to confusion and often a resulting lack of faith in the mentor. For example one student was told by her mentor:

I think I'm going to have to fail you and I can't write a reference for you but having said that you know I think you'd make a good teacher.

If the mentor fails to explain things clearly this can lead to students misinterpreting the information and thus result in a number of potential problems for the dyadic relationship. For example, students reported examples of how misinterpreted comments by their mentors resulted in personal problems for the student such as poor self-image, confusion concerning one's teaching ability, self-denial and a resulting lack of faith and respect for the mentor. Mentors therefore need to be aware of how their comments might be misinterpreted by the trainees and avoid 'overloading' the student with an excess of negative comments relating to their teaching performance. Although it is realised that it is vital for criticisms to be candid in order for the trainee to recognize and develop their teaching skills, discretion and empathy can relieve the tension of post lesson debriefings of teaching performance. The mentor needs to recognize that he/she is not only responsible for the appraisal of the student — but also for the appraisal of themselves in that they have a professional responsibility and a moral duty to put their 'mentoring' practice under scrutiny.

The quality of mentoring is as important as the quality of teaching. Ways of dealing with students, their successes and problems is an integral part of the all encompassing role of mentor which includes a plethora of skills and duties. In fact, data from the study suggests the state of the relationship between the student and mentor can enrich or mar the trainees' experience of school, teaching and even physical education.

It is the nature of the role of mentor that makes the task a complex one, however. The mentor engages in and is responsible for a wide range of duties — not least the education of children. The role of mentor itself suggests the need for diverse, multifarious skills of both professional and personal capacity. The task can involve the key skills of teaching, assessing, negotiating, counselling and facilitating — not all of which are complementary in nature. Pinpointing and defining the role of mentor is difficult and is, to some extent, reliant upon the individual student-mentor relationship. The mentor's vocation is partly shaped by the needs of the mentee and as Menter (1995) suggests:

> ... inductees' needs are idiosyncratic — everyone's needs are quite different. (p. 21)

Thus, there is no one model of mentoring. Although the trainees' commented upon what they thought a good mentor should do, the success or failure of the mentor role is also dependent upon the distinct nature of the unique dyadic relationship between an individual mentor and their trainee.

This is not to say, however, the mentoring process should not lack a common structure that might apply across different teacher education partnerships, or that we should not strive for a set of common principles and standards for the mentoring role that might act as a benchmark for the development of quality in initial teacher education.

This study's findings of trainees' views of the mentoring process in physical education suggest that there may be positive and negative aspects of the mentoring process as experienced by trainees. These may be summarized as follows:

*Positive factors*
The trainees indicated the following qualities as positive factors in a mentor:

— A mentor able to carry out both a professional and personal role.
— A mentor able to demonstrate competency in physical education through performance, understanding of material, competency in teaching skills and approaches and a knowledge of PE.
— A mentor with interpersonal and communication skills.
— A mentor who acts as an identifier of need and as a facilitator of teacher development.
— A mentor who provides positive, constructive feedback.

— A mentor who shows flexibility in allowing and fostering the development of individual teaching style and approach.
— A mentor who freely gives of their time and is 'willing to listen'.
— A mentor who offers collegial support to students.
— A mentor who is committed to the profession of teaching physical education.

*Negative factors*

The trainees indicated the following qualities as negative factors in a mentor:

— A mentor who is too authoritarian in approach.
— A mentor who lacks flexibility.
— A mentor who provides negative, contradictory feedback or no feedback at all.
— A mentor who is a bad professional role model and does not set good examples.
— A mentor who is overworked and cannot find time to talk to or interact with the trainee.
— A mentor who demonstrates a lack of commitment to their position and profession.

## Internal and External Factors Affecting the Mentoring Process

The mentoring process, however, cannot be viewed in isolation. There are many internal and external factors affecting the mentoring process during all stages of the training of a teacher within a school-based partnership scheme. Mentoring needs to be seen within the wider context of school life. The quality of the training experience is reliant upon a multifaceted complex network of relationships within the partnership including tutors, mentors, trainees and significant others. The student teacher's experience of the mentoring process is also largely dependent upon the 'type' of school placement and school mentor to which they are assigned. Schools can vary in status, size, age and ethos. Similarly, the mentor's views of their role can differ from school to school. The student-mentor relationship is unique and complex in terms of its combination of both professional and personal aspects. The very nature of learning to teach is both subjective and objective. Teaching develops and fails within social interactive situations. The teacher in the class acts in both proactive and reactive ways and bases his/her decisions in the teaching context upon the pupils actions, reactions and responses. In a similar sense the student-mentor relationship is reliant not only upon the ability to ascertain competencies and skills, but the ability to adapt and respond to changing circumstances and, as importantly, the ability to communicate and work effectively with one another to create positive support systems for learning. Evidence from this study suggests that some trainees are immediately on the 'wavelength' of their mentor. In other cases one or both partners require a degree of adaptability to relate to each other, whilst other mentor dyads are clearly antagonistic in nature for reasons varying from differences in philosophy to personality clashes, as Haggarty (1995) points out.

> . . . whilst mentors cannot be chosen for their personalities alone, it is important at the very least that mentors are teachers who are actively sympathetic to the needs of the learner teachers. (p. 40)

Evidence from this study suggests that 'problems' within the student-mentor relationship seemed more likely to emerge as a result of differences in personal opinion concerning incidents that had occurred within the classroom, or to differences in attitude and philosophy to school in the wider context.

It was also recognised the student-mentor relationship could also be potentially hindered by teacher 'workload'. To facilitate those 'teachers as mentors' the image of mentoring as an added responsibility and an extra burden to daily school life must be dispelled and an increase in awareness of the full implications of the role must be recognized. Fullan (1993) reinforces this point when he states that:

> . . . a situation where the mentors teach full-time and 'fit their mentoring in and around the edges' does not permit staff development to flourish. (p. 44)

'Mentor time' needs to be stressed. The availability of 'mentoring time' is essential for mentors to be able to fulfil their duties to the trainees. The results of the study suggest that some teachers are not afforded either the time or status for the role and so consequently are unable to carry out all of their duties effectively. The quality of training offered by the subject mentor is not only dependent upon their own individual ability to manage, assess and support students, but also upon the importance attached to the mentoring process within the school itself. In this study the differing experiences of trainees during the school practice was partly due to 'teacher mentors' receiving inconsistent (if any) rewards for their new position. For example, in some schools mentors received a variety of different benefits ranging from financial remuneration, free periods within the timetable, a reduction in other school duties, to extra equipment or capital expenditure for the department. However, in other schools mentors received nothing for the additional mentoring duties. The standardization of mentoring for students within and across schools may be facilitated by consistent incentives for the job.

The study findings suggested that a variety of approaches and procedures were practised by mentors which in one case revealed differences in assessment procedures for students within the same school. Although this example may partly be a result of a lack of 'institutionalized' mentor training, it is important that schools take into account the need to identify mentor aptitude and suitability for the post. Mentors must also be clear about their roles and responsibilities and negotiate and agree upon a teacher education programme (with the HEI) which ensures quality and consistency in training. Although there may be professional and personal aspects to the role of being a mentor, in all dyadic relationships the essential and critical question the mentor must continually ask is 'am I providing the support and training for this trainee to become a good teacher of physical education?' This is the basis for quality in education and all partners are accountable and obliged in their given roles to facilitate quality learning in ITE through partnership.

The research suggests that the quality of the mentoring process may play a significant part in the initial training of teachers of physical education. In fact, the student-mentor relationship may be seen as the pivotal point and fundamental element underpinning the whole philosophy of partnerships in teacher education. Although it is recognised that *both* mentor and student are going through a 'learning experience' during the mentoring process, the outcomes for the mentor do not hold the same implications or present the same consequences as they do for the student teacher, however. The learning curve for both partners is ongoing and continual in nature and can easily extend beyond that of the postgraduate training year. However, in the short term the trainee will ultimately pass or fail — be successful or unsuccessful in gaining qualified teacher status. The mentors (despite their levels of competence in their new found position) are not assessed or exposed in the same way and so evidence of the rate at which they are developing as 'mentors' is unclear and not evaluated or appraised synonymously with that of the student.

Thus, it is essential that the views, opinions and experiences of those in training are taken into account when planning school-based initial teacher education (ITE) courses and mentor training if the quality of teacher training in physical education is to improve and develop. The voices, opinions and first hand experiences of the trainee teacher are a crucial element in examining, reviewing, studying and analysing the mentoring process.

Both the issues and successes of mentor training highlighted in this chapter allow us to respond positively to improving the teacher training process. 'Mentoring' needs to take into consideration selection procedures, training needs, effective management strategies, and adequate resourcing and conditions to further advance and improve the quality assurance of teacher education through partnership in the future.

## References

Brawdy, P. and Byra, M. (1995) 'Supervision of pre-service teachers during an early field teaching experience', *The Physical Educator*, **52**, 3, pp. 147–58.

Cameron-Jones, M. (1993) 'Must a mentor have two sides?', *Mentoring*, **1**, 1, pp. 5–8.

DEPARTMENT OF EDUCATION AND SCIENCE (1989) *Initial Teacher Training: Appraisal of Courses*, (Circular 24/89), London, HMSO.

DEPARTMENT FOR EDUCATION (1992) *Initial Teacher Training* (Secondary Phase) (Circular 9/92), London, HMSO.

EDITH, J. (1995) 'Mentoring: A universal panacea for staff development?', *Journal of Teacher Development*, **4**, 3, pp. 41–7.

FULLAN, M. (1993) *Change Forces*, London, Falmer Press.

GRABER, K.C. (1995) 'The influence of teacher education programs of the beliefs of student teachers: General pedagogical knowledge, pedagogical content knowledge, and teacher education course work', *Journal of Teaching in Physical Education*, **14**, 2, pp. 157–77.

HAGGARTY, L. (1995) 'The complexities of effective mentoring in initial teacher education', *Mentoring and Tutoring*, **2**, 3, pp. 32–41.

JACQUES, K. (1992) 'Mentoring in initial teacher education', *Cambridge Journal of Education*, **22**, 3, pp. 337–51.

MENTER, I. (1995) 'What newly qualified teachers really need: Evidence from a support group', *Journal of Teacher Development*, **4**, 3, pp. 15–21.

MILES, S., EVERTON, T. and BONNETT, M. (1994) 'Primary partnership matters: Some views from the profession', *Cambridge Journal of Education*, **24**, 1, pp. 49–63.

PUTMAN, K., BRADFORD, S. and CLEMINSON, A. (1993) 'An analysis of the role of mentor in professional education: A comparative study', *Mentoring*, **1**, 1, pp. 9–14.

YAU, C.K. (1995) 'From a student standpoint: My views on mentoring', *Mentoring and Tutoring*, **3**, 2, pp. 45–9.

*Part Three*

# *Issues Concerning the Role of the Mentor*

# 8    Physical Education Mentors' Needs

*Ros Phillips, Ann-Marie Latham and
Joanne Hudson*

## Introduction

This chapter is about the professional needs of physical education (PE) mentors in secondary schools, as perceived by themselves. It is based on research which focuses on secondary school higher education institution (HEI) partnerships and on physical education mentors in particular. The growing body of evidence from this study, other local projects and from national studies by the Office of Her Majesty's Chief Inspector of Schools (OHMCIS, 1995b), suggests that much of what we are discovering, in terms of models of practice and continuing professional development needs, can be applied across all subjects and the following areas of teacher pre-service and in-service education:

- secondary school-HEI partnerships;
- school-centred schemes (OHMCIS, 1995a);
- primary schools (though there are particular issues in primary school mentoring which are developed by Mick Mawer in his chapters in this book);
- mentoring the newly qualified teacher (or the probationary teacher if the probationary year returns).

But we also believe that PE mentors and students have particular views to offer to the partnership debate and also particular needs to be acknowledged and dealt with by the managers of initial teacher education (ITE) in schools; hence the research in which we are engaged, and reported in this chapter.

Our purpose is to review and analyze how mentors talk about their role, and in particular the ways in which they balance the demands of the role against all the other expectations, including the requirements of their prime responsibility as teachers of children. We hope that this will be of interest to all those involved in the induction of PE teachers into the profession, including headteachers, professional tutors/co-ordinators, teacher education tutors in HEIs and the mentors themselves. We hope that the issues we identify will help those working with mentors to understand the role from the mentors' perspective and that mentors will realize that the problems they face are not theirs alone, but are shared by many others, and that colleagues are working to identify the difficulties and provide an improved structure for their task.

To explain the nomenclature we use: the title 'co-ordinating mentor' describes the teacher who has responsibility for the management of the school's involvement in ITE and the support of students' induction into whole school issues. Elsewhere these teachers are called 'professional tutors'. The title 'subject/PE mentor' is given to teachers with specific responsibility for inducting the student into his/her role as a teacher of PE.

The chapter starts with a brief description of, and rationale for, the research project on which the data used in this chapter are based. This leads to clarification of the concept of mentoring as it is developing within initial teacher training partnerships. The research data so far analyzed is then used to explore mentors' perceptions of mentoring. From this a model of mentors' needs is developed and tentatively proposed as the starting point for further, focused research and for the means of addressing these needs.

## The Research Project

The work on which the material in this chapter is based is part of a case study of two ITE school-university partnerships. The project was developed jointly by the PE departments at the University of Brighton and Liverpool John Moores University (LJMU) with a view to evaluating, and thus providing a quality audit and development plan for, the partnership in teacher education schemes developed by the physical education departments in the two universities.

The research team was initially interested in the extent to which the differences in geographic and institutional context might manifest themselves in the development of partnership, including students' and mentors' responses to it. The comparative data analysis carried out so far in this respect is not complete enough to be formally reported at this stage, but the evidence gathered to date suggests that there is much greater similarity than there are differences, and as the national picture emerges (OHMCIS, 1995b) it would appear that there are many issues that are common to all partnerships in the early stages of development.

The research focuses on the Postgraduate Certificate in Education (PGCE) and four year BEd/BA undergraduate courses in PE at the two institutions. The subjects who are taking part in the research are students, school PE mentors, university tutors and headteachers in a cross section of schools within the partnership schemes. A wide range of data is being obtained and analyzed using both quantitative and qualitative methods. The data used for this chapter were obtained from mentors by (i) a written questionnaire; (ii) structured interviews as a follow-up and expansion of the questionnaire data; and (iii) life history interviews to elicit information about PE mentors' own professional development. A further investigative protocol, using dyadic interaction analysis techniques (Jones, 1980), is currently being developed. The formal reporting of the research is ongoing and appears elsewhere (for example, Hudson and Latham, 1995; Yau, 1995, Phillips, 1994).

## Mentoring in Initial Teacher Education

*The Concept of Mentoring*

A great deal has been written, since the introduction of the reforms in ITE, about partnerships between teacher training institutions and the schools who provide teaching experience for trainees. Issues which emerge from this literature can be categorized into discussions of:

(i)    organizational challenges;
(ii)   the curriculum content of the joint courses;
(iii)  the processes of teaching and learning;
(iv)   the nature of teaching competence;
(v)    mentoring as an educational/training strategy.

Models of partnership are developing and the concept is becoming both more flexibly interpreted and situation specific. Implicit in all the models, however, is the central role of the mentor. Models of mentoring have been adapted for teacher training purposes from other professional settings, but this has generated some conflict of opinion in terms of what a mentor is and thus what (s)he can and should contribute to a student's learning to teach. Nor does there seem to be consensus on how mentors might be chosen and prepare themselves for the role. Research is only just beginning to address these issues, yet they are fundamental if teacher education is going to successfully prosper in schools (Haggarty, 1995).

In introducing the concept of mentoring in ITE it is important to distinguish it from previous models of teacher/student contact. Perhaps the language we use does not help us in this respect. Laker (1994), and much of the literature from the USA (Smith, 1992), still uses the term 'supervising teacher', and whereas the mentoring process may be implied in this, the fundamental change in role from pre-partnership arrangements to the current situation is not best served by the concept of supervision as it has been used in ITE (i.e. observing, analysing and commenting on teaching performance). The training and assessing role required of mentors in ITE is broader than this. This raises a problem for ITE mentors, that is the conflict inherent in the role which involves both support and assessment. It appears to be a particular potential difficulty in the PE context because of the friendly working relationships which often develop within PE departments between mentor and students.

*Role conflict*

The concept of mentoring in its generic sense and in the way in which it is used in business, industry and Higher Education refers to the mentor as a trusted, experienced colleague, whose prime role is to *support* in the particular enterprise in which the mentee is engaged (Race, undated). It is unusual in these contexts for the mentor to have other than a peripheral role in the formal assessment of the mentee's competence, other than, of course, the formative assessment concomitant with assisting in the development of a colleague's competence in the job. However, in teacher education, an additional task has been added, that of formal, summative assessment of competence. McIntyre *et al* (1994) suggest four main elements to the teacher-mentor's role:

- working directly with the student teachers in various ways (e.g. collaborative teaching; observation and feedback; discussion);

- managing the student teachers' learning about teaching, in collaboration with the HEI, and drawing appropriately on departmental colleagues classes and their expertise;

- assessing the student teachers' classroom teaching and their capacity to evaluate and develop their teaching for formative and summative purposes;

- providing personal support for the student teachers, who will often experience both insecurity and failure, perhaps on a scale and in a more personal sense than ever before. (p. 16)

It is the juxtaposition of these last two elements of the role which are the most difficult for mentors to manage effectively and which create the greatest role conflict for them. In the previous teacher-training system, before the formation of the Circular 9/92 partnerships (DFE, 1992) the university tutor(s), in close consultation with supervising teachers, made the judgment as to whether a student-teacher was sufficiently competent to be awarded qualified teacher status. Currently, however, whereas the formal awarding of qualified teacher status is the responsibility of the HEI (within a partnership arrangement), in practice it is the mentor, and usually the subject mentor, who has the task of summatively judging competence. The co-ordinating mentor and the university tutor normally support and moderate, but the PE mentor is at the forefront of the assessment process. There are a number of important implications, for both the mentor and the system, which derive from this. Firstly, the mentee is acutely aware of the power of his/her mentor to hold the key to their qualification. And yet the mentoring process encourages the mentee to raise problems, discuss difficulties openly and frankly, and explore alternatives. In instances where the student is confident, reasonably competent and where a good relationship has been established between mentor and student, then this does not appear to present any major difficulties. However, even the most effective student prefers, where possible, to hide mistakes from his/her mentor in case an otherwise good impression is marred. But where the student is having many, perhaps deep-seated difficulties, such openness is less easy to effect. Mentors have commented on the difficulty of sustaining the support role in these cases and evidence suggests that they welcome the involvement of the university tutor as mediator (Shilling *et al*, 1995).

### PE Mentors' Views of Partnership and the Mentoring Role

#### On partnership

In spite of the difficulties and frustrations of the early days of partnership, PE mentors are generally enthusiastic about the opportunity to be involved in the schemes. They see partnership as an improvement on the previous 'teaching practice' model. They welcome the opportunity to play a more central role in the development of students' skills; they believe that they can give students a more realistic picture of what teaching is like, and how to do it, than can the HEI. There are some, however, who feel that the balance of responsibility has swung too far towards the schools and that they are being asked to do more than they can possibly deliver, given that their prime responsibility is to their pupils and the National Curriculum. Some suspect a 'hidden agenda'; that what they will be asked to take on in terms of ITE will continue to expand 'until we are doing everything'. This, of course, is the essence of school-centred schemes, but none of the mentors we talked to appeared to be interested in accepting total responsibility for teacher training. The extent to which this response is a reflection of their real feelings, or of the fact that the researchers were university-based, is impossible to assess in this investigation (and is a question to be answered when discussing the validity of the findings in another forum). Other mentors regret the considerable lessening of contact with HEI tutors at subject level, a feature of most (though not all) partnership schemes. Our analysis of what PE mentors say in this respect suggests that ITE managers have underestimated the reciprocal benefits in terms of information, support and professional/subject development inherent in the 'old' system of teaching practice supervision visits to schools by HEI subject tutors. The majority of PE mentors see the positive benefits of a closer formal association with the ITE courses in the institutions and welcome the opportunity to be involved in interviewing, in course planning and for some, in contributing to HEI-based teaching. Students have always been welcomed into schools as sources of new ideas, different teaching strategies and youthful enthusiasm; PE mentors recognize that partnership extends these opportunities and helps the student to feel even more a part of the school and thus to increase his/her commitment to it. Mentors report a greater involvement by students in extra-curricular activities than previously and a willingness to take the initiative in introducing new clubs or projects.

#### On mentorship

All PE mentors see their role as very demanding and a great responsibility. The majority tend to invest a great deal of their professional 'self' in the role. They identify the major demands as being related to their pedagogical and subject knowledge, yet on the whole they feel confident about their interactional skills and evidence from the students, in most instances, tends to support this view (Hudson and Latham, 1995; Yau, 1995). They speak less frequently of their role in the management of students' learning and this may be an area to focus on in professional development work with mentors. They identify the following elements of their role and further research is needed to indicate the priority they ascribe to these:

- facilitator (of experiences and access to people and resources);
- evaluator/assessor;
- reviewer and goal-setter;
- teacher and role model;
- encourager;
- pastoral supporter;
- setter of targets and tasks.

They recognize the 'assessor/supporter' conflict discussed earlier and some find this difficult to manage, but on the whole they do not espouse a simplistic view of mentoring. Underpinning their model of mentoring is the clearly identifiable view that mentoring must be a flexible process and that it must take account of the individuality of students and of their changing needs as their experience grows. This is an interesting and important point, for it indicates that whereas PE mentors seem to be asking for a clear prescription of their role and more information about its associated procedures and practices, yet some also seem to recognize that their task goes beyond this prescription.

### On recognition and resources

As indicated previously, PE mentors tend to make a heavy self-investment in the role and they are disappointed when they perceive it to be undervalued by their colleagues. Some of these colleagues are themselves involved in the students' training as supervising teachers and thus there are practical implications of this concern. Where the articulation of partnership, the mentor role and a whole school approach to ITE has not been made explicit and publicized within the school, an element of 'passive resistance' by their non-mentor colleagues has been reported by a few mentors. The place of mentoring within the overall career structure of teaching is discussed later in this chapter. Currently there is no clear pattern in terms of how mentorship fits into the range of responsibility posts within schools, but mentors wish to see it formalized, with publicized selection procedures, a job description, clear incentives and supportive networks. The early difficulties of fund transfer which the HEIs had to face had a negative effect on mentors' perceptions of the efficacy of the partnership scheme. There was (and remains some) considerable suspicion that the HEIs were holding back funds to protect teaching posts. Some mentors still see the schemes as relying too much on 'goodwill', perhaps failing to recognize that the intention of Circular 9/92 was that funds should only be transferred for responsibilities over and above those undertaken in the past (OHMCIS, 1995b). Nevertheless, without exception mentors perceive their role to be under-resourced, largely in terms of the time for contact with the student and for training. This issue is discussed further later in the chapter.

## On preparation and training

The majority of PE mentors are heads of department or experienced teachers and only a small minority have limited experience of teaching. In our sample the mean length of experience of the PE mentors was thirteen years. In some departments mentorship is shared between the boys' and girls' sections and this seems to allow a closer contact between student and mentor, though it means that resources must be divided. On the whole mentors initially felt confident about the role, particularly in the light of their previous experience of supervising students, of pastoral care of pupils and of the processes of staff appraisal, but as they become aware of the implications of partnership, some said that they feel less secure and there is now a greater recognition by the mentors of the need for professional development in mentoring. They suggest three categories of training, prioritized as follows:

- information about the course, processes and procedures;

- training in particular skills, i.e. observation, assessment, analysis, providing feedback, reviewing;

- longer term professional development, i.e. consideration of mentoring within career structure, theoretical perspectives, the process of learning to teach, etc.

Mentors comment favourably on the improvements they have seen in training and in the documentation and materials provided by the universities, particularly in terms of the timing of its arrival in school and in its presentation. Some mentors feel overwhelmed by the amount of documentation and the increased paperwork for themselves which accompanies it. There is still some concern, however, that they are not well enough informed about the content of the PE courses which the students are following at the university and the expectations for students' teaching performance at various stages in the course.

Both universities in the study have established useful programmes for the development of mentoring skills, but these are costly to deliver at subject level and the most appropriate means of providing PE subject mentors with an extended skills training programme has yet to be decided. Also, it remains to be seen what the long term take-up of extended professional development courses will be.

Mentors' views on the quality of their training so far varies. Much of it has had a cross-curricular, generic emphasis and they see greater value in the input from university subject specialists and welcome the opportunity to meet PE colleagues from other schools.

## On mentoring as an aspect of career development

The notion of teaching as a career is a complex one. Whereas some (Lyons, 1981) see a career in teaching as being a linear progression from novice through increasing responsibility into senior management, others (Becker, 1970; Ozga, 1988) discuss the horizontal aspect of career progression (that is moving between posts at the same level), a path which for some teachers assumes greater importance than vertical promotion. Such teachers do not see their work in terms of career, but as an interesting, challenging, worthwhile and convenient job. Mentors do not appear, as yet, to have come to any clear decisions about mentoring as an aid to career advancement. The vast majority certainly see it as an invaluable aspect of professional development and indicate that the role has given them a great deal of personal and professional satisfaction. They perceive the task of helping students however, to be of questionable value, for career progression and for its status to depend on the extent to which partnership is viewed positively by headteachers and governors. Some mentors were quite clear in their minds that the route into senior management (deputy headships and headships) was via curricular and financial responsibility, not the 'softer' jobs of pastoral care or mentoring.

## On theory and practice

An interesting issue which developed in discussion is the extent to which PE mentors recall their own experience of learning to teach and build their mentoring around the positive and negative aspects of this. Life history methodology, which formed part of the research, identified 'critical incidents' (Measor, 1985) which mentors recounted and which seemed to change or amplify what they saw to be important in teaching. It is these experiences which seem to be informing mentors' 'theories in use' (i.e. the personal guidelines which practitioners develop about their work), which derive partly from empirically-based theory passed on during training and largely from experience gained 'on the job'. Each mentor has formulated, and is able to articulate to a greater or lesser extent, such 'theories in use' and we believe it is these which they pass on to their mentees. We do not know a great deal about how such theories develop and further work is needed in this area if we are to know what student teachers are learning from mentors. Mentors differ in terms of their acceptance of and interest in current theories of teaching. The variables which seem to most affect this are age and type of training (i.e. BEd or PGCE). More experienced mentors are more likely to reject a theoretical analysis of children's learning in PE and to stress craft knowledge, yet at the same time they appear to value their higher education-based training (which for the majority of those we interviewed was by means of a Teaching Certificate or

BEd and took place in colleges and polytechnics) and to compare it favourably with what they perceive to be the structure and content of current courses. They have particular concerns about PGCE courses. The small number of more recent graduates were more likely to refer to educational theory in their discussion with students and in talking to the researchers about how they conduct review sessions.

On the basis of what we are learning about how PE mentors perceive their role and the demands it makes on them, in the following section we tentatively propose a model of mentors' needs which can be used as a basis for further research and analysis or for developing mentor-support policy.

## A Proposed Model of PE Mentors' Needs

The model shown in Box 1 below has been derived from what mentors say about their work and what they feel is needed to assist them in developing quality in mentoring. Its hierarchical structure reflects more well known models (Maslow, 1954) in that it is suggested that in planning to support mentors it might be useful to work from the bottom up, that is by ensuring that resources and support are in place before making demands on the development of mentoring competence. But it must be emphasized that the model is hypothetical; it is derived from our own work with mentors but needs further empirical verification. Each element of the model is expanded and justified in the following sections.

*Box 1: A Model of Mentors' Needs*

| |
|---|
| Continuing Professional Development |
| Professional Recognition and Status |
| Opportunity for Critical Reflection |
| Competence in the Role |
| Professional Support |
| Personal Support |
| Resources |

### Resources

At the current stage of the development of school-based teacher education, this is one of the topics most often mentioned by PE mentors as being an area of concern, as it was in research by Back and Booth (1992) much earlier in partnership development. There are a great many resource issues which the school as a whole must take into account in deciding whether or not (or to how many students) to offer ITE, in addition to the impact on pupils' learning. Space in the staff room, study and IT facilities, impact on photocopying and consumables are all 'costs'. However, the resource most often commented on by PE mentors is that of 'time'. There will probably never be enough time to do the job as mentors would wish to do it, but it is important to recognise that PE mentors have a particular difficulty in this respect, a problem that is common to those teaching practical subjects in which clearing up from one lesson and preparation of a practical area for the next class takes up what little time exists between lessons. Changing room tasks (lost property, 'notes', kit, extra-curricular notices, control) require the undivided attention of both mentor and student. Extra-curricular activities make claims on time which would be otherwise available for informal discussion. PE mentors need 'quality' time to be made available in the timetabling process and for this time to be inviolate, that is not liable to be taken for 'substitution' and other duties. The problem for school managers is that the time needed to mentor appropriately is not constant, either throughout the school year or between students. More time is needed early in the student's school experience, particularly the first few days in school, and mentors comment that a student who is having difficulties later in the course requires an unexpected amount of attention if failure is to be turned into success.

In addition to time spent with students face-to-face, effective mentors need to plan carefully both the student's programme and the teaching which accompanies it. It has yet to be fully recognized that in school-based ITE, (and particularly in PE where students may lack some subject knowledge as well as inexperience in applying that knowledge to teaching the National Curriculum) the mentor's role includes developing the student's knowledge about PE activities and about how to teach them as well as responding to a student's teaching performance. The little that has been written and researched on mentoring in PE has tended to focus on the supervisory element of the role (Laker, 1994) and to ignore tutoring, which requires planning, thought and imagination as well as an understanding of the process of learning to teach. It is an aspect previously undertaken almost exclusively by the HEI, but the transfer of time allocation to schools has lessened the time available for this, and mentors will need to take up the task if students are to maintain their knowledge base and show the improvement in teaching effectiveness which the new system is designed to develop. Planning for tutoring students will involve identifying their needs, devising strategies to help them develop particular skills, planning a programme of subject knowledge expansion, structuring reviews and action plans and providing feedback. All this requires time which is in addition to basic supervision of the student and to school teaching duties such as curriculum planning, lesson preparation, marking etc. Mentors believe more cognizance must be taken of this is in the calculation of a mentor's normal teaching load.

### The Need for Personal Support

Mentoring in PE may bring many rewards, including the arrival of new ideas and youthful enthusiasm into a department; a change of focus from teaching children to training future professional colleagues; the opportunity to articulate one's ideas about teaching to a receptive colleague and thus test them out. But the role also brings stresses and conflicts which have been referred to previously and which stem from resource constraints, interactional requirements or simply the uncertainty about ones own effectiveness which everyone feels when undertaking a new role. Whereas part of the the mentor's role is to provide support and guidance to the young PE teacher, so the mentor themselves will need the support of more experienced and senior colleagues. Such support will need to be in the form of resource provider, adviser, listener and sharer of problems and involve offering mediation in the event of disagreement or conflict with other mentors or with the student. Mentoring can be very time consuming and stressful. When all is going well, mentors feels positive and confident, but if a student is not making progress, then the mentor's self-confidence may be lowered. Our research has shown that PE mentors invest a great deal of personal ambition in their mentees. They take pride in their successes, but equally tend to take responsibility for their failures. If difficulties persist, and particularly if colleagues begin to comment negatively on the effect that a particular student is having on the discipline and progress of their classes, then there is a danger that the mentor will experience self doubt, both in terms of their ability as a mentor and in extreme cases in terms of his/her own teaching ability. In such cases, the mentor will need a trusted friend to help objectify the situation.

### The Need for Professional Support

Such objectification of the student/mentor relationship is very important if the interactions are to remain on a professional footing and if both are to retain confidence in the educational setting. This is not always easy, because of the immense investment of self in the process by both student and mentor. Each have expectations of the other and tensions mount if the student does not appear to be fulfilling these, particularly if the mentor perceives the student not to be at the expected level of competence. Analyzing the reasons for this and discussing the difficulties with the student demands a sophisticated level of pedagogical and interactional skill on the part of the mentor and most need to feel that their decisions about, and strategies for, dealing with the situation have the support of other staff, particularly the co-ordinating mentor and the HEI tutor. PE mentors report feeling most confident when they are given scope to develop their own mentoring relationship with the student, but also feel part of a mentoring team, able to share 'triumphs and disasters' with others playing the same role. They thus value contacts with PE mentors in other schools as well as regular meetings with their own school's team.

### The Need to Feel Competent in the Role

One of the most common questions we faced from the mentors themselves when we talked to them about PE mentoring was 'do you think I'm doing this job properly?'. There is not the space in this chapter to analyze in detail what is meant by 'mentor competence' in the context of ITE, but we suggest three categories of competence needs as identified by mentors: to be informed of process and procedures; to be effectively trained to observe, assess and report the progress of the student; and to have confidence in one's own teaching ability.

## The need to be informed and in control

Partnership has thrown into sharp relief the need for communication systems between school and HEI to be effective, and effective at the appropriate level. Each member of the partnership role set (the headteacher, the co-ordinating mentor, the subject mentor, the student, the HEI tutor) has different requirements in terms of what they need to know and it is important to ensure that information is targeted directly at those who will be making direct use of it as well as informing those ultimately responsible for the operation of the system. One of the most challenging tasks which partnership has placed on both schools and HEIs is the need for both partners to make the processes, materials and content available in a readily accessible form to each other. Partnership implies that all such materials, and the programme itself, will have been jointly planned by schools and HEI. Such joint planning gives all those concerned empowerment and control. Most partnerships are working towards this ideal, but in practice such collaboration is an immensely time consuming process. Whatever their involvement in it has been, PE mentors need procedural detail, but also welcome subject specific information which tells them what the students will be doing in their HEI-based PE sessions and what can reasonably be expected of them at any given point in the term. Particularly crucial in this respect is the timing of courses in those activities in which the students have little experience, such as gymnastics or dance. If this information can be made available early, in time for careful planning of the student's programme and related to his/her particular strengths and needs, mentors feel in control of the process and students feel cared-for.

Both partnerships in the study have recognised the need for efficient communication networks to be set up between the HEI and schools. Electronic mail may well have an important role to play in this respect in the near future. In the meantime, a Partnership Unit, dedicated to the management of school-university communication in whatever form is appropriate, has proved invaluable in helping mentors to feel 'in touch'.

## The need for effective training

It would be fair to say that much of the early training of mentors focused on procedures, to ensure that the transfer of responsibility passed smoothly from HEI to school. What mentors themselves now recognize is that the role demands a range of skills which is not necessarily directly transposed from children to adults. Their well-established abilities to observe, assess, record and report on children's progress in PE must now be adapted to the needs of a young adult learning to teach PE. The processes are the same, but the depth of analysis and the interactional style required differ significantly. Another focus for training is the integration of students' knowledge of sport with National Curriculum requirements and teaching strategies. Mentors are the catalysts in this process of integration and need to understand how it can be developed.

There appears to be a need for mentor training materials which deal with generic issues in mentoring but which also focus on PE as a subject area. There is currently a shortage of good video footage, both of students' lessons and of the subsequent review sessions.

### Self-confidence

To develop confidence in others a teacher must have confidence in him/ herself. One of the functions of mentor training must therefore be to reinforce mentors' confidence in themselves as effective, reflective professionals. One of the justifiable criticisms of HEI-based training has been that HEI tutors did not necessarily have to demonstrate their ideas in practice. The best, of course, often did so, very effectively, but it was not a daily requirement as it is for mentors. PE mentors are very aware of their task as a role model, particularly in the early part of a school attachment, when the student is spending a lot of time observing; most take it seriously and it adds some stress to the job. They know that their teaching, their organization, their management, their relationships with colleagues and pupils, their personal presentation will all be under scrutiny by the student. To be able to challenge a student to achieve more when one is only too aware of one's own limitations takes a particular kind of self-belief which training can help foster.

### The Need for Professional Recognition and Status

As mentioned previously, PE mentors' have a need for professional recognition and status. There is both a personal and an instrumental facet to this. Recognition by colleagues of the worth of the task that one is involved in enhances self-belief and acts as a strongly motivating factor. Recognition by senior management in a school usually results in at least some of the resources necessary for the task. As has been argued, both these are essential if mentoring is to be effective. Recognition by colleagues of a job being well-done can be acquired through one's own efforts. Alternatively the role itself can have status ascribed to it. Ideally mentors would wish for both types of recognition, for the latter brings immediate benefits whilst the former takes time to establish. However, our research showed that there is some variation in ascribed status for mentors. This status is at its highest where there exists a whole-school commitment to ITE, when the co-ordinating mentor is a senior manager and when the PE mentor works within a well-co-ordinated team.

### Opportunity for Critical Reflection

This chapter is not the place to enter into the 'competence-capability-reflective practice' debate which has accompanied the development of competence-based models of teacher training (Eraut, 1989). The two partnerships involved in this study espouse the notion that if teachers are to be fully professional (rather than 'merely' competent) they need to have developed a critically reflective approach to their work. It is important to recognize Williams' (1993) point, however, that the notion of reflexivity in teaching is not a unitary concept and may best be represented as a continuum of definitions from a utilitarian mechanism for improving teaching skills at one end to a view of education as being essentially problematic and in need of reconstruction at the other (*ibid*, p. 137). Where the two partnerships lie on this continuum in terms of their view of PE teachers as critically reflective practitioners needs to be addressed. Our experience of partnership to date suggests it might be difficult to refute Williams' claim that

> . . . much of initial teacher education in physical education remains concerned with initiation into a particular culture in which a perform-ance based pedagogy, underpinned by scientific knowledge and rein-forced by personal experience, dominates thought and action. (*ibid*, p. 142)

Nevertheless, younger mentors, those trained on concurrent courses during the last ten years, claimed familiarity with the notion of critical reflection as such, were prepared to work on its development with their students and appeared to recognize value in the process. One mentor made the point that in helping the student to become more reflective about his teaching, she had begun to question and revise her own practice in a quite radical way. Herein lies the basis of a most significant 'quality circle', which may well have an important contribution to make to the raising of the standard of PE teaching in both newcomers to the profession and those already established in it.

### Continuing Professional Development

One of the aspects of mentoring which we discussed with teachers during our research was their perception of mentoring within their professional 'life his-tory' (Sparkes and Templin, 1992). As indicated in a previous paragraph, many mentors perceive that the skills and values they are developing in working with students within partnership arrangements add value to both their own teaching and to their professional development, but they feel the need for these to be channelled and legitimated. Few express an immediate interest in award-bearing courses, but the majority welcome 'mentor training' which is purposeful and, most particularly, subject-specific. The two obvious questions to be asked in relation to this need are (i) how is such training to be resourced; and (ii) who is to co-ordinate it? Each partnership will address these questions in relation to their own particular circumstances; what is important is that coherent provision of training and support for mentors is enhanced by, and does not become a victim of, competition in the market place between those agencies able and willing to provide it. There are several models of good practice (Kinder and Earley, 1995) that provide a basis for a partnership to build a network of support provision that might include the school, the HEI, the LEA and possibly other training agencies outside education. The HEIs' contribution to developing and co-ordinating such a network is seen by many as an important part of their revised role.

In spite of the sustained attack on the ITE provided by HEIs in the past, (encapsulated in the 1992 reforms) and together with the growing self-belief of the schools in their ability to do the job asked of them, PE mentors in particular recognize that there is a wealth of teacher education experience and PE expertise remaining in the HEIs which they value and wish to remain in contact with. One way of ensuring this, which several partnerships have instigated, is the setting up of subject mentor planning groups as the means by which teachers and university tutors can meet to plan and review partnership issues from a subject perspective whilst at the same time keeping in touch with subject development. Such groups, informal though they may be, may well have an important place alongside more structured forms of mentor training. Both are important if mentors are to feel supported and empowered in their role.

### Conclusion

This chapter has presented a discursive analysis of some preliminary research findings which indicate what PE mentors say about mentoring. We now need, if we are to fully understand what mentoring involves, to know more about the action theories which mentors bring to their role, and to examine its behavioural components: what mentors actually do, how they do it and how they explain and justify their actions. Therefore the next stage in the research is to develop a form of 'dyadic interaction analysis' to study the interactions between mentors and mentees (Jones, 1980).

We have argued, and provided some tentative evidence for, the idea that the development of effective partnership in initial teacher education is best served by a strategic approach to addressing the needs of mentors which might start with the provision of resources, fiscal and human, and develop through integrated and progressive programmes of continuing professional development. In terms of mentoring, these programmes should be based on a careful needs analysis. Such an analysis should take into account criteria from a number of contexts: the requirements of the Department for Education and Employment (DfEE) and the Teacher Trianing Agency (TTA); the demands of the National Curriculum and the teaching profession; mentor competence criteria, in particular the practical skills of evaluating, monitoring and providing instructional feedback. The main argument in this chapter has been that in carrying out such a needs analysis it is important to include the perceptions of the people doing the job. These perceptions cannot be the only basis for the strategy, but they should perhaps be a starting point and at the time of writing, a coherent, shared plan for mentors' professional development has yet to emerge, though individual partnerships and the Teacher Training Agency are working in this direction.

A second plea emerging from the research is for such professional development of mentors at secondary school level to be firmly rooted in the subject. Whereas all recognize the generic nature of teaching, of tutoring and of mentoring, and that much is to be gained from working with mentors in other subject areas, PE students and mentors need also to develop their skills within a subject-specific context. Managing and assessing pupils' learning in PE makes peculiar demands on student teachers, largely because of the transitory nature of action performance. Mentors therefore need particular guidance in the complex process of integrating students' knowledge of the structure of the activities with their ability to observe and analyse children's movement responses and levels of achievement. This can only be done using subject specific examples.

Another argument for resources to be available for subject-specific mentor development in PE is the changing nature of the PE teacher's role (Shenton, 1994). The integration of ITE partnerships with partnerships between primary/secondary schools and national/community agencies in sport/dance provision for children and young people, advocated by Shenton in her article and currently being pioneered in the North West of England, has enormous potential. But the concept is new. If particular PE student teachers are to be effectively trained in the role of sport/dance co-ordinators in a school, and if all are to be cognizant of the importance of the role, PE mentors need to understand it and to develop the knowledge base and networking skills which it demands. Without their support, and the training needed to generate and sustain that support, a very significant innovation will struggle to make ground.

The 1992 reforms to ITE in England and Wales, (DFE, 1992) which formalized the notion of partnership between school and HEI, have had and will continue to have far reaching effects on the quality of teaching in our schools. Central to this quality is the role of the mentor, both in ITE and beyond. PE mentors now have a clearer picture of what the role is and what its demands are. They are the main agents of what is potentially a radical and positive change in the way in which teachers are trained. For the goals of partnership to be achieved, mentors must understand and believe in the worth of the change they are being asked to instigate. They are very aware of the costs and benefits to themselves (and to their pupils) of the new system and currently appear to be prepared to invest in it. The extent to which they are able to translate the rhetoric of partnership into reality will in large part depend on whether they continue to see the benefits outweighing the costs (Sparkes, 1991). Their analysis of what is needed to do the job effectively, so as to produce highly competent, effective and proactive teachers, without prejudicing the physical education of children, deserves the most careful attention of those whose responsibility it must be to satisfy these needs.

## References

Back, D. and Booth, M. (1992) 'Commitment to mentoring' in Wilkin, M. (Ed) *Mentoring in Schools*, London, Kogan Page, pp. 29–42.

Becker, H.S. (1970) 'The career of the Chicago public school teacher' in Becker, H.S. (Ed) *Sociological Work: Method and Substance*, Chicago, Aldine, pp. 165–75.

Department for Education (1992) *Initial Teacher Training (Secondary Phase)* (Circular 9/92) London, DFE.

Eraut, M. (1989) 'Initial teacher training and the NVQ model' in Burke, J.W. (Ed) *Competency Based Education and Training*, London, Falmer Press.

Haggarty, L. (1995) 'The complexities of effective mentoring in initial teacher education', *Mentoring and Tutoring*, **2**, 3, pp. 32–41.

Hudson, J. and Latham, A-M. (1995) 'PE and dance students' perceptions of mentoring under the partnership scheme', *Mentoring and Tutoring*, **3**, 1, pp. 23–30.

Jones, G. (1980) 'The ideology of partnership in the supervision of teaching practice: An interpretative analysis of case-study material', unpublished MEd thesis, University of Liverpool.

Kinder, K. and Earley, P. (1995) 'Key issues emerging from an NFER study of NQTs' in Kerry, T. and Mayes, A.S. (Eds) *Issues in Mentoring*, London, Routledge, pp. 164–70.

Laker, A. (1994) 'A teacher's guide for supervising student teachers', *British Journal of Physical Education*, **25**, 4, pp. 31–3.

Lyons, G. (1981) *Teacher Careers and Career Perceptions*, Slough, NFER/Nelson.

McIntyre, D., Hagger, H. and Burn, K. (1994) *The Management of Student Teachers' Learning: A Guide for Professional Tutors in Secondary Schools*, London, Kogan Page.

Maslow, A.H. (1954) *Motivation and Personality*, New York, Harper and Row.

Measor, L. (1985) 'Critical incidents in the classroom: Identities, choices and careers' in Ball, S.J. and Goodson, I.F. (Eds) *Teachers' Lives and Careers*, Lewes, Falmer Press, pp. 61–77.

Ozga, J. (1988) 'The teaching career' in Open University (1988) *EP228 Frameworks for Teaching: Teachers' Work and Careers*, Milton Keynes, Open University Press.

Office of Her Majesty's Chief Inspector of Schools (OHMCIS) (1995a) *School-centred Initial Teacher Training 1993–4*, London, HMSO.

Office of Her Majesty's Chief Inspector of Schools (OHMCIS) (1995b) *Partnership: Schools and Higher Education in Partnership in Secondary Initial Teacher Training*, London, HMSO.

PHILLIPS, C.R. (1994) 'The effects of the 1992 teacher education reforms on the career perceptions of mentors: A life history approach', unpublished paper, Liverpool John Moores University.

RACE, P. (undated) 'Mentor support', unpublished paper, University of Glamorgan.

SHENTON, P.A. (1994) 'Education and training through partnership — A possible way forward', *British Journal of Physical Education*, **25**, 4, pp. 17–20.

SHILLING, H., WILLIAMS, A. and WOODHOUSE, J. (1995) 'Partnership in physical education' in WILLIAMS, A. (Ed) *Partnership in Secondary Initial Teacher Education*, London, David Fulton, pp. 83–93.

SMITH, M. (1992) 'The supervision of physical educators: A review of American literature', *British Journal of Physical Education Research Supplement*, **11**, pp. 7–12.

SPARKES, A.C. (1991) 'Exploring the subjective dimension of curriculum change' in ARMSTRONG, N. and SPARKES, A. (Eds) *Issues in Physical Education*, London, Cassell.

SPARKES, A.C. and TEMPLIN, T.J. (1992) 'Life histories and physical education teachers: Exploring the meanings of marginality' in SPARKES, A.C. (Ed) *Research in Physical Education and Sport: Exploring Alternative Visions*, London, Falmer Press, pp. 118–45.

WILLIAMS, A. (1993) 'The reflective physical education teacher: Implications for initial teacher education', *Physical Education Review,* **16**, 2, pp. 137–44.

YAU, C.K. (1995) 'From a student standpoint: My views on mentoring', *Mentoring and Tutoring,* **3**, 2, pp. 45–9.

# 9 Supporting the New Generalist Teacher in the Teaching of Physical Education in the Primary School

*Mick Mawer*

## Introduction

Whereas there is a developing UK research literature concerning the mentoring process in secondary physical education from the trainee's perspective (see Hardy 1995; Hudson and Latham 1995, and other chapters in Part 2 of this text), there has been very little examination of the process of supporting generalist student teachers with the teaching of physical education (PE) in the primary school.

A number of studies (Yeomans and Sampson, 1994; McNamara, 1993; Davies and Harrison, 1995; Campbell, 1995) have investigated various aspects of mentoring in UK primary schools, but these studies have examined primary teaching in general, and have not specifically looked at an individual curriculum area such as PE. In UK primary schools, it is the classteacher who generally undertakes the role of supporting or mentoring student teachers who are learning to teach all aspects of the primary school curriculum, including PE. Primary schools already in 'partnership' with teacher training institutions such as universities and colleges, may have a member of staff who is the designated 'mentor' of all trainees on school placement, but such a role may not necessarily involve the mentor also being the trainee's classteacher (Davies and Harrison, 1995). Therefore, the main 'supporting' member of staff for trainees in many primary schools is likely to be the classteacher. But, what do primary generalist classteachers consider should be the school's role in the training of student teachers to teach PE, and what part do they feel they, as classteachers, should play in that training?

This chapter presents the results of a preliminary small-scale study that attempts to provide answers to these and other questions by consulting the classteachers themselves. It is hoped that the issues that are raised, will not only provide an insight into the present perceived role of the primary classteacher in supporting trainees with the teaching of PE, but that it will also be of value to those who are designing partnership courses, school-based training programmes, and courses of mentor training.

### The Study

The twenty primary school teachers who had acted as the main supporting member of staff for the twenty PGCE trainees who took part in the study described in chapter 6, were interviewed using a semi-structured interview schedule. The teachers varied considerably in terms of their responsibility in the school, and their age and teaching experience. Two of the teachers were teaching headteachers in small primary schools, several were deputy head-teachers, two were curriculum co-ordinators for PE (CCPE) and four were originally PE specialists. The teachers' years of teaching experience ranged from three years to over thirty years, with the majority having between ten and twenty years of service.

The interview schedule was designed to ascertain the views of the teachers on the following topics:

- What should a student teacher be able to do as far as the teaching of PE is concerned by the end of the PGCE year?
- What parts should the university and the school play in the training of the student teacher to teach PE?
- What do classteachers see as their role in supporting student teachers in the teaching of PE?
- What knowledge and skills do classteachers feel they need to fulfil their role in supporting student teachers with the teaching of PE?
- What training do classteachers feel they need in fulfilling their role in supporting student teachers with the teaching of PE?
- What help do classteachers feel they need from other staff in supporting student teachers with the teaching of PE?
- What personal benefit did the classteachers feel they gained from supporting a student teacher with the teaching of PE?

The data from the interviews was transcribed and analyzed using a content analysis procedure.

### Teachers' Views of What a Trainee Should be Able to do Concerning the Teaching of PE by the End of the PGCE Course

The majority of the teachers in this study (70 per cent) expected trainees to be able to plan lessons and teach all the activities in the primary school PE National Curriculum (which includes gymnastics, dance, games, athletic activities, and outdoor and adventurous activities), although a number of teachers were uncertain about the necessity for trainees to be able to teach swimming, as in many schools this was generally taught by qualified instructors at the local pool. A knowledge of the procedures used by schools when they take children swimming was considered to be sufficient by many teachers. In addition the teachers also expected trainees (with percentage of teachers mentioning the issue in brackets):

- to be aware of safety issues (80 per cent);
- to be able to organise a PE lesson (65 per cent);
- to have a good knowledge of progression in each PE activity area (35 per cent)
- to be able to observe pupils' movements and give appropriate feedback (30 per cent);
- to be able to control and manage a class in PE — including having good class positioning to monitor pupils' work and being aware of management rules and routines (25 per cent).

Other, less frequently mentioned teaching skills that teachers expected of trainees included an ability to demonstrate skills; provide a class (or pupil) demonstration; have good communication skills, such as being able to explain well and adapting one's language to the age of the children; a good knowledge of game rules; know how to assess children in PE; be aware of health and other cross-curricular issues in PE; and have a knowledge of childrens' development.

### The University Role

Teachers expected that the university course in the teaching of PE should provide trainees with information in the areas discussed above, and three-quarters of them felt that the course should give trainees a 'good grounding' in all areas of the the PE National Curriculum except swimming. However, several teachers felt that a knowledge of a 'core' of activities, such as gymnastics and games, was all that was needed and was realistic in terms of the length of the university course, which was twenty-four hours in duration. Also, teachers considered that the university course should:

- teach trainees how to plan lessons in all areas of PE (80 per cent);
- cover safety issues for all areas of PE (80 per cent);
- make trainees aware of organization and management skills in PE (75 per cent);
- provide trainees with a knowledge of progression in each PE activity (30 per cent);
- have schemes of work for trainees to consult (25 per cent).

In addition, some teachers felt that the course should provide trainees with the opportunity to watch children being taught PE either live or on video, and give information on teaching skills such as 'how to observe and give feedback to children on their performance', and the use of the voice for clear communication.

Occasional mention was also made of the need to discuss such areas as the aims of PE, assessment, differentiation, different types of school equipment and facilities, resources (including recommending books and guidelines for teaching the various activities), rules of games, and to provide trainees with the opportunity to take additional courses in the teaching of a variety of sports.

There was a strong feeling that the university should be providing the trainee with most of the 'knowledge' about teaching PE, as one classteacher pointed out:

> Well, I would expect you to be more of the specialist — I'm talking about the subject help — and the teacher in the school would do more of the organisational and safety side. I don't have a great deal of knowledge or background in the subject so I would feel you (the University) were more qualified.

### The School's Role

As far as the schools' role in the partnership was concerned the comments of the teachers centred around the following issues:

- providing experience of observing teaching;
- providing background knowledge for teaching;
- assistance and advice with the planning for teaching;
- providing experience of practising teaching;
- supervision in the development of the trainee's teaching skills.

The school's role in providing experience of observing teaching was seen by 40 per cent of the teachers as 'giving demonstration lessons', and by two teachers as 'showing an example of good practice', and to 'observe other staff with particular expertise'.

Just over a quarter of the teachers felt that trainees needed to be provided with information about the school's schemes of work for PE, the resources that were available for teaching PE, and 55 per cent saw it as important for trainees to be aware of the school policy for safety in PE, and the school rules and regulations for PE lessons (for example, clothing, barefoot work, etc). Provision of background knowledge about management rules, routines and procedures, the school PE policy, or assessment in PE, were mentioned by some teachers. Four teachers considered it important for trainees to meet the school CCPE.

Six (30 per cent) of the teachers mentioned that the school should provide assistance with the planning of lessons, but three of these teachers implied that they should 'check' the trainees planning rather than help them with it.

There was unanimous agreement that schools ought to provide trainees with the opportunity to experience teaching all areas of the PE curriculum during their training year, eight (40 per cent) teachers considered it important for trainees to attend a residential, and four felt that trainees should be aware of the school's procedures for taking children to the swimming pool. However, some teachers thought that providing the opportunity to teach each PE curriculum area could be problematical because schools had their own PE scheme (including only certain activities) for each term. Also, some small rural primary schools lacked an indoor space for gymnastics and dance. Some teachers felt that one of the answers to this problem might be for the first school placement to attempt to provide the trainee with experience of teaching gymnastics, dance and winter games, and the second placement offer summer games, athletic activities and outdoor and adventurous activities. Most teachers agreed with the idea of a professional development 'profile' following (or preceding) the trainee to the second placement school to help staff to identify any 'gaps' in a trainee's teaching experience in PE.

A quarter of the teachers felt that the schools' supervisory role should entail staff working alongside the trainee in a collaborative teaching approach in the development of their teaching, observational, and feedback skills, and suggesting ways to improve their teaching.

Although about a third of the teachers seemed to have a clear vision of the role of the school in complementing the work done on the university PE course, the majority of the teachers appeared to see the role of the school as being 'the provider of opportunities to practise', rather than to build on and extend the knowledge provided by the university.

### What Classteachers Perceived as the Role of a Mentor Supporting Trainees with the Teaching of PE

The twenty teachers identified seventy different aspects of the role of a classteacher supporting a trainee with the teaching of PE, and these were grouped into the following broad categories in order to provide an image of what these teachers perceived as the mentoring role and skills required of the supporting classteacher:

- providing the trainee with the opportunity to observe teaching and acting as a 'role model' and 'guide' for the understanding of teaching;
- providing the trainee with the background information and support for preparing to teach;
- to work with the trainee in a collaborative approach to learning to teach;
- a supervisory role in the development of the trainee's teaching skills.

### A 'Guide' and 'Role Model' for Understanding Teaching

The majority of teachers (70 per cent) stated that a mentor should take demonstration lessons for the trainee to observe, and five other teachers mentioned the importance of 'being a good role model' or 'good teaching example'. But, simply observing the teaching act does not necessarily mean that the trainee will be able to understand the significance of the various teaching behaviours on display. Maynard and Furlong (1993) suggest that this 'apprenticeship' model of mentoring or learning to teach does require an 'interpreter' to enable the trainee 'to see', or make sense of teaching in conceptual terms and appreciate the significance of certain classroom events and behaviours (Furlong and Maynard, 1995, p. 71). As Maynard and Furlong (1993) point out, trainees need:

> ... to be able to model themselves on someone. Such a model can also act as a guide, articulating and presenting 'recipes' that will work. (p. 79)

One of the classteachers in this study reinforced this view:

> I would hope to be a good example, a role model, to guide them and answer any queries and help with planning ... suggestions and praise.

But, although the teachers did appear to see the mentoring role including 'modelling' teaching for the apprentice to see and possibly copy, did they appreciate the importance of being an 'interpreter' or 'guide' to enable the trainee to understand the complexities of teaching? Four of the teachers did seem to appreciate that it was important for a mentor to 'explain their teaching' or 'talk through their class organization and planning', and their 'class rules and routines' with the trainee. One teacher explained how this would be done:

> ... I would show them how I do things, and I would point out to them safety aspects because different teachers have different kinds of rules — I would show what I expect from children because that's my class and they're used to working a certain way, and I would show them how I would develop something over a shorter period of time just so they could see it.

Another teacher felt it was important for the trainee to initially be able to see them working with a class:

> ... so they would have the opportunity to observe the children working and then discuss afterwards any points they wished to raise about why I'd done certain things and why things were done in certain ways throughout the lesson.

These teachers seemed to appreciate the importance of articulating to the trainee their professional knowledge or 'situational understandings' that they had built up over years of experience; and some consider this to be the 'central task' of mentoring (Wilkin, 1992). However, one can appreciate why other teachers in this study did not immediately think of this as being an essential aspect of the mentoring role because, as Furlong and Maynard (1995) discovered in their research in primary schools, teachers 'often found it difficult to articulate their "taken-for-granted" practical professional knowledge' (p. 167). This may be particularly true of those primary teachers who, having had little training in the teaching of PE themselves, still feel underconfident about teaching certain aspects of the subject. The majority of the primary teachers in this study felt "underconfident" about teaching at least one aspect of the primary school PE curriculum, and 55 per cent of them had felt 'underconfident' about teaching PE when they had completed their training. It is therefore possible that many of the classteachers who act in the role of mentor to trainees may have difficulty articulating their pedagogy in PE because, as far as this subject is concerned, they may still be 'learning to see' themselves.

### Provider of Information and Advice to Support Planning

Only half of the teachers stated that the role of a mentor should involve 'help with the planning of lessons', or to 'check lesson planning', and this point was reinforced by the 60 per cent of trainees being supported by these teachers (see chapter 6) who 'never' had help with their planning or had their lesson planning checked before teaching.

Less than a quarter of the teachers mentioned that the mentoring role should entail the provision of the various items of background knowledge of resources, facilities, equipment, children's abilities and experiences, safety, and schemes of work that are essential for planning lessons. Yet trainees saw these issues as being areas that they needed particular help with from their mentor (see chapter 6). It was surprising that so few teachers mentioned that the mentor's role should entail informing trainees of safety issues when 75 per cent of them had seen this as an important aspect of the school's role in the training process. Maybe they expected trainees to 'pick up' this information as they become more familiar with the school's procedures.

### Collaborative Teaching

A definite 'thread' running through the statements of teachers was the importance of mentors using a collaborative approach to learning to teach during the trainee's early teaching experiences. When asked if they could visualize appropriate 'stages' in learning to teach PE and the experiences that trainees should have at each stage, the majority of teachers saw collaborative approaches to learning to teach being a second stage following lesson observation and the university course. Half of the teachers saw collaborative teaching as a part of the mentor's role, and a further four teachers mentioned 'working out the lessons together' and 'planning together', for teaching. Maynard and Furlong (1993) view the term 'collaborative teaching' (see Burn, 1992; Tomlinson, 1995) as a 'powerful' substitute for the term 'apprenticeship', in that the trainee is involved in the teacher's planning (they plan together), has a role in the teaching of the lesson (having a responsibility for some part of the lesson) as well as the evaluating of the lesson, and thus by becoming:

> ... an 'insider' to the planning and execution of the lesson, the student has the opportunity to model the teacher's teaching at a level of great detail. (Furlong and Maynard, 1995, p. 184)

Two of the teachers saw the mentoring role as very much a 'partnership', and they viewed the mentor-mentee relationship in a similar way to that described by some of the primary teachers in the Bedford TEAM Project (Yeomans, 1994), in that the relationships described by Yeomans, 'acquired some of the qualities of a relationship between equals' (p. 110).

One teacher thought that the mentoring role should entail alternating between 'acting as follower and leader yet still very much in charge', thus giving the trainee the opportunity to take further responsibility for teaching as they became more confident, yet always being ready to offer appropriate advice.

### The Supervisory Role

Most of the teachers suggested that the third stage in learning to teach PE might involve the trainee taking whole lessons by themselves with the mentor observing and later providing feedback on the lesson at a debriefing meeting afterwards.

One teacher felt that the role of the mentor during an observed lesson ought to be negotiated with the trainee, but two teachers considered it important to intervene if necessary, particularly if there were safety problems. However, two other teachers felt that the mentor should not interfere during a trainee's lesson.

There was little mention of advice on lesson content and whether the trainee should follow the school's scheme of work, although one teacher suggested that the mentor should provide the trainee with the 'opportunity to experiment'.

All the teachers felt that an important aspect of the mentor's role would be to provide feedback following observation of the trainee's lesson. Three teachers actually stated that this should be in the form of written feedback, but the large majority of teachers felt that because of time constraints oral feedback would suffice. Teachers felt that post-lesson meetings might involve the mentor in offering 'alternatives and solutions', 'advice and suggestions on how to improve', and 'suggestions on how the lesson might be developed'. However, 80 per cent of the teachers suggested that during lesson debriefings they ought to 'pose questions' in order to 'get the trainee to think about the lesson', and nine (45 per cent) of the teachers appreciated the importance of mentors encouraging trainees to 'be reflective'. In the TEAM Project's primary study, Sampson and Yeomans (1994) noted the use of questioning by mentors as an 'educator' strategy to promote trainee independence and develop in trainees a 'self-analytic' strategy which may later lead to 'reflective analysis' (p. 90). One teacher explained why she used this approach to de-briefings:

> I think it's important that they see the need to reflect on why they've done the lesson that way. I think there's a way of asking questions — 'Why did you do that?' . . . or 'Did you think of doing it another way?' or, 'Did you think of involving so and so?' — but it's asking questions rather than saying 'You should have done this', or, 'You should have taken it that way'.

Teachers had differing views of how a post-lesson conference should be conducted, but the majority of teachers tended to mention the same strategies as the following teacher:

> Talk through the lesson with the student — ask them first what they thought — get them to reflect on the lesson. Then talk about what was good and what needs to be improved — balancing the strengths and weaknesses, the positive and the negative aspects of the lesson. But they have got to be told if it's unsafe — you have to be honest . . .

At least half of the teachers felt it was important to 'be honest' in the post-lesson conference even though they considered that the mentor should 'be positive', 'encourage', and try to 'build confidence'. There is evidence (Borko and Mayfield, 1995) that classteachers may place a priority on being positive with trainees in order to build their confidence and 'maximize comfort and minimize risks in the student teaching experience' (p. 516), but it may also be because mentors find the 'supporting' role easier (Jayne, 1995). However, as Cameron-Jones and O'Hara (1995, p. 197) also point out, sometimes a concentration on being 'supportive' and 'encouraging' with trainees might not 'challenge' them in the same way that forcing the trainee in discussion to 'defend a decision' or 'prove a point' might do (p. 197). One teacher commented upon the mentoring skills needed to balance being honest with being supportive, and challenging the trainee:

> These are really personal qualities — you've got to tread a fine line between support and constructive criticism. You've got to maintain a

certain level of confidence in them, they've got to be aware of where they are going wrong and what they need to do to improve it. I say 'Do you think you should have done that?', or 'What did you think about that?' I wouldn't just give a list of compliments or criticisms, I make them think for themselves.

The majority of teachers did feel it was important to question trainees about their lessons and to be honest in lesson de-briefings. However, we know very little about the types of questions they asked, whether they were attempting to encourage the trainee to think about their teaching skills (or what is referred to as 'performance pedagogy'), whether they were challenging the trainee to reflect on pupil learning, or to consider such wider issues (for example, equality of opportunity, sexism, etc) in keeping with what has been termed a 'critical pedagogy' (Kirk, 1986; Tinning, 1992).

One teacher saw the post-lesson conference reflecting a 'partnership' relationship with the trainee:

> . . . the whole thing's a partnership, it's not becoming the heavy-handed thing, 'This is wrong, that is wrong' — no, we're doing it together, . . . we went into it together in the first place . . . so together we reflect on it, together we look at alternatives . . .

Quite a number of teachers mentioned the need for mentors to have certain 'attributes' or 'personal qualities'. For example, the need to have 'empathy' with the trainee was mentioned by nearly half of the teachers (45 per cent), others mentioned such qualities as being 'positive', 'supportive', and 'enthusiastic', 'sympathetic', 'approachable', to be 'encouraging' and be a 'good listener'. There was also individual mention of such qualities as 'having patience', 'being confident', 'being sensitive', 'tactful', 'accessible', 'helpful', and being able 'to relate' and develop 'good relationships' with trainees. 'Not being overbearing', 'having a sense of humour', 'making the trainee welcome', being a 'point of reference', and 'being prepared to give time' were also mentioned by individual teachers. Most of these personal qualities and skills might be considered to be valuable in a 'counselling' role, and a quarter of the teachers did mention the need for mentors to have 'counselling skills'.

A 'personal' or counselling dimension to the mentoring role does imply that mentors ought to be aware of trainees' concerns and changing needs. Only three of the teachers referred to these issues as part of the mentoring role, and when asked what they considered to be the training 'needs' of the student teacher they had supervised the previous term, very few teachers were able to accurately state a 'need' that matched the concerns and difficulties experienced by their trainee. Those who were aware of their trainee's concerns and difficulties were noticeably considered to be 'effective' or 'very effective' mentors by their trainees.

## Fulfilling the Mentoring Role: Mentors' Training Needs

Classteachers were asked whether they felt that they needed training to fulfil any aspects of the mentoring role in supporting trainees with the teaching of PE. Sixteen (80 per cent) of the classteachers considered that they did need training, and a variety of aspects of mentoring in PE were mentioned, including the following:

- Mentoring skills generally — six teachers mentioned different aspects of mentoring such as 'knowledge of the mentoring role', 'general mentor training', and 'mentoring skills'. Two others teachers referred to 'adult learning techniques' and 'learning to communicate my teaching'.
- Lesson observation and debriefing skills — nine teachers mentioned different issues related to this aspect of the mentoring role. These included 'what to look for in the observation of lessons', 'evaluating lessons', 'how to record observations', 'giving feedback', and 'how to de-brief students'.
- Updating knowledge of PE — seven teachers mentioned such issues as 'becoming more up to date with PE', 'filling gaps in my knowledge of PE', 'get to know more about PE', and specific reference was made to such areas as dance, outdoor and adventurous activities, gymnastics, and athletics.
- Background information — four teachers felt it would be useful to be given more information about the University course, and two teachers mentioned knowledge of 'competencies', and 'what students are expected to do'.

The classteachers were also shown a list of the the help and assistance that their trainees had requested of their mentors. The teachers were asked to indicate if they felt 'confident' or 'needed training' to provide that assistance. Most of the teachers felt confident about giving trainees information about use of facilities and equipment, safety, and class management. They were also happy about providing schemes of work, helping with planning of lessons, giving demonstration lessons, and observing lessons and giving written feedback in games (although five preferred to do this orally), but up to a third of teachers were less confident about gymnastics, dance and athletics, and half felt underconfident about providing such help with outdoor and adventurous activities (OAA). In fact, about a quarter of teachers felt schemes of work should be provided by the school CCPE. The majority of teachers were confident to work in a collaborative teaching format with trainees in all activities except OAA, and a third felt they needed training in 'helping trainees with the use of a variety of teaching styles and strategies in PE'.

This lack of confidence on the part of some classteachers to support trainees with the teaching of such activities as gymnastics, dance, athletics and OAA, does seem to reflect their own initial training. When asked if they had felt confident with the teaching of PE when they left training, 55 per cent said that they had not, three had no training in the teaching of PE at all, and two attended courses of less than ten hours duration. About a third had received no training in the teaching of athletics, and a half no training in OAA. Up to a half considered that their training to teach gymnastics, dance, athletics and OAA had been 'not adequate' or 'poor'. These results continue to support the findings of studies of inadequate initial training in the teaching of primary school PE published in the last fifteen years (Mawer and Head-Rapson, 1984) and more recently reported by Carney (1995).

As far as this sample of classteachers is concerned, it would appear that a lack of confidence in teaching the subject could lead to what Parker (1990) suggests may be an 'uncertainty of enacting the role of mentor' (p. 18), and therefore some of them may need training or additional support with the role. The teachers were actually asked if they were 'happy to support trainees with the teaching of PE alone' or whether they felt that 'other staff should be involved'. Sixteen of them (80 per cent) preferred to have other staff involved, the remainder being either a CCPE themselves, were PE trained, or a head-teacher, and felt more confident in the mentoring role. When asked which col-leagues they would like to have involved, 75 per cent mentioned the school CCPE, with the remainder wanting either 'other staff with particular expertise' (for example, dance) or a combination of such staff and the CCPE. One teacher mentioned that she would like 'everyone' involved, and hinted at the notion of 'the mentoring school' (Kelly *et al*, 1992) in which, as Campbell (1995) sug-gests 'everyone mentors each other' (p. 8) and staff collaboration and consul-tation are part of the self-supporting ethos of the school.

When the teachers were asked what they would want 'other staff' to do in supporting the trainee, the majority wanted the CCPE to do what appeared to be a large part of the mentoring role in PE including, providing schemes of work, helping with lesson planning, demonstration lessons, observing trainees teaching, debriefing, etc., although some teachers just needed help with areas of activity in which they were less confident.

The notion that a number of teaching staff might be involved in various aspects of mentoring a trainee in the primary school is not new. Stephenson and Taylor (1995) noted that a 'mentoring matrix' may exist in primary schools in which the trainee's environment during school experience contains:

> . . . not only the mentor (nominally responsible for the student teacher's development): but other people (who may be co-mentors or minor mentors, or mentor-like in some of the things they do to help the student teacher's development). (p. 5)

Watkins and Walley (1993) also refer to 'multiple mentors' being involved in a whole school view of the mentoring process, including the further profes-sional development of all staff in the school (p. 137).

The classteachers in this study appeared to prefer to be part of a 'matrix' of mentoring support as far as PE is concerned. However, one classteacher did feel that there was a danger that if too many people were involved in supporting the trainee in a mentoring way, then the trainee might become confused with the 'stream' of advice coming from different sources. Even 'shared mentoring' by two teachers supporting a trainee has been known to fail if the two teachers have different classroom styles and approaches to teaching (Dart and Drake, 1993).

## Staff Development: Benefits of Supporting a Trainee

Several authors have suggested that acting in the role of mentor for a trainee may have considerable staff development benefits, such as opportunities to reflect on one's own practice, developing an insight into personal professional developmental needs, learning and using specific mentoring skills (for example, listening, observing practice, providing feedback), opportunities to discuss one's pedagogy with others, the chance to learn new ideas from contact with student teachers in training — all of which might enhance and develop a teacher's own teaching and be transferable to other professional situations (Kelly *et al*, 1992; Shaw, 1992a; Magliaro *et al*, 1994).

The majority (85 per cent) of the classteachers considered that they had benefited professionally from supporting a trainee. The most frequently mentioned benefits had been to do with new ideas and approaches to teaching the subject, such as: 'I saw how lessons were done that I felt less confident about', 'Ideas — the way she broke lessons down and structured the development of skills', 'Ideas for outdoor and adventurous activities', 'Saw new teaching approaches and learned about cricket teaching skills'. One teacher said that she '. . . drew knowledge from the university course that the student had attended'. Very few teachers mentioned that they had become more reflective about their teaching, although one commented that 'I was able to look at my own teaching, and this made me more reflective'.

## Implications

Although it is difficult to draw any clear implications from what is a preliminary, small-scale investigation, the fact that there is very little research literature on the topic of classteacher support or mentoring of trainees in PE in primary schools in the UK, whatever information we do have, ought to some degree guide our future practice and planning of partnership teacher training and mentor training programmes.

The results of this study have also identified some suggestions for the mentor training of those teachers who are likely to be involved in supporting a trainee with the teaching of PE, and for the liaison that ought to occur between the two 'partners' in the training process — the school and the university.

There are therefore three main issues that have been raised by this study concerning the school-based support of generalist trainees in their preparation for teaching PE:

- the need for clear communication between school and university concerning the training 'entitlement' of the student teacher;
- planning the trainee's programme of professional learning experiences;
- the training of mentors to support the trainee with the teaching of PE.

### *The Trainee's Entitlement: The School and University in Partnership*

Both partners in the training process need to be clear about what each other should be doing in order for the trainee to receive the training that will enable them to feel confident about the teaching of all aspects of the PE National Curriculum to their classes as newly-qualified teachers. Because of the limited time now available for initial university-based courses in the teaching of PE, a greater responsibility is now placed on the school to provide not only the necessary experience of teaching all aspects of the primary school PE curriculum, but also to plan a school-based training programme to 'top up' or extend the trainee's knowledge beyond what was covered in the university. To ensure that the trainee does receive their training 'entitlement', there may be a case for a more a formative professional training 'profile' that records the knowledge and teaching experiences provided during the training year. This ongoing, formative profile may be added to (or become) the proposed 'summative' document or 'career entry profiles' being trialled by the Teacher Training Agency in the UK in 1996. This would enable schools 'hosting' PGCE students for their second period of school experience to identify trainee strengths and weaknesses, or 'gaps' in their knowledge and teaching experience, and to plan a professional training programme to match the individual trainee's needs. The profile would contain details of the professional training programme provided for the trainee in both periods of school placement and might then follow the trainee into the first year of teaching to provide information for those acting in a mentoring capacity to identify the PE in-service needs of the newly-qualified primary teacher.

### *The school-based professional training programme*

Wilkin (1992) has suggested that when devising a programme of school-based training for a student teacher, the following principles should be considered (pp. 86–9):

- the school and the university should negotiate the agreed training responsibilities of the school;
- the planned programme for the trainee should be developmental and build upon the individual trainee's previous experience and progress;
- the training programme should be clearly articulated to all concerned and should include provision for assessment of the trainee;
- the mentor should be accountable for ensuring their training work with the student teacher is planned according to the trainee's needs, and that records are kept of the trainee's progress.

Evidence from this study (and that reported in chapter 6) suggests that the training of the student teacher to teach PE may not always be clearly articulated and planned or based on the trainee's needs at that time, and in some cases can result in a rather 'hit and miss' process. As Watkins and Whalley (1993) also suggest, the training programme should be 'appropriate for a particular learner teacher at a particular stage' (p. 135).

Student teachers need to be treated as individuals with their own concerns, apprehensions and learning needs (see chapter 6). Evidence from this study would suggest that classteachers may have difficulty identifying the training needs of their student teachers. Therefore, a starting point for planning a trainee's programme of learning experiences may be a process of 'needs analysis' (Shaw, 1992b) with the mentor discussing and negotiating with the trainee what they feel they have achieved and are confident about, and what they are ready to move onto. Such 'identified needs' may then be translated into a set of progressive, planned learning experiences and professional targets.

The teachers in this study had initial difficulties in identifying the 'stages' that a trainee may go through in the process of learning to teach PE, and in articulating the appropriate learning experiences for each stage. But the majority did visualize a training process similar to what Tomlinson (1995) refers to as 'progressively collaborative teaching' in which the trainee 'engages in teaching with another, usually more experienced/mentor teacher, initially staying very much within the mentor's framework and undertaking limited aspects with support, but progressively trying out and taking a wider range of more extensive aspects of teaching' (p. 197). This process might entail:

(i)   guided observation of the mentor's teaching and introduction to the mentor's immediate and long-term planning, and an opportunity to share the mentor's post-lesson reflection;
(ii)  trainee to be involved in some limited planning of part of the lesson in collaboration with the mentor, and to teach part of the lesson or a group of children within the lesson. Reflection on the lesson continues to be shared;
(iii) trainee gradually takes over more of the planning and teaching of the lesson with the mentor observing and joining the trainee in joint analysis and reflection.

Although the advantages of collaborative teaching are well documented (Burn, 1992; Tomlinson, 1995), and trainees themselves see the value of this approach (see chapter 6), there are dangers that those planning such an arrangement need to be aware of. First of all, collaborative teaching needs planning and this takes time. Secondly, the mentor needs to be prepared to put their practice under scrutiny, be open and flexible, and able to articulate their teaching to the trainee. Thirdly, mentors should guard against viewing the trainee as an extra 'pair of hands', as several trainees in the study discussed in chapter 6 felt they had gained very little by being given a group of children to practise on, and having no help with planning, or feedback of their lesson. Mentors also need to appreciate when the trainee should progress from working alongside the teacher, to being given more independence in planning and teaching. Tomlinson (1995) is also of the opinion that trainees would benefit from engaging in collaborative teaching with several teachers who may have contrasting teaching styles.

### Training of Mentors to Support Trainees in the Teaching of PE

There are many classteachers in the UK who, regardless of their limited training in the teaching of PE, have been doing their best to support student teachers with their teaching of the subject. But, as schools enter into partnerships with universities and colleges, and a greater role is demanded of the generalist classteacher, there are doubts whether the classteacher alone is able to provide the extended knowledge base and support that the trainee needs. As the majority of classteachers in this study felt 'underconfident' about teaching several of the PE National Curriculum activities, a point also noted by OFSTED (1995):

> Many primary classteachers lack subject knowledge in physical education, and are not confident that they can meet the requirements of the National Curriculum. (p. 14)

— then we could be creating a situation in which 'the blind are really leading the blind'!

The results of this study do suggest that some generalist classteachers would prefer to be part of a team or 'matrix' of staff supporting the student teacher, but the majority wanted the school CCPE to be assisting with the task or possibly acting in the role of 'mentor for PE' for all trainees in the school. In some schools there may therefore be a case for the CCPE being the person who plans the PE training programme for trainees and possibly trains other staff (such as the classteacher) to fulfil aspects of the support process. In this case it would be the CCPE that might attend 'mentor training' courses for PE, so what might such training entail? On the basis of the findings from this study, mentor training for PE might include discussion of such issues as:

- general mentoring skills and the role of the mentor in supporting a generalist trainee with the teaching of PE;
- student teachers as adult learners;
- knowledge of teaching competencies to teach physical education;
- identifying individual trainees' needs and understanding their concerns;
- planning the school-based professional training programme;
- awareness of trainees' stages of development in learning to teach PE and the need to adapt the mentoring role accordingly (see Furlong and Maynard, 1995, p. 181):

  *Stage 1* — Mentor as 'role model' with focussed trainee observation of mentor's lessons (for example, management rules and routines)

  *Stage 2* — Mentor as 'collaborator' within progressively collaborative teaching format (see Tomlinson, 1995, pp. 196–201)

  *Stage 3* — Mentor as 'coach' and 'facilitator' systematically observing trainee teaching, giving feedback on teaching performance, and initiating trainee reflection of the lesson

  *Stage 4* — Mentor as 'critical friend', observing trainee lessons and helping the trainee to focus more on pupil learning through effective teaching

  *Stage 5* — Mentor as 'co-enquirer' and partner in investigations and teaching experiments related to developing different approaches and teaching styles for pupil learning

- mentoring skills and strategies for each of the above mentor roles:

  — articulating teaching and professional knowledge;
  — planning trainees focused observation of mentor's lessons;
  — working with the trainee in a collaborative teaching format;
  — structured observation of trainee's lessons;
  — supervision and debriefing feedback skills (see Watkins, 1992);
  — assisting critical analysis and reflection;
  — acting in the role of 'critical friend' and 'co-enquirer';
  — interpersonal skills such as 'befriending and counselling' (Wilkin, 1995);

- the use of a formative professional training profile to monitor trainee progress in the development of experiences and competencies to teach PE.

### A Final Point

Before the trainee professional development programmes and profiles, and mentor training programmes suggested in this chapter can be developed, an appropriate 'infrastructure' needs to be in place to enable effective school-based primary training in PE to flourish. That basic infrastruture needed to raise the profile of primary school PE is hinted at in the Teacher Training Agency's (TTA, 1995) proposals for 'increasing Key Stage 2 teacher's subject knowledge', and 'specialist teaching in the primary phase, focusing on subject co-ordinators'; and in the Government's blueprint for the future of sport in schools 'Raising the Game' (Department of National Heritage, 1995), in which it is stated that:

> . . . initial teacher training courses will ensure that new primary teachers . . . have the skills to deliver the strengthened commitment to sport set out in this Policy Statement . . . (p. 14)

Although the job description and work of primary PE co-ordinators appears to need attention (OFSTED, 1995), many classteachers in the study described in this chapter have suggested that the involvement of the specialist PE co-ordinator in the mentoring of generalist student teachers is essential, and it may therefore be appropriate that mentor training in PE be directed towards this 'key player' in the school-based training process.

## References

BORKO, H. and MAYFIELD, V. (1995) 'The roles of the co-operating teacher and university supervisor in learning to teach', *Teaching and Teacher Education*, **11**, 5, pp. 501–18.

BURN, K. (1992) 'Collaborative teaching' in WILKIN, M. (Ed) *Mentoring in Schools*, London, Kogan Page.

CAMERON-JONES, M. and O'HARA, P. (1995) 'Mentors' perceptions of their roles with students in initial teacher training', *Cambridge Journal of Education*, **25**, 2, pp. 189–99.

CAMPBELL, A. (1995) 'The mentoring school: Tensions and dilemmas for primary schools', *Mentoring and Tutoring*, **2**, 3, pp. 6–13.

CARNEY, C. (1995) 'Initial teacher training and the delivery of National Curriculum physical education in Key Stages 1 and 2', paper presented at the annual conference of the Physical Education Association UK, April.

DART, L. and DRAKE, P. (1993) 'School-based teacher training: A conservative practice?', *Journal of Education for Teaching*, **19**, 2, pp. 175–89.

DAVIES, J. and HARRISON, M. (1995) 'Mentors' roles in a primary articled teachers' scheme', *Mentoring and Tutoring*, **3**, 1, pp. 49–56 and 65.

DEPARTMENT OF NATIONAL HERITAGE (1995) *Sport: Raising the Game*, London, HMSO.

FURLONG, J. and MAYNARD, T. (1995) *Mentoring Student Teachers: The Growth of Professional Knowledge*, London, Routledge.

HARDY, C. (1995) 'The organisation of mentoring in school-based initial training courses: Perceptions of pre-service physical education teachers', *Bulletin of Physical Education*, **31**, 1, pp. 55–61.

HUDSON, J. and LATHAM, A-M. (1995) 'PE and dance students perceptions of mentoring under the partnership scheme', *Mentoring and Tutoring*, **3**, 1, pp. 23–31.

JAYNE, E. (1995) 'Mentoring: A universal panacea for staff development', *Teacher Development*, **4**, 3, pp. 41–8.

KELLY, M., BECK, T. and THOMAS, J. (1992) 'Mentoring as a staff development activity' in WILKIN, M. (Ed) *Mentoring in Schools*, London, Kogan Page, pp. 173–80.

KIRK, D. (1986) 'A critical pedagogy for teacher education: Towards an inquiry oriented approach', *Journal of Teaching in Physical Education*, **5**, pp. 230–46.

MAGLIARO, S.G., NILES, R.A., WILDMAN, T.M., WALKER, D.C. and MADDEX, J.S. (1994) 'Challenges, changes, and chances for professional development in the 90's', paper presented at the annual meeting of the American Educational Research Association, New Orleans, April.

MAYNARD, T. and FURLONG, J. (1993) 'Learning to teach and models of mentoring' in MCINTYRE, D., HAGGER, H. and WILKIN, M. (Eds) *Mentoring: Perspectives on School-based Teacher Education*, London, Kogan Page, pp. 69–85.

MAWER, M. and HEAD-RAPSON, B. (1984) 'Professional courses in physical education for non-specialist primary and middle school teachers' in MAWER, M. and SLEAP, M. (Eds) *Physical Education within Primary Education*, London, Physical Education Association, pp. 14–21.

MCNAMARA, D. (1993) *Student Teachers' Classroom Practice: The Influence of Their Tutors and Mentors*, Report of a Mentor Teacher Training Project, The University of Hull.

OFFICE FOR STANDARDS IN EDUCATION (OFSTED) (1995) *Physical Education, A Review of Inspection Findings 1993/94*, London, HMSO.

PARKER, M.B. (1990) 'Adolescent dancing and the mentoring of beginning teachers', paper presented at the annual meeting of the American Educational Research Association, Boston, April.

SAMPSON, J. and YEOMANS, R. (1994) 'Analyzing the work of mentors: The role' in YEOMANS, R. and SAMPSON, J. (Eds) *Mentorship in the Primary School*, London, Falmer Press, pp. 62–75.

SHAW, R. (1992a) 'Mentoring' in SHAW, R. (Ed) *Teacher Training in Secondary Schools*, London, Kogan Page, pp. 173–80.

SHAW, R. (1992b) 'Can mentoring raise achievement in schools?' in WILKIN, M. (Ed) *Mentoring in Schools*, London, Kogan Page, pp. 82–95.

STEPHENSON, H.J. and TAYLOR, M.I. (1995) 'Diverse views of the mentoring process in initial teacher training', paper presented at the International Mentoring Association Annual Conference, San Antonio, Texas, April.

TEACHER TRAINING AGENCY (1995) 'The Continuing Professional Development of Teachers'. Advice to Secretary of State for Education and Employment, July.

TINNING, R. (1992) 'Teacher education pedagogy: Dominant discourses and the process of problem setting' in WILLIAMS, T., ALMOND, A. and SPARKES, A. (Eds) *Sport and Physical Activity: Moving Towards Excellence*, London, E & FN Spon, pp. 23–40.

TOMLINSON, P. (1995) *Understanding Mentoring: Reflective Strategies for School-based Teacher Preparation*, Buckingham, Open University Press.

WATKINS, C. (1992) 'An experiment in mentor training' in WILKIN, M. (Ed) *Mentoring in Schools*, London, Kogan Page, pp. 97–115.

WATKINS, C. and WHALLEY, C. (1993) 'Mentoring beginner teachers — Issues for schools to anticipate and manage', *School Organization*, **13**, 2, pp. 129–38.

WILKIN, M. (1992) 'The role of the training institution in mentor development', paper presented to UCET Conference, November.

YEOMANS, R. (1994) 'Relationships: Mentors and students' in YEOMANS, R. and SAMPSON, J. (Eds) *Mentorship in the Primary School*, London, Falmer Press, pp. 101–21.

YEOMANS, R. and SAMPSON, J. (Eds) (1994) *Mentorship in the Primary School*, London, Falmer Press.

# 10 Working Together: Roles and Relationships in the Mentoring Process

*Joanne Hudson and Ann-Marie Latham*

With the reforms detailed in Circular 9/92 (DFE, 1992), teacher educators in schools and universities are facing a number of ideological and tangible challenges to their current practice and ideologies. The introduction of school-based mentoring, which has resulted from these reforms, presents a challenge of some magnitude to mentors themselves and their student protégés. Mentoring itself is not a new concept and, if Homer's *Odyssey* bears true testimony, has existed since the ancient world. Nor is teacher education a stranger to mentoring, as Monaghan and Lunt's (1992) discussion of the history of mentoring indicates. Indeed, some authors have placed mentoring at the heart of the educational process (for example, Moses-Zirkes, 1993). However, we cannot rely purely on historical sources to establish an understanding of contemporary mentoring in School-based Teacher Education Partnerships (STEPs) if we wish to improve, and build upon, its quality. Based on recent research findings and writings which are discussed below, we can begin to build a picture of the challenges and demands which contemporary mentoring in initial teacher education (ITE) offers. Following this overview of the conceptions of mentoring which can be identified in recent literature, we would then like to offer conceptions of mentoring in the context of physical education and dance ITE. These have emerged from our own research which is discussed in more detail in a subsequent section of this chapter.

### What is Mentoring?

McIntyre, Haggar and Wilkin (1994) discuss mentoring as a mechanism of counselling, educating and socializing the student into the school environment. A summary of the conception of mentoring employed in the partnership structure at the University of Brighton reads as follows: the mentor's role involves the support, guidance, assessment and induction of students, in helping them to develop their teaching plans and competences (University of Brighton, 1994). Jacques (1992) supports this notion in her description of the mentor's role as one which encompasses instruction, counselling, assessment and the transmission of practice and principles. Similarly, Corbett and Wright (1994) suggest that mentoring requires the following skills: organization; communication; counselling; support; monitoring; collaboration, and problem-solving.

### Personal Attributes of the Mentor

Providing an exhaustive list of appropriate attributes for mentoring would be a difficult task. However, some helpful suggestions made by a number of authors are offered in both this and the following section. Shaw (1992) describes the ideal mentor as someone who is able to listen, who is encouraging, empathetic, organized, reflective, analytical and approachable.

According to Smith and Alred (1994), the unique and complex qualities which mentorship requires are based on the kind of person the mentor is rather than any of their personal skills or competences. This view is shared by Williams (1994a) who sees the interpersonal skills of supportive listening and critical evaluation of performance as important as, if not more so than, subject expertise. Competence and knowledge, however, are attributes which should not be overlooked, a belief which is widely held by, for example, Haensly and Edlind (1986), who state that the mentor must possess skill, expertise and knowledge in their own specialist area. To some extent, the mentor's personal attributes shape their relationship with the student and the role which is defined for the student within this relationship.

The success of the student/mentor relationship depends on the student's willingness to seek help, which in turn requires that the student feels comfortable and able to communicate with their mentor (Tellez, 1992). Haensly and Edlind (1986) suggest that for the student to function successfully in their role the mentor must be a trusted colleague and guide who is flexible, possesses a good sense of humour and is a good communicator. Effective communication, according to Haensly and Edlind (*ibid*) involves active listening and the ability to engage in the mutual exchange of feedback with the student. In a similar vein, Maynard and Furlong (1994) advocate that the mentor should be open-minded and able to confront personal beliefs and values if the student is to be helped to develop as a reflective practitioner. As a result, a reciprocal student/mentor relationship is likely to develop, involving the active participation of both the student and mentor, a mutual exchange of information and willingness to adapt individually held beliefs when faced with novel approaches and perspectives. A core component of shared power, competence and self (Bolton, 1980), is repeatedly favoured in the literature on mentor-protégé relationships. Characterized by mutual empowerment, active involvement and the mutual exchange of information, the student/mentor relationship requires that the roles of co-enquirers are adopted rather than those of pupil and instructor (Maynard and Furlong, 1994). The mentor should however, provide an appropriate role model which will guide the student's standard and style of behaviour and simultaneously encourage the development of interdependence (Clawson, 1980). Jacques (1992) captures the mutuality of the student/mentor relationship by describing it as one which is '. . . dynamic and fluid' (p. 348).

The personal attributes, requirements of the mentor's and the student's roles and characteristics of the student/mentor relationship, discussed above, are largely accepted as prerequisites for an effective relationship. However, the individuality of this relationship must not be ignored as Hardy (1994) describes this as one of its most important characteristics. This is reflected in the personal nature of the mentor-protégé relationship, the variation in experience between different dyads and the endogenous principles which he suggests govern each student/mentor relationship. These principles create a uniqueness which shapes that mentor's role and consequently the definition of 'mentor' within that particular relationship (Monaghan and Lunt, 1992). As such, no universal definition of 'mentor' can be formed as no universal 'mentor' is in existence. A mentor can only be defined within the context of their own student/mentor relationship. In essence, Monaghan and Lunt (*ibid*) suggest that 'mentoring' and 'mentor' are dynamic definitions which can only be understood in relation to the context of individual mentoring relationships and the individuals which share them.

Adopting a broader perspective, Dunne and Harvard (1994) discuss mentoring as the combined impact of a number of individuals, for example, lecturers, school-based staff, and experts in a given field. We would not dispute that the mentoring of the trainee teacher involves input *from* individuals such as the professional and link tutors, school and university personnel, respectively, however, whether their roles are part of the process of mentoring *per se* or whether and how their roles impinge on the mentoring process seems to be, as yet, undetermined. Undoubtedly, if it is to prove effective, the student/mentor relationship is dependent on a supportive framework of outside agents such as the professional tutor in the school and the link tutor from the university. Having examined mentoring from the perspective of current literature, the discussion now considers previous research which has examined the student's perspective of mentoring.

### Student Views on Mentoring: Previous Findings

Although conceptions of mentoring and perceptions of the mentor are widely discussed, and research which examines partnership and mentoring is increasing, what is lacking at present, is research which allows us to monitor the possible strengths and weaknesses of the mentor role and its implementation (Jacques, 1992). Perhaps more importantly, research is scarce which examines conceptions of mentoring from the perspective of the focal point, or the third party of partnership, that is, the student (Booth, 1993; Williams, 1994b; Williams, Butt and Soares, 1992). Only by reviewing the needs of the student can we attempt to describe the role of the mentor (Wilkin, 1992). The small body of research which has investigated mentoring from the student's perspective is described below.

Williams (1994b) examined how twenty-seven postgraduates from a variety of subject specialisms and institutions perceived the roles and responsibilities of those involved in their training. As may be expected, although a consensus on the value of mentoring was demonstrated, students were concerned about variation in the quality of the experiences which different schools offered. Where some received oral and written feedback, had regular progress meetings and were involved in negotiating the focal points of the mentor's observations, others felt that their mentors had little time for them and seemed only to see their support as necessary if the student was at risk of failing. Lack of support and professional criticism was not always wholly attributed to the attitude of the mentors but instead to the fact that mentors were allocated insufficient time and training to fulfil their role. Students also commented that the level of commitment required by the mentoring role greatly impinged on the mentor's prime concern of educating children.

In a study conducted by Booth (1993), English, geography and history postgraduate students completed questionnaires before and after their first school experience. The latter of these asked the students to report on the frequency with which different areas relevant to teaching were discussed in student/mentor interactions. The students also described how much they felt their confidence had increased in these areas compared with their perceived levels of confidence prior to their school experience. They reported greater increases in confidence in those areas which dominated student/mentor interactions than in those which were discussed with relatively less frequency, for instance, cultural matters and special education issues. As a result, Booth (*ibid*) suggested that mentors were instrumental in increasing students' confidence in: lesson preparation; teaching materials; schemes of work, and, discipline and the control of pupils. The qualities which students valued in their mentors included being supportive, accessible, sympathetic, and positive. They also favoured a student/mentor relationship which allowed them to adopt an active role and which gave them some degree of empowerment, rather than one in which the mentor adopted a dictatorial role and they a passive one. Booth suggests that this research demonstrates the 'crucial importance' (*ibid*, p. 194) of the mentor, a view which is shared by other authors, for example, McIntyre, Haggar and Wilkin (1994), who state that,

> . . . the quality of school-based initial teacher education will depend crucially on the work of teachers in the role of mentors. (p. 11)

Although this view appears to exist as a consensus and Jacques (1992) has stated that the validity of the mentor role is universally approved, the role of the mentor and the meaning of 'mentoring' are, as yet, undetermined (McIntyre *et al*, 1994).

It is apparent from the research discussed above that the main focus of inquiry and discourse about mentoring in secondary ITE has been on perceptions and interpretations of the mentor's role. Interest and research efforts have increasingly been directed towards an examination of student interpretations and experiences of mentoring. However, recent research (for example, Hudson and Latham, 1995) has indicated that we are unable to build a comprehensive picture of mentoring and the student/mentor relationship if the focus remains solely on the role of the mentor. The mentor is part of a relationship with the student where the function and role of one is influenced, if not defined, by that of the other. Hence, an attempt to understand the role of the mentor in the context of STEPs must consider this in relation to the mentoring *relationship* and to the role of the student within this relationship.

## The Study at the University of Brighton

We conducted interviews with the first cohort to experience formal mentoring in physical education and dance at the University of Brighton, who were postgraduate students from the 1993/1994 cohort group. The line of inquiry focused on the students' perceptions of the role, function and attributes of the mentor. However, in describing their perceptions of the ideal student/mentor relationship, and of their own experiences of mentoring, these students emphasized the reciprocity which must underpin this relationship if it is to prove successful.

We do not offer this as a completely novel concept, on the contrary, we recognize that this is a somewhat 'obvious' statement to make in the light of the fact that mentoring is a process which involves two individuals and therefore undoubtedly requires input from both of these individuals to ensure its success. Nevertheless, in some instances it is the obvious which needs restating and reconsidering, and this appears to be one of those instances. The comments which were made by students in the study described above have provided an initial indication that without full consideration of the student's part in mentoring and the mentoring relationship we are likely to limit the extent of our understanding of mentoring.

This issue was, therefore, subject to further investigation in a subsequent study which provides the framework for the remainder of this chapter and comprises responses from both mentors and students in order to obtain a relatively balanced perspective. Of the seventeen mentors who were involved in the study, five provided written responses to open-ended questions which they received through the post, whilst twelve of these took part in individual semi-structured interviews. All the students, twenty-three of whom were fourth year BA(QTS) students, and eight of whom were postgraduates, made their contribution to the research by attending individual semi-structured interviews. The undergraduate students attended only one interview following their final professional semester spent in school whilst the postgraduate students attended two, one following each of their two school placements. Implementing this design allowed that differences in response could be identified and explored between the following: students and mentors; postgraduates and undergraduates, and, postgraduate perceptions subsequent to their first and second school experiences. Analysis of the responses provided by each of these groups indicated that little difference existed between them. Therefore in the discussion which follows these are treated cumulatively as one data set except where specifically indicated.

## The Mentoring Partnership

Without exception, the successful student/mentor relationship was described as one which is characterized by reciprocity in a number of different areas. First, in relation to the tangible contributions which the student and mentor can make to the mentoring experience. By virtue of their relative positions and qualifications for entering into the relationship, there is a necessary imbalance between what the student and mentor can offer. The mentor possesses a range of relevant skills and experiences which they can contribute to the mentoring process, for example, counselling and student support and alternative teaching styles and strategies with which the student can experiment. The student also brings their own, often unique, skills and competences which can be of benefit to both themselves and their mentor. They may specialize, for instance, in one of the department's weaker areas, may offer a new philosophy for the mentor to consider and evaluate, or simply, a fresh pair of legs:

> I mean the students are a positive effect on the PE department, they're very very positive for us in that we get fresh views, a fresh pair of legs etc. etc . . . I mean the student we've got has got a completely different philosophy to teaching gym than I've got and both have got a part in education so now I will add that to my teaching and it means that he will add what I've got to his as well and that's the way it should go. It's a partnership between the two of us and he brings a lot in and we give him a lot.

In some cases the student makes a contribution to the mentor's development, regardless of whether or not they themselves are aware of it. A number of mentors suggested that through their mentoring experiences, they revisited their own teaching practices and philosophies and therefore made some gains in their own professional development, as is illustrated by the quotation cited above.

Factors of a more personal nature were also felt to be essential in developing a successful and reciprocal relationship. A relationship defined in this way should be based on respect, not just the student's respect for the mentor's position of authority but mutual respect for each other's individual needs and opinions. For instance, both the student and the mentor must recognize that they may adopt styles and subscribe to philosophies which are fundamentally different. The successful relationship is underpinned by the concept of individuality and respect for the individual. Without this basis, neither the mentor nor the student are likely to reap any benefit from the relationship.

Alongside respect, there is a need for trust and honesty in all aspects of the relationship, for instance in the communication which takes place between the student and their mentor. A relationship which is built around a framework of honesty, trust and respect is then likely to facilitate a two way communication channel, also frequently cited in interview responses as a factor which contributes to success. Effective and open communication involves more than the mentor imparting information to the student and the student's passive receipt of this information (see Hudson and Latham, 1995). Instead, it involves the mutual sharing of information and of listening to, interpreting and acting upon, this information.

These comments appear to indicate that the successful mentoring relationship rests not only on the investment of time, effort and expertise by both the student and the mentor. It also depends upon the investment of self, reflecting Bolton's (1980) suggestion that self, power and competence should be shared facets within the effective mentoring relationship. For the mentor and the student alike this self-investment has potentially positive or negative repercussions. For example, the emotional consequences of mentoring were highlighted in one mentor's discussion of her experiences with two different students, from which the following excerpt is taken:

> I learnt from her as well because she came in with all these new ideas and that made me rethink my own teaching and I looked again at the way I taught in the light of what she was saying to me. So it was very exciting. In the second it was exhausting and it was taking taking taking and there was nothing coming back. But it wasn't anybody's fault. She was inappropriate for the course really.

Although mentoring demands a high degree of personal and often emotional investment, mentors and students stressed the importance of an underlying professional basis to their relationship.

Moreover, it was important to the students, in particular the undergraduates, that they were allowed opportunities to develop, and hold, a certain status within the mentoring relationship and the school as a whole. They wanted the school staff and the pupils to perceive them not as a student but as, respectively, a fellow colleague and a *bona fide* teacher. This is likely to be associated to the students' need to develop a sense of belonging within the school, a finding which echoes that revealed by previous research (for example, McNally, Cope, Inglis and Stronach, 1994). The majority of students felt that they had achieved this and their status as a teacher, which is demonstrated in the following comment made by an undergraduate student.

They didn't treat us like students at all. I just literally felt like a teacher there, I was like a new teacher.

Based on the responses of a number of students, it seems safe to assume that the extended period of time spent in school made some contribution towards developing this status.

## Defining a Role for the Student

The data discussed above indicate that the student should not just be a part of the mentoring process but should be an instrumental and integral part of this process. As a result, what we will now consider is how the student can fulfil their role and contribute towards the success of their own mentoring experience.

The student involved in mentoring should be at least in partial control of their own development as a teacher. In no way can we view the mentor as active informer and decision maker and the student as a passive recipient of this information. The students find themselves in a relationship which is likely to differ from any they will have previously experienced in educational contexts. The roles in these relationships are likely to have been defined in terms of pupil and teacher, with the student cast in the pupil's role. Roles within the student/mentor relationship, of which they are now a part, are defined instead in terms of coenquirers (for example, Maynard and Furlong, 1994), placing new and increased demands on the student.

First, the student must meet the challenge of accepting responsibility for not only the pupils' learning but for their own learning throughout the school-based element of their education and training. With the mentor's guidance and direction, the students themselves must ensure that they gain as much benefit from this experience as it can possibly offer. Some fourth year students who were interviewed believed that in comparison with their previous placement in school, they took more responsibility for their own development and learning. The following quotation demonstrates this belief:

I think you should be more reflective on what's going on in a school and actually working with the mentor and working with your lecturer and working with professional tutor if you've got it (a professional tutor). I don't think you should be going in and teaching the lesson and leaving. There is a different role there I think, it's a role of actually being part of the school.

However, at this juncture we cannot state whether or not this is an artefact of the extended period of time spent in school which the partnership model of ITE offers or of the increasing competence and maturity which is likely to accompany the student's progress through their course. Whichever explanation offers the more accurate interpretation, student responsibility is an integral feature of successful mentoring.

As previously mentioned, it is essential that the student gets involved in the life and running of the school and the Physical Education Department. For instance, by assisting with, and running, extra-curricular activities for the children. For the physical education or dance student this appears to have particular implications for the image which they project to their mentor and to other departmental staff, and in some cases, their assessment, as the mentor's comment below demonstrates:

> I mean, some students come in with a completely alien view of what education's all about, well, what my opinion of PE is all about, in that they come in and they think well I'm going to teach from 9 o'clock to 3.20 and then I'm going home and they just can't do it. I mean, that gets people's backs up as well in the department. I mean we expect as a PE Department that we will be working until 5 o'clock every night, and that's what we'd expect from the students, but we also tell them that when they come through the door, so it's up to them whether they take it or leave it, but if they leave it, then it's recorded.

Involvement in extra-curricular activity also presents the student with an opportunity to give something back to the mentor and the department, reflecting an increasingly reciprocal relationship between the student and their mentor. Some fourth year students felt that to some degree the extended period of time spent in school as a result of the partnership model acted as a facilitator of their involvement in both departmental and wider school life. It was suggested that the extended period of time now spent in school allowed students the time to initiate their own extra-curricular activities with a long term focus and purpose, for instance, fixtures, tournaments or performances. This was also seen by some of these students as a means of more firmly establishing themselves, with teachers and pupils, in their role as teacher rather than student:

> You get a chance to be responsible I think without being told. I guess I felt with it being a longer time you felt that you had more chance to experiment with different ways of doing things, using worksheets and organizing your small tournaments and to get clubs going and then obviously it was better because you were working within that school and you didn't feel like you were a part of college you felt like you were away and you dealt with things within that school within your department and you were treated as if you were in the department.

Again, this study cannot clearly identify whether or not the student's increased involvement and perceived identity as a teacher is attributable to the partnership model itself or to developmental changes which can be expected throughout the student's education. We may speculatively state that partnership is likely to represent one of a number of factors which contributes towards the student's level of involvement in school and departmental life.

Part of being responsible for one's own learning involves recognizing and acting not only on one's strengths, for instance, through establishing extra-curricular clubs and activities, but recognizing and acting also on one's weaknesses. Not only is it the student's responsibility to identify weaknesses but to then seek support from their mentor rather than waiting for it to be offered, which echoes comments made by Tellez (1992). On receipt of advice, guidance or ideas from the mentor, it is important that the student then acts on this information. From the mentor's perspective, nothing is more frustrating than repeatedly offering the same piece of advice for it to be repeatedly ignored by the student. However, it is imperative that the student does not accept the validity of this advice without question. They must assess whether or not this advice is compatible with their own educational philosophies, their teaching approach and the children and context at which it is aimed. If it is not, they must modify the advice and strategies offered to meet their own needs and the demands of their current context. The student must also critically examine their own ideas, practices and attitudes, neither moulding themselves unquestioningly on their mentor nor on their own *a priori* conceptions of teaching and physical education. If the mentor adopts a similar analytical perspective (as Maynard and Furlong (1994) advocate), then they and the student can cultivate a relationship in which problem-solving becomes a joint venture for both student and mentor. In some instances this may also prove to be an exercise which is mutually beneficial for both parties. The mentor needs therefore to allow the student sufficient status within the relationship so that they may offer their opinion and assess and analyze the mentor's suggestions and educational philosophies. The mentor and the student alike should recognize that the student, although in need of constant professional, and at times personal, support, also needs their autonomy. To this end, they should be allowed, and prepared, to express their opinion and experiment with their own and others' ideas in practical settings.

## Concluding Comments

This evidence supports the notion (for example, Monaghan and Lunt, 1992), that it is the individuals within the relationship itself who define the roles and responsibilities involved in this relationship and not any outside agent. Without an approachable mentor, the student cannot actively seek support and guidance on their own initiative. If the student is not allowed the freedom to express their own ideas, to analyze critically and experiment with these and others' ideas, they will have no opportunity for independent inquiry, personal and professional development. Succinctly stated, these are the roles which the student needs to adopt if the mentoring relationship and process are to prove worthwhile and beneficial. That is, as an autonomous, active and analytical partner in a working relationship and a developmental process.

It is imperative that the student is made aware of the significance of their own role in mentoring. They must also be equipped with some of the necessary skills to fulfil this role (for instance, independent and analytical inquiry). It seems that training for mentoring should not be the sole reserve of the mentor. Students should also be educated into their role to enable them to be the autonomous, active and analytical learner which successful mentoring requires. This responsibility lies with a number of individuals including the mentor, university personnel and the students themselves.

Outlined below are suggestions of how we may begin to develop the student's role in the mentoring process. We offer these as a starting point around which initiatives in ITE in physical education and dance may be initially developed. Although through debate and research the nature and structure of these initiatives is likely to undergo considerable change, we believe that the principles outlined below should nevertheless remain.

Before any practical initiatives can be implemented, we need first to ensure that all those involved in mentoring and teacher education share similar perceptions of the student's role. At a fundamental level, this may mean increasing awareness that the student does have an active and complementary role to play in mentoring and their own professional development. It is important that students, mentors and university tutors view the student as an active part of the mentoring process and not one which is passive. If perceptions of the student's role are inaccurate or if we fail to develop common perceptions of the student's role throughout all relevant personnel, then it is likely that any practical steps taken will have less than their desired impact.

Fazey (in press) provides recommendations for fostering student autonomy in higher education and the discussion now offers these as guidelines for fostering student autonomy in physical education and dance ITE and mentoring. Fazey suggests that student tutoring is an effective means of developing student autonomy and identifies principles on which this tutoring should be based. In the context of ITE, it seems that these principles offer appropriate guidelines for both mentoring the student within the school and for their tutoring within the university. Those principles which Fazey outlines and which are of most relevance here are concerned with the concept of individuality, with reflection and action planning and with student ownership.

## Individuality

At a fundamental level, one-to-one discussion between the student and their university tutor or mentor is required if this process is to work effectively. However, the emphasis on the individual does not end there. The focus of the tutoring or mentoring process should be placed firmly on the student, reflecting and responding to their needs. It is important to recognize that students in the same year group may have reached different developmental levels and may bring different strengths and weaknesses to the mentoring situation.

## Reflection and Action Planning

It is essential that students engage in regular goal setting and reviews of the progress made towards achieving these goals. The structure and focus of future learning experiences can then be determined on the basis of this review procedure. The tutor, or mentor, has a facilitating role to play in this process, for instance, guiding the student towards appropriate learning opportunities or resources, the review and goal setting process should be centred around the student's own self-reflection, assessment and action planning.

This principle brings to prominence the notions of the reflective practitioner of physical education and dance and of student profiling. More than ever before, it appears that one of the primary aims of ITE courses in physical education and dance should be to develop students' skill of self-reflection and analysis if they are to benefit fully from the potential gains which mentoring offers.

Similarly, comments made by Fazey (*ibid*) appear to emphasize the need to bring student profiling to the top of the agenda in physical education and dance ITE. This profile could focus on three different facets of the student's development: personal development; academic or subject knowledge; and professional and teaching competence. The discussion below expands upon possible interpretations of these areas. These are not offered as definitive, the reader's interpretations may differ from ours, and they may identify different focal areas for the profile, however, what is offered here are ideas for a general underpinning framework.

*Personal Development*: broadly speaking, self-reflection and target setting are the basic skills of effective profiling, these processes are also likely to effect an increase in the student's personal knowledge and understanding. Not only does profiling increase personal knowledge and self-awareness but it can also encourage communication and critical thinking. All these skills, or attributes, are commensurate with the development of learner autonomy, and, whilst beneficial experiences *per se*, are also likely to have a positive influence on the student's experience of school-based mentoring. This association between the skills which are required for, and can be developed through, profiling and mentoring, serves to indicate how the student's experiences in school and university can and do complement each other.

*Academic and Subject Knowledge*: this section of the profile could be used to reflect upon, and further, progression and development in two distinct areas: academic skills and subject knowledge. The former refers to the skills necessary to fulfil the requirements of an academic degree, for instance, writing assignments, presenting seminars, critical analysis of theoretical arguments, and, the correct use of references. Subject knowledge can be sub-divided into at least three further areas (although the reader is likely to identify more): pedagogy; subject specific knowledge; and subject discipline knowledge. Here, pedagogical knowledge is referred to as the student's knowledge about teaching and child development and the relationship between the two. Subject specific knowledge refers to knowledge about specific curriculum areas, such as gymnastics, dance, netball and rugby, the student's knowledge of the different skills required in these areas, and, the rules and language which are peculiar to each area. Knowledge about the subject discipline is taken here to mean the knowledge which underpins both theory and practice in physical education such as biomechanics, anatomy and physiology, and, psychological factors in sport and exercise. It is important that the student appreciates the relationship which exists between these three areas and can identify their strengths and weaknesses in relation to each, in order that maximum gains can be made in their understanding of their subject and their application.

*Professional and Teaching Competence*: this section of the profile could be incorporated, or used in support of, part of a more formal assessment procedure which reflects the competencies of Circular 9/92 (DFE, 1992), therefore meeting government requirements. Here, students should be encouraged to analyze not only their personal teaching performance but how their role and their actions influence the learning environment for the pupils. Developing greater understanding of this relationship can then help the student to ensure that they are able to create effective learning environments for all the pupils.

*Self-evaluation*: as part of the process of profiling, the student is required to provide evidence of any self-assessments they have made in different areas of competence, such as the ones outlined above. They must also assess their achievements and progress in relation to the targets or goals they previously set for themselves. From this, they can then outline suitable and worthwhile targets or goals in areas of most relevance, which they can aim for in the future. When evaluating teaching and professional competence, the focus of this evaluation should be placed firmly on specific teaching episodes and the outcomes of these episodes. The tutorial discussion involved in lesson evaluation is a key element in the overall process of profiling as it stimulates the student to engage in a variety of activities such as: articulation of thoughts and ideas; goal-setting; critical analysis of own and other's perspectives and interpretations, and, identification of personal strengths and weaknesses.

Not only may these episodes be used to provide evidence in support of the student's developing professional and teaching competence, they may also be used as a source of evidence in support of gains in subject and academic knowledge. For instance, if the student is able to explain the way in which they organized and progressed the lesson or a series of lessons, they are able to demonstrate their understanding of how the subject material can, and should, be progressed in relation to the development and developmental level of the children involved.

## Ownership

Fazey (in press) states that students should take ownership of the decision-making process, taking control of the decisions made and dealing with the consequences of these decisions. The tutor, or mentor, has to allow the student the option of accepting, or declining, advice which is offered (unless of course this advice is essential, for instance, regarding the safety of the children in their care) and of making decisions which may be at odds with tutor's or mentor's own beliefs or value system.

It seems then that both the schools and the university must work together, through adopting the principles discussed above, to encourage the student to become active, autonomous and analytical learners which will enable them to work together with their mentor as this partnership dictates.

## References

BOLTON, E.B. (1980) 'A conceptual analysis of the mentor relationship in career development of women', *Adult Education*, **30**, pp. 195–207.

BOOTH, M. (1993) 'The effectiveness and role of the mentor in school: The students' view', *Cambridge Journal of Education*, **23**, 2, pp. 185–97.

CLAWSON, J.G. (1980) 'Mentoring in managerial careers' in DERR, C.B. (Ed) *Work, Family and the Career*, New York, Prager, pp. 144–65.

CORBETT, P. and WRIGHT, D. (1994) 'Issues in the selection and training of mentors for school-based primary initial teacher training' in MCINTYRE, D., HAGGER, H. and WILKIN, M. (Eds) *Mentoring: Perspectives on School-based Teacher Education*, London, Kogan Page, pp. 220–3.

DFE (1992) *Initial Teacher Training* (Secondary Phase) (Circular 9/92), London, HMSO.

DUNNE, R. and HARVARD, G. (1994) 'A model of teaching and its implications for mentoring' in MCINTYRE, D., HAGGER, H. and WILKIN, M. (Eds) *Mentoring: Perspectives on School-based Teacher Education*, London, Kogan Page, pp. 117–29.

FAZEY, D.M.A. (in press) 'The role of the tutor in developing autonomy in learning', *Guidance and Learner Autonomy Network Newsletter: Higher Education Projects*, **3**, Sheffield, DfE.

HAENSLY, P.A. and EDLIND, E.P. (1986) 'A search for ideal types in mentoring' in GRAY, W.M. and GRAY, M.M. (Eds) *Mentoring: Aid to Excellence in Education, the Family and the Community*, Vancouver, BC, International Association for Mentoring.

HARDY, C.J. (1994) 'Nurturing our future through effective mentoring: Developing roots as well as wings', *Journal of Applied Sport Psychology*, **6**, pp. 196–204.

HUDSON, J. and LATHAM, A-M. (1995) 'PE and dance students' perceptions of mentoring under the partnership scheme', *Mentoring and Tutoring for Partnership in Learning*, **3**, 1, pp. 23–30.

JACQUES, K. (1992) 'Mentoring in initial teacher education', *Cambridge Journal of Education*, **22**, 3, pp. 337–50.

MCINTYRE, D., HAGGER, H. and WILKIN, M. (Eds) (1994) *Mentoring: Perspectives on School-based Teacher Education*, London, Kogan Page Limited.

MCNALLY, J., COPE, P., INGLIS, B. and STRONACH, I. (1994) 'Current realities in the student teaching experience: A preliminary inquiry', *Teaching and Teacher Education*, **10**, 2, pp. 219–30.

MAYNARD, T. and FURLONG, J. (1994) 'Learning to teach and models of mentoring'. in McINTYRE, D., HAGGER, H. and WILKIN, M. (Eds) *Mentoring: Perspectives on School-based Teacher Education*, London, Kogan Page, pp. 69–85.

MONAGHAN, J. and LUNT, N. (1992) 'Mentoring: Person, process, practice and problems', *British Journal of Educational Studies*, **40**, 3, pp. 248–63.

MOSES-ZIRKES, S. (1993) 'Mentoring integral to science, practice', *The Monitor*, **24**, 7, p. 34.

SHAW, R. (1992) *Teacher Training in Secondary Schools*, London, Kogan Page.

SMITH, R. and ALRED, G. (1994) 'The impersonation of wisdom' in McINTYRE, D., HAGGER, H. and WILKIN, M. (Eds) *Mentoring: Perspectives on School-based Teacher Education*, London, Kogan Page, pp. 103–16.

TELLEZ, K. (1992) 'Mentors by choice not design: Help-seeking by beginning teachers', *Journal of Teacher Education*, **43**, 3, pp. 214–21.

UNIVERSITY OF BRIGHTON (1994) *Partnership in Education Handbook.*

WILKIN, M. (1992) 'On the cusp: from supervision to mentoring in initial teacher training', *Cambridge Journal of Education*, **22**, 1, pp. 79–90.

WILLIAMS, A. (Ed) (1994) *Perspectives on Partnership: Secondary Initial Teacher Training*, London, Falmer Press.

WILLIAMS, A. (1994a) 'The mentor' in WILLIAMS, A. (Ed) *Perspectives on Partnership: Secondary Initial Teacher Training*, London, Falmer Press, pp. 134–50.

WILLIAMS, A. (1994b) 'Roles and responsibilities in initial teacher training-student views' in WILLIAMS, A. (Ed) *Perspectives on Partnership: Secondary Initial Teacher Training*, London, Falmer Press, pp. 93–108.

WILLIAMS, E.A., BUTT, G.W. and SOARES, A. (1992) 'Student perceptions of a secondary postgraduate certificate in education', *Journal of Education for Teaching*, **18**, 3, pp. 297–309.

# 11 Pedagogical Content Knowledge and Critical Reflection in Physical Education

*Tony Rossi*

## Introduction

The purpose of this chapter is to discuss the nature of pedagogical content knowledge (hereafter referred to as PCK) for, and critical reflection in, teaching physical education. In a chapter of this length, it is inevitable that a significant amount of the vast body of literature related to these topics will be excluded. This is not judgemental, simply an acknowledgment of space limitations. There will also be an attempt throughout to consider how a mentor might support the development of PCK and critical reflection in pre-service teachers.

In any expert-novice situation, it is sometimes assumed that sage knowledge and 'tricks of the trade' can be passed on unhindered and unchallenged. It is acknowledged that the development of PCK is more complicated than this. Wilson, Shulman and Richert (1987) suggest that for successful teachers, PCK cannot simply be an intuitive understanding of subject matter. They argue:

> Successful teachers cannot simply have an intuitive or personal understanding of a particular concept, principle, or theory. Rather, in order to foster understanding, they must themselves understand ways of *representing* the concept for students. They must have knowledge of the ways of transforming the content for the purposes of teaching. (p. 110)

### Pedagogical Content Knowledge

Significantly, PCK has proven elusive to clarify (Marks, 1990). Metzler (1992), has argued that PCK may be considered as follows: 'In many ways it is the heart of teaching, encapsulated in those lessons when a teacher knows a good deal about the topic or skill *and* knows how to teach it effectively to a class of students in a particular context' (p. 154). However, this may fall short of a satisfactory definition and possibly does not capture the ambiguity inherent in the term pedagogical content knowledge which Marks (1990) claims is derived from the broad conceptualizations of it.

Shulman (1986) coined the term pedagogical content knowledge as a way of conceptualizing that essential knowledge required to be able to teach subject content knowledge. He describes PCK as:

> . . . the most useful forms of representation . . . the most powerful ana-
> logies, illustrations, examples, explanations and demonstrations — in
> a word, the ways of representing and formulating the subject that make
> it comprehensible to others. (p. 9)

Shulman's conceptualization has been useful in so far as it has enabled an understanding of the knowledge base for teaching to develop. Moreover, it has served as the impetus for acknowledging the link between subject content knowledge (or discipline knowledge) and knowledge for teaching. For some, however, Shulman's conceptualization does not fully capture the *essence* of PCK. For example Cochran, DeRuiter and King (1993) describe PCK as follows:

> PCK differentiates *expert teachers in a subject* area from *subject area
> experts*. PCK concerns the manner in which teachers relate their sub-
> ject matter knowledge (what they know about what they teach) to
> their pedagogical knowledge (what they know about teaching) and
> how subject matter knowledge is a part of the process of pedagogical
> reasoning. (p. 263)

Using a constructivist perspective, Cochran *et al* (*ibid*) have attempted to go beyond Shulman's conceptualization which they regard as too static. They regard PCK as neither complete or absolute but dynamic and ever evolving. Drawing on the work of Lerman (1989) in mathematics education, Cochran *et al* (1993) indicate that '. . . knowledge is actively created by the knower and not passively received in an unmodified form from the environment . . .' (p. 265). Cochran *et al* therefore prefer to refer to the knowledge for teaching subject content as pedagogical content *knowing* to emphasize the dynamic qualities of coming to know.

My own work (Rossi, 1994, 1995 and 1996) has taken a similar turn. Drawing on the constructivist traditions of Kelly (1955), it has become appar-ent that knowledge for teaching physical education is a dynamic process with lifeworld experiences of student teachers contributing to the development of PCK. It might be that Cochran *et al's* (1993) work and my own could be perceived as the *process* or the *acquisition* of PCK. However, it can only be perceived in this way if knowledge (including PCK) is considered to be com-plete and absolute. What I am arguing, is that PCK will to continue to be reshaped or reformed by teachers and students teachers and is unlikely to be static or complete. Rather, it is knowledge which is constantly in 'transit' and thus may represent what a teacher understands about PCK *at a particular time* in a career span. This may well be a 'process', but it is knowledge nonetheless. Some of the experiences which appear to shape PCK clearly have greater impact than others and it would come as no great surprise that for pre-service teachers, the practicum is located as a site where much 'knowing' takes place, supporting work done elsewhere (Rovegno, 1992; Barrow, 1990; Hargreaves, 1984; Graber, 1989).

## Pedagogical Content Knowledge for Physical Education

Tinning (1992a) has also attempted a reconceptualization of Shulman's ideas to demonstrate the dynamic qualities and to indicate the need to emphasize the subject specific nature of PCK. Tinning argues that the nature of physical education — its experiential qualities, determines that PCK requires special treatment in special 'methods' courses. He argues that such courses should complement general courses in pedagogy. Like other researchers, Tinning identifies PCK as being concerned with the 'how to teach', in other words the adept use of the best analogies, representations, examples and demonstrations. However, he extends Shulman's idea by suggesting that PCK in physical education can be seen as having practical *and* theoretical dimensions. In other words it is possible to know about pedagogy in physical education but not know how to apply such knowledge in the practical setting. To explain, Tinning argues that PCK can be learnt about for the purposes of, say, passing an exam. This is quite different, however, to knowing *how* to use such knowledge in a practical way to bring about desirable learning in children. Hence it is possible to regard PCK itself as being forms of both knowing that *and* knowing how.

Schempp (1993) suggests, supporting the work of Cochran *et al* (1993) that teachers' knowledge is 'living', it is not inorganic but grows in certain directions in accordance with the synthesis between the many and varied views of teaching. Certainly in Schempp's study, the participant saw the development of professional knowledge as coming from the distilled wisdom of practice. He took the view that what he knew about teaching he had learned on the job. Moreover in his view, he felt that most of the learning about how to teach had been in the real situation and this knowledge accrual had occurred as a result of *experience* rather than *thinking or theorizing* about the experience. Furthermore, he argued that 'new knowledge' (in other words things that he didn't already know), should be of a practical kind, that is, to serve a utilitarian purpose. This view may well be consistent with the view of many teachers (Rossi and Nicholls, 1994) and indeed many student teachers whose appetite for the 'how to' of teaching physical education is often insatiable. How is the mentor to function in this situation? If support is provided for this kind of teacher development, is a mentor aiding and abetting the development of what Giroux and McLaren (1987) refer to as pedagogical clerks whose practice is simply a list of technical procedures requiring little professional judgment or reflection?

Many texts on physical education pedagogy deal in large measure (though not exclusively) with the technical and functional aspects of pedagogy (for example, Siedentop, 1991; Rink, 1985; Mosston and Ashworth, 1986; Wall and Murray, 1990). Much of this work does go beyond simple instructional skills. However, it does represent a considerable contribution to the literature on technical aspects of teaching. For example, nearly all of Mosston and Ashworth's chapters include a section on 'how to do it'. The importance of this 'knowing how' should not be understated. The National Curriculum documents in the UK, for example, indicate a that range of 'teaching styles' should be used implying in the first instance, that teachers actually know what different styles there are and secondly how they might be differently used, in other words for what purposes and in what contexts. It would not be unfair to argue that most teachers of physical education use a teacher-centred command/practice approach. Certainly neophyte teachers and student teachers teach very close to the command end of Mosston's spectrum as there is a desire for security and safety afforded by tightly disciplined lessons (Rossi, 1995).

It could be argued that the notion of learning to teach 'on the job' could be better captured in the collaboration between intern and mentor. The traditional expert-novice relationship can be construed in such a way as to allow the participants to actively construct PCK which will be both personal and practical, rather than rely on a model of 'hand me down' knowledge. In this way, student teachers would begin to become 'educational craftspersons' (Tinning, Kirk and Evans, 1993) where reflective practice is an inextricable part of physical education PCK. Tinning, Kirk and Evans describe an educational craftsperson as someone who bases the knowledge for their practice on observation and experimentation, rather than the more usual authoritative forms of knowledge found in, and priviledged by the academic community. Tinning *et al* do not deny the importance (and indeed value) of distilled knowledge of research on teaching and the conventions of collective wisdom. However, as they argue, such knowledge is better considered as '. . . directions for practice rather than tenets' (p. 204).

### Drawing from Recent Research

Process-product research studies in the 1970s and early 1980s whilst narrow in their function and application, have nonetheless created an epistemological base upon which some broad considerations about PCK in physical education can be made. There is some commonality in the findings with regard to what is considered PCK in physical education.

### Being a manager

It does seem that this is important in teaching, and particularly in physical education (Boyce, 1992; Graham *et al*, 1993; Mawer, 1995; Solmon *et al*, 1991;

Mosston and Ashworth, 1986; Rink, 1985; Siedentop, 1991). I have indicated elsewhere (Rossi and Nicholls, 1994; Rossi, 1994 and 1995) the importance that is attached to management (in particular class management) by PE teachers and student teachers. Management activities are diverse and range from how children may enter the learning environment (the field, gym or pool, etc) to managing complex learning arrangements for a broad range of abilities, and the need to employ a range of teaching approaches to more than one task. Again all of these are highly contextual. For example, one assumes we would have strict guidelines about how a group of learners might enter the pool and engage in certain activities for a swimming lesson. Within such a lesson there might be a strict management protocol for the obvious safety reasons. Conditions might be similar for a lesson on javelin throwing. For a lesson on soccer, however, the managerial tasks might be of less importance. However, there is a tendency for novice and pre-service teachers to have a very tight management structure in all lessons and all facets of lessons. Indeed Behets (1990) has indicated that the major concerns for pre-service physical education teachers are organization and pupil control. In effect, these are manifested as management techniques, as organization most often refers to resource management which might include; giving out equipment, placing of equipment, organizing groups and work arrangements, return of equipment. Pupil control is often translated as behaviour management, the management of noise levels and keeping learners on task and the processes of admonishment for those who are off task.

## Planning as a management task

Inherent in the managerial responsibilities of the teacher is the necessary planning for lessons. Much time is spent on this in teacher preparation courses and some neophyte teachers go into their lessons with plans that are almost scripts which must be rigidly followed. Tinning (1992a) has argued that we expect student teachers to plan in certain ways knowing that teachers in their everyday lives do not plan in the *same* way. It cannot be argued that teachers do not plan, but how they do is manifestly different to the way student teachers are asked to plan. It may simply be that the course requirements placed on students to plan in highly prescribed ways requiring highly prescriptive written lesson plan statements bear little resemblance to the idiosyncratic ways that teachers actually do plan. Barrett, Sebren and Sheehan (1991) found that planning was important for converting subject matter into what Shulman (1987) has called pedagogically powerful reasoning. Barrett *et al* (1991) argue that this is justification enough to consider planning as an element of PCK. Moreover, they argued that novices tend to be heavily plan dependent and that experienced teachers work from plan-in-memory and that written plans appear only to be superficial. Solmon *et al* (1991) also noted that planning was considered by a group of student teachers as a characteristic of good teaching. There are important dimensions here for the mentor-student teacher interaction. If there is a perception of the importance (and indeed value) of planning, mentors will need to discuss why as veterans or experienced teachers, the necessity to plan meticulously has either largely disappeared or changed significantly. This will have much to do with how a student is inculcated into the life of a school and the lifeworld of a physical education teacher. Barrett *et al* (1991) argue that time and an improved ability in mental planning are factors as to why *written* planning decreases with experience. This is important as Dodds' (1994) analysis drawing on the expert-novice literature suggests that expert teachers' plans are more developed, contain more detail and strategies for the unseen or unanticipated events in lessons. What Dodds does not indicate is whether such planning is made, totally at least, in writing. It is evident that planning is perceived as highly important and as such can be viewed as PCK. Therefore it seems appropriate that a mentor might discuss the issue of planning with student teachers and indicate that planning for teaching is knowledge that appears to be idiosyncratic and resides in the personal domain.

## Instruction

In many respects this represents only a part of teaching, though it is often viewed as teaching. It would be fair to regard it as the *essence* of teaching. Having said that, what then is it that is included in the notion of instruction? Is it instructional style, or format, or strategy? Indeed is there any difference between any of these? Writers would argue for example, that teaching style is often used as a catch all term for what takes place in any given lesson or at least the instructional related activities. Siedentop (1991) argues that style is quite different from format, he says:

> ... *instructional format* refers to the way a teacher organizes and delivers instruction and provides practice for students. *Teaching style* refers to the managerial and instructional climate of the learning environment, especially as reflected in the interaction patterns of the teacher. (p. 226)

Perhaps what is important to ask is whether teachers perceive there to be any difference between style and format, and just as importantly, do they care and does it make any difference to what they do? As Locke argued in 1977, teaching styles represented a data free excursion into making claims for certain forms of instruction. Since then, there has been an increase in the studies specifically testing Mosston's spectrum (see Boyce, 1992; Beckett, 1991; Goldberg and Gerney 1990, as examples and for good literature reviews of the work in this field). For the most part, the results confirm that command/practice styles (more often a combination of the two) yield the best results for motor skill acquisition and these represent the most common styles. Mosston's (1972) original claim that student growth and development would occur as the student moved from command to discovery has been significantly modified as it became more and more apparent that choice of style was closely associated with context (Siedentop, 1991).

As for strategy and format; Rink (1985) describes a strategy as a delivery system for getting the content (subject matter) to the learner. She refers to this as an instructional framework which in turn is referred to as a teaching strategy. As indicated above, format as described by Siedentop (1991) '. . . refers to the different ways teachers organise for the delivery of instruction and, particularly, how the student role changes as a result of the changing format' (p. 228). It is not hard to see why a teacher might regard the differences between strategy, format and style as much ado about nothing. Moreover, as Metzler (1992) has argued, teachers use very little of published research on teaching to guide their own practice, clearly they use other forms of knowledge. Lawson (1990) has indicated that a form of tacit knowledge guides practice which appears to be based on a lesson-by-lesson account and knowledge for instruction seems to rest with an understanding of descriptive terms of skills, topics, key words, demonstrations and the setting up of worthwhile practices (Graham *et al*, 1993). Tinning (1992a) asks whether a detailed knowledge of formats or style is strictly necessary. He acknowledges as I have indicated elsewhere, that the skills of organizing the conditions and environment so that learning can take place should include consideration of the pupil characteristics, safety, and contextual factors. Since student and novice teachers of physical education (and other subjects) have a view of teaching that tends to be custodial and authoritarian, and that given that the biography of most physical education teachers is likely to be steeped in the traditions of competitive sport, it is no real surprise that the discovery end of any spectrum of teaching strategies might remain largely untouched.

*Demonstrating*

Demonstrating falls within the broad understanding of instruction and is an interesting facet of PE teaching that warrants analysis. As a young student, I was a member of a practical soccer class that was taught not by university staff but by a local teacher (Ted — a pseudonym) who at the same time, was the top football (soccer) coach in the South West of England. We all liked this person largely for his unique turn of phrase and interesting demeanour. During the mini-teaching sessions he used to set up for us we would all diligently describe the skill to be learned to our small group of learners using intelligent and appropriate language (or so we thought). Ted would watch our performance from the sidelines pacing up and down, raising his eyebrows and tutting with disgust until he could contain himself no longer whereupon he would bellow 'show them!' at the top of his voice (which was considerable). Of course we had been taught the virtues of good demonstrations in our college program and indeed Mawer (1990 and 1995) drawing from considerable literature has indicated the *potential* value of quality demonstrations as an aid to learning. Of course this is undeniable, but how imperative is it that the teacher can actually perform the skills in order to provide a demonstration to the class. Shulman's (1987) analysis would seem to indicate that for PE teachers, skill performance should be the subject matter content and as such, could logically be considered part of a teacher's PCK (Dodds, 1994). The power of the earlier vignette made an indelible mark on me until I entered my first teaching post and found that I had been called upon to teach hurdling during the track and field season, an activity I had always struggled with as a student. I found of course that I could actually teach it quite well without having to provide what would have been a very poor demonstration.

Tinning (1992a) has considered this issue with clarity. The substantive content of physical education he argues, has its basis in practical knowledge or knowing *how* (to do something). Academic subjects have their basis in what is known as propositional knowledge, this represents knowing *that*. The distinction in the nature of knowledge is quite apparent particularly in the case of physical education . . . or is it? Tinning (*ibid*) continues his discussion by drawing on an analysis by Arnold (1988) who suggests that practical knowledge may be distinguished as being 'weak' or 'strong'. Arnold argues that knowing how in the *weak* sense refers to someone who can perform some physical task (a handstand or hammering a nail), but who is unable to articulate exactly how it was done. Knowing how in the *strong* sense seems to have two facets to it according to Arnold's analysis, both involve an understanding of how physical tasks are performed and accomplished, but a person may or may not be able to actually perform the tasks. It would seem then that this is inextricably linked to PCK for physical education teachers. Knowing how is clearly essential in the strong sense but the necessity to be able to demonstrate (in other words actually do the task) would not appear to be crucial. What does emerge as crucial, however, is how information is provided, what information is provided, how and what tasks are set, what the practice arrangements might be, how feedback is provided.

### Giving information, giving feedback, providing practice opportunities

Giving information to learners in physical education will largely depend on the context and on the teacher's orientation to knowledge. First, it would be seen as highly irresponsible to teach elements of abseiling using a discovery approach by setting very open tasks and giving learners only limited information. Such an approach, however, has been used consistently in educational gymnastics and other forms of free movement. The teaching for understanding approach to games (see Bunker and Thorpe, 1982; Spackman, 1983) also reappraised what information should be given and why, in an attempt to teach for understanding during skill and game development sessions, and to base the lesson on the needs of individuals which in itself is part of a broader emancipatory pedagogy. Laws (1994) has argued that this approach to pedagogy has emerged as a form of rhetorical justification and that for the most part, even under the auspices of child-centred pedagogy, authoritarian and didactic forms of teaching are, for a whole host of reasons, still in evidence.

Feedback and practice go almost hand in hand. Mosston and Ashworth (1986) link the two very closely. The complexity of teaching make it almost impossible to identify what might be considered as good practice that could be consistently employed with any confidence across a range of situations. Indeed a mentor would have great problems (as indeed would teacher educators) in saying 'in this situation do this or that'. As far as feedback and practice go, it would fair to say that teachers again do not operate from a research base. This is interesting as one assumes that young student teachers of PE may well be (or have been) engaged in the study of motor learning for example, where the topics of practice scheduling and feedback may have been the subject of some analysis. Suffice it to say that such study seldom appears to inform teacher practice. Rather, teachers tend to operate from an implicit theory or from time honoured practices (which may characterize an implicit theory) possibly irrespective of outcomes.

The language of information giving is also important. Mosston and Ashworth (*ibid*) deal with this extensively and it has long been a feature of Mosston's spectrum. In many respects the use of language can involve a hidden complex code which will result in a number of hidden learnings which might be of an oppressive nature; it may well be that the learnings are unintended. However, unless language use is critically examined, such hidden learning is unlikely to be exposed. The nature of hidden learnings will be dealt with later but to give a simple example in language, how many teachers (student teachers in particular) use the phrase 'what I want you to do . . .' when setting a task? On the surface this may seem completely innocuous. However, what potential message is coming across here? Does it not beg the question why should the child do this for the teacher? Is the task being set not inherently worthwhile without the teachers' claim of ownership? This may seem trivial, but a school lifetime of this kind of language use I think casts a very clear message about who is in control of knowledge, what knowledge is most worthwhile but more importantly, that the acquisition of knowledge/ skills are for the pleasure of the teacher not the development of the child. Ask any teacher if this is what they set out to mean, the answer would of course be no, however, the potential for such unintended learning is great.

## Pedagogical Content Knowledge in Physical Education as Being Problematic: The Case for Reflective Teaching

Given that there is no 'one size fits all' pedagogy (Lawson, 1990) in the day-to-day lives of teachers and their practice, the necessity for reflective teaching becomes paramount. By collecting data about one's own practice, it becomes possible to seek improvements in teaching physical education. The idea of reflection as epistemology can then fit within the broader parameters of PCK for physical education. This is not to say that it is unique to physical education, rather that it represents an indispensable facet of it.

Clearly the skilled use of teaching techniques is a legitimate concern and worthy of competent mastery. However, such teaching skills alone do not constitute PCK for teaching physical education, at least not if teaching is viewed as having something to do with learning. This approach to teaching is characterized by its mechanistic nature. It is a process or a performance which like factory tasks has a number of cues that indicate a change or adjustment in the task performance behaviour. Such behaviour conforms to the observance of a strict set of rules (Grundy, 1987). This form of teaching in physical education has been described as technocentric (Charles, 1979), and technocratic and rationalist (Tinning, 1992a; Sparkes, 1993; Macdonald, 1992; Gore, 1990). Tinning (1991) also refers to this form of teaching as 'performance pedagogy' where the purpose of the teaching activity is the measurable improvement or accretion of performance levels in learners. Moreover, Tinning has argued that it is the dominant paradigm in physical education teaching and that for the most part its greatest success is keeping children 'busy, happy and good' (Placek, 1983). Tinning has argued elsewhere (Tinning, 1987a) that such forms of teacher work in physical education '. . . is more likely to be physical *miseducation*, characterized by unjust competition, long periods of inaction for most children . . .' (p. 10). Dodds (1994) has indicated that physical education is perhaps the site for the greatest degree of social injustice including motor elitism, sexism and racism. Physical education is also implicated (whether we like it or not) in the issue of body shapism or what Tinning (1985) has referred to as the cult of slenderness. As cultural practices in the form of multi-media entertainment endorses such a cult and at the same time engages in a form of victim blaming, the necessity to stamp out the 'ugly isms' in our gyms (Dodds, 1986), must manifest itself in our actions and our use of language signifiers. Language therefore is inherently a part of PCK for teachers and in particular physical education teachers.

It appears then, that much of what a teacher of physical education does and says leads to hidden learnings which may be a more powerful form of learning than what appears in the overt curriculum. How is this to form part of the knowledge for teaching physical education? Tinning (1990) argues that one way of considering this is to problematize the nature of teaching and teaching work. This however, is not without difficulties and certainly Tinning has suggested that to problematize the nature of teachers' work, to consider the unseen or the not-so-obvious is viewed with great suspicion by student teachers, novice teachers and veteran teachers.

In physical education, there has been much work done which challenges the conventions of performance pedagogy, notably by Kirk (1986 and 1988), Tinning (1987a, 1990, 1991 and 1992a), Gore (1990), Kirk and Tinning (1990), Macdonald (1992) and Petit (1992). Some have taken their work into the feminist field (see Wright, 1990; Scraton, 1990 and 1992; Humberstone, 1990), and some are more overtly political (see Evans, 1988). These efforts, which represent a small portion of the work going on, indicate the importance of reflection or reflective teaching as being fundamental to alternative forms of educational practice in physical education. But as Gore (1990) points out, even reflection can be a technical rather than contemplative and thought provoking process. In her study, some of the participants had little or no interest in reflection and saw the whole process as meaningless, and Macdonald and Brooker (1993) have noted a similar phenomenon. Tinning (1993) has also noted the difficulties in trying to 'teach' students to be reflective when reflecting on his own teaching. The process or method of reflection as integral to teaching has been the subject of much theoretical and research literature which is far too expansive to cover here. It is important to note however, that Schon's (1983) oft cited work has generated much of it.

### Reflection as Epistemology

It is not uncommon as Gore (1987) has indicated and as has already been discussed to regard 'reflection' as a technical process. Indeed the term 'reflection' could be regarded as very overworked. At the superficial level (perhaps the most common) it serves purely as a functional process to improve individual *technical* practice. This form of reflection addresses a limited range of questions that relate to technical aspects of teaching, such as; 'did my voice reach all the group?', 'were my instructions clear?', 'did the equipment come out in an organised and efficient fashion?' and so on. Don't misunderstand me, these are important questions but it would not be unreasonable to suggest that they are narrow in the extreme. For a start, nowhere in the above examples is there any consideration of pupil learning. A reasonable starting point in reflective teaching might be 'what learning took place, and more importantly, why?'.

Zeichner and Tabachnick (1991) have indicated that the range of reflective discourse has come to include nomenclature such as action research, reflective teaching, teacher-as-researcher. As a consequence, 'reflection' has come to mean many things to many people and as such the term has been appropriated and used in different ways. Therefore as Tinning (1993) argues it is not so much how we reflect that is important but rather the kinds of questions we are asking ourselves. Tinning takes the social reconstructionist position and believes that schools should have a broad mission which is to transmit the best of culture and to eliminate those practices which are unjust and oppressive. Zeichner and Tabachnick (1991) concur suggesting that reflection of this nature must take account of the social and political ramifications of schooling. Therein lies a problem. For the most part student teachers only focus on their own performance as teachers. This is hardly surprising given the traditional power triad of university lecturer or supervisor, the supervising (or cooperative) teacher and the student teacher. For reflective practice to reach its full potential, in other words, reflection on a number of planes and levels as characterized by the work of Zeichner and Tabachnick (*ibid*), the mentor-intern/student teacher relationship clearly needs to function at a collegial level.

### Forms of Reflection

Drawing on a broad range of literature, Zeichner and Tabachnick (*ibid*) have identified four varieties of reflective practice. They argue that no one form of reflection is adequate on its own. Moreover, for them reflection does not necessarily make for better teaching. As they say: 'We do not accept the implication that exists in much of the literature, that teachers' actions are necessarily better, just because they are more deliberate or intentional' (p. 2). The limits on space prevent a full analysis of Zeichner and Tabachnick's position. Suffice it to say the forms of reflection are closely related to academic, social efficiency, developmental or constructivist, and social reconstructionist perspectives of teaching. A number of things are apparent in Zeichner and Tabachnick's analysis. First, that reflection in its simplest form is not a panacea for poor educational practice or indeed a guarantee of good educational practice. Secondly, reflection is a complex process that operates on several levels and requires the collection of good data for it to be in any way meaningful. Good data is always a contentious term particularly in the qualitative paradigm. The issues of validity and reliability do have a place here though the interpretation of them may vary. Tinning (1987a) provides a good discussion on this issue with particular regard to gathering data about one's own practice in physical education (pp. 38–41).

In reporting on an attempt to teach for reflection, Zeichner and Liston (1987) argued that a teacher education program should emphasize:

> . . . the preparation of teachers who are both willing and able to reflect on the origins, purposes, and consequences of their actions, as well as on the material and ideological constraints and encouragements embedded in the classroom, school and societal contexts in which they work. (p. 23)

The program drew on the distinction made by Dewey between reflective action and routine action. The latter being governed by external authority and heirachy, tradition and circumstance, the former as described by Zeichner and Liston '. . . entails the active, persistent and careful consideration of any belief or supposed form of knowledge in the light of the grounds that support it and the consequences to which it leads' (*ibid*, p. 24). The designers of the program then, were committed to an approach which problematized educational practice rather than took it for granted. Furthermore, this particular program was guided by Van Manen's (1977) concept of three different levels of reflectivity which in short refer to technical reflection, reflection on the educational consequences of practical action, and critical forms of reflection which relate to forms of action which are underpinned by the principles of social justice, liberation and anti-oppressive educational practice. Again, the point is made that all levels of reflection are important and inextricably linked. However, for truly *critical* reflection to occur then an action research model of enquiry which is guided by the tenets of critical theory offers some genuine possibilities in this regard.

### Reflection as Action Research and Action Research as Epistemology

It would be an oversimplification to suggest that action research is simply reflection. The emphasis in action research is on *action*. However, for reflection to be meaningful, effective, and relevant then action research offers a very comprehensive form of reflection that can be undertaken. It can be argued then that action research as epistemology can be considered as a necessary component of PCK because inherent in action research is the theory of critique; the challenge to everyday assumptions. In this case, a mentor would have quite different requirements with regard to PCK. The mentor as action researcher would be quite a different role to that of the traditional supervising teacher. It is not possible here to comprehensively discuss action research as epistemology. Tinning (1992b) has provided an excellent analysis of this concept in physical education and there are many examples of action research as epistemology available (see Carr and Kemmis, 1986; Kemmis and McTaggart, 1988). However, here it is appropriate to discuss how such epistemology might radically change the role of the mentor to what I would argue is a far more educationally defensible role and one that would enhance student teacher growth rather than stifle it. Action research as a form of reflection is not new either to physical education or teaching more generally. The Faculty of Education at Deakin University in Australia has perhaps led the field in this regard and this is certainly so in physical education (see Tinning, 1987a and 1987b; Tinning, Kirk and Evans, 1993). Perhaps what has not been explored so thoroughly is how an action research structure might function in a mentor/intern situation. A starting point might be to suggest that a mentor should not assume to have 'all the answers'. This is not to suggest that the distilled knowledge of years of experience should be discarded, rather that mentors might use the opportunity to ask *themselves* some questions too. A mentor can then begin to collaborate (rather than dominate) with the intern/student teacher to collect data about educational practice in which they are both engaged and upon which it would be a fruitful learning experience to both reflect. This, of course, assumes that a mentor will have an understanding of action research. It may well be that this represents a role for the university, to make action research a part of mentor preparation programs. Implicit in this suggestion then, is that action research be considered as part PCK in physical education.

As a point of professional coalescence, action research could not be more appropriate for a mentor and student teacher. The essence of reflective educational practice can therefore be framed in a collaborative effort where knowledge (including PCK) is actually produced jointly by student teacher and mentor rather than simply implemented or reproduced by the mentor alone.

## Can a Teacher Assume this Mentor Role? Some Final Comments

It is likely that mentors will be drawn in large measure from the teachers who already carry a range of responsibilities in schools. The demon that conspires to thwart the kind of professional practice described here is time, a commodity in extremely short supply in schools. With prospective mentors often in middle management roles (in secondary teaching), spending time with a student teacher is often invasive on the day-to-day routine activities in which teachers are involved. However, assuming time is created, the question then becomes are teachers *able* to perform such a role? This is a more difficult question. The oft cited reluctance of teachers to 'use' anything that relates to research and the preference for teaching knowledge as mastery of multiple *practical* rules of thumb tends to suggest that a cultural change might be necessary. It is appropriate that the first change ought to occur in the university-school relationship. Moves are being made here almost universally and the nuance of partnership is being redefined. It also requires a change from the expert-novice paradigm of handed-down commonsensical knowledge and a move towards a collegial approach to the *production* of PCK, rather than an uncritical acceptance of time honoured practices which hold privilege with an 'expert'. This then, would represent the move towards teachers (student teachers and practising teachers alike) becoming educational craftspersons as described earlier. Such teachers regard knowledge for teaching as having dynamic qualities constantly in need of being tested out, reflected upon and further acted upon in the day-to-day realities of school life. It is here that a mentor can truly support the development of beginning teachers.

## References

ARNOLD, P. (1988) *Education, Movement and the Curriculum*, London, Falmer Press.

BARRETT, K.R., SEBREN, A. and SHEEHAN, A.M. (1991) 'Content development patterns over a two-year period as indicated from written lesson plans', *Journal of Teaching in Physical Education*, **11**, 1, pp. 79–102.

BARROW, R. (1990) 'Teacher education: Theory and practice', *British Journal of Educational Studies*, **38**, 4, pp. 308–18.

BECKETT, K. (1991) 'The effects of two teaching styles on college students' achievement of selected physical education outcomes', *Journal of Teaching in Physical Education*, **10**, 2, pp. 153–69.

BEHETS, D. (1990) 'Concerns of preservice physical education teachers', *Journal of Teaching in Physical Education*, **10**, 1, pp. 6–75.

Boyce, B.A. (1992) 'The effects of three styles of teaching on university students' motor performance', *Journal of Teaching in Physical Education*, **11**, 4, pp. 389–401.

Bunker, D. and Thorpe, R. (1982) 'A model for the teaching of games in the secondary school', *Bulletin of Physical Education*, **18**, 1.

Carr, W. and Kemmis, S. (1986) *Becoming Critical: Education, Knowledge and Action Research*, Geelong, Deakin University Press.

Charles, J.M. (1979) 'Technocentric ideology in physical education', *Quest*, **31**, 2, pp. 277–84.

Cochran, K.F., DeRuiter, J.A. and King, R.A. (1993) 'Pedagogical content knowing: An integrated model for teacher preparation', *Journal of Teacher Education*, **44**, 4, pp. 263–72.

Dodds, P. (1986) 'Stamp out the ugly "isms" in your gym', in Pieron, M. and Graham, G. (Eds) *Sport Pedagogy*, Champaign, IL, Human Kinetics, pp. 140–50.

Dodds, P. (1994) 'Cognitive and behavioral components of expertise in teaching physical education', *Quest*, **46**, 2, pp. 153–63.

Evans, J. (1988) 'Body matters: Towards a socialist physical education' in Lauder, H. and Brown, P. (Eds) *Education in Search of a Future*, London, Falmer Press, pp. 174–91.

Giroux, H. and McLaren, P. (1987) 'Teacher education as a counter public sphere: Notes towards a redefinition' in Popkewitz, T.S. (Ed) *Critical Studies in Teacher Education: Its Folklore, Theory and Practice*, London, Falmer Press, pp. 266–97.

Goldberg, M. and Gerney, P. (1990) 'Effects of learner use of practice time on skill acquisition of fifth grade children', *Journal of Teaching in Physical Education*, **10**, 1, pp. 84–95.

Gore, J. (1987) 'Reflecting on reflective teaching', *Journal of Teacher Education*, **38**, 2, pp. 33–8.

Gore, J. (1990) 'Pedagogy as text: Beyond the preferred reading' in Tinning, R. and Kirk, D. (Eds) *Physical Education, Curriculum and Culture: Critical Issues in the Contemporary Crisis*, London, Falmer Press, pp. 101–38.

Graber, K. (1989) 'Teaching tomorrow's teachers: Professional preparation as an agent of socialization' in Templin, T. and Schempp, P. (Eds) *Socialization into Physical Education: Learning to Teach*, Indianapolis, Benchmark Press, pp. 59–80.

Graham, K.C., Hohn, R.C., Werner, P.H. and Woods, A.M. (1993) 'Prospective PETE students, PETE students, and clinical model teachers in a university teacher education program', *Journal of Teaching in Physical Education*, **12**, 2, pp. 161–79.

Graham, G., Manross, M., Hopple, C. and Sitzman, T. (1993) 'Novice and experienced children's physical education teachers: Insights into their situational decision making', *Journal of Teaching in Physical Education*, **12**, 2, pp. 197–214.

Grundy, S. (1987) 'Critical pedagogy and the control of professional knowledge', *Discourse*, **7**, 2, pp. 21–36.

Hargreaves, A. (1984) 'Experience counts, theory doesn't: How teachers talk about their work', *Sociology of Education*, **57**, 4, pp. 244–54.

Humberstone, B. (1990) 'Warriors or wimps? Creating alternative froms of physical education' in Messner, M. and Sabo, D. (Eds) *Sport, Men and the Gender Order*, Champaign, IL, Human Kinetics, pp. 201–10.

Kelly, G. (1955) *The Psychology of Personal Constructs*, New York, Norton.

Kemmis, S. and McTaggart, R. (1988) *The Action Research Planner*, Geelong, Deakin University Press.

Kirk, D. (1986) 'A critical pedagogy for teacher education: Toward an inquiry-oriented approach', *Journal of Teaching in Physical Education,* **5**, 4, pp. 230–46.

Kirk, D. (1988) *Physical Education and Curriculum Study: A Critical Introduction,* London, Croom Helm.

Kirk, D. and Tinning, R. (Eds) (1990) *Physical Education, Curriculum and Culture: Critical Issues in the Contemporary Crisis,* London, Falmer Press.

Laws, C. (1994) 'Rhetorical justification for new approaches to teaching games — Are physical education teachers deluding themselves?', Proceedings of the 10th Commonwealth and International Scientific Congress, 'Access to Active Living', Victoria, BC, August, pp. 175–80.

Lawson, H.A. (1990) 'Sport pedagogy research: From information gathering to useful knowledge', *Journal of Teaching in Physical Education,* **10**, 1, pp. 1–20.

Lerman, S. (1989) 'Constructivism, mathematics and mathematics education', *Educational Studies in Mathematics,* **20**, pp. 211–23.

Locke, L. (1977) 'Research in physical education: New hope for a dismal science', *Quest,* **28**, pp. 2–16.

Macdonald, D. (1992) 'Knowledge, power and professionalisation in physical education teacher education: A case study', unpublished doctoral thesis, Deakin University, Geelong.

Macdonald, D. and Brooker, R. (1993) 'Reaching for excellence in physical education teacher education', paper presented at the 19th ACHPER National/International Conference, Darwin, July.

Marks, K. (1990) 'Pedagogical content knowledge: From a mathematical case to a modified conception', *Journal of Teacher Education,* **41**, 3, pp. 3–11.

Mawer, M. (1990) 'It's not what you do, it's the way that you do it! Teaching skills in physical education', *British Journal of Physical Education,* **2**, summer, pp. 307–12.

Mawer, M. (1995) *The Effective Teaching of Physical Education,* London, Longman.

Metzler, M.W. (1992) 'Bringing the teaching act back into sport pedagogy', *Journal of Teaching in Physical Education,* **11**, 2, pp. 3–11.

Mosston, M. (1972) *Teaching: From Command and Discovery,* Belmont, CA, Wadsworth.

Mosston, M. and Ashworth, S. (1986) *Teaching Physical Education,* Ohio, Charles Merrill.

Petit, A. (1992) 'On bridges, roads and pathways: A personal journey toward "Tikkun"', paper presented at the AARE/NZARE joint conference, Deakin University, November.

Placek, J. (1983) 'Conceptions of success in teaching: Busy, happy and good?' in Templin, T. and Olson, J. (Eds) *Teaching in Physical Education,* Champaign, IL, Human Kinetics, pp. 46–56.

Rink, J. (1985) *Teaching Physical Education for Learning,* St. Louis, MO, Mosby.

Rossi, A. (1994) 'Constructing knowledge for teaching physical education: The genesis of a collaborative project', paper presented at the 10th Commonwealth and International Scientific Congress, 'Access to Active Living', Victoria, BC, August.

Rossi, A. (1995) 'Researching the lived experience of student teachers: Identifying constructed knowledge for teaching', paper presented at the First International Conference 'Understanding the Social World: Towards an Integrative Approach.' University of Huddersfield, July.

Rossi, A. (1996) 'Making active connections: Knowledge growth in pre-service primary physical education specialists', paper presented at the 20th Biennial ACHPER National/International conference, University of Melbourne, January.

ROSSI, A. and NICHOLLS, J. (1994) 'The value of theoretical course work: What teachers think', *British Journal of Physical Education, Research Supplement,* **15**, pp. 12–18.

ROVEGNO, I.C. (1992) 'Learning to teach in a field-based methods course: The development of pedagogical content knowledge', *Teaching and Teacher Education,* **8**, 1, pp. 69–82.

SCHEMPP, P.G. (1993) 'Constructing professional knowledge: A case study of an experienced high school teacher', *Journal of Teaching in Physical Education,* **13**, 1, pp. 2–23.

SCHON, D. (1983) *The Reflective Practitioner,* New York, Basic Books.

SCRATON, S. (1990) *Gender and Physical Education,* Geelong, Deakin University Press.

SCRATON, S. (1992) *Shaping Up to Womanhood: Gender and Girls' Physical Education,* Buckingham, Open University Press.

SHULMAN, L. (1986) 'Those who understand: Knowledge growth in teaching', *Educational Researcher,* **15**, 2, pp. 4–14.

SHULMAN, L. (1987) 'Knowledge and teaching: Foundations of the new reform', *Harvard Educational Review,* **57**, pp. 1–22.

SIEDENTOP, D. (1991) *Developing Teaching Skills in Physical Education,* Mountain View, Mayfield.

SOLMON, M.A., WORTHY, T., LEE, A.M. and CARTER, J.A. (1991) 'Teacher role identity of student teachers in physical education: An interactive analysis', *Journal of Teaching in Physical Education,* **10**, 2, pp. 188–209.

SPACKMAN, L. (1983) *Teaching Games for Understanding,* Curriculum Development Centre, College of St. Paul and St. Mary, Cheltenham.

SPARKES, A. (1993) 'Challenging technical rationality in physical education: The potential of a life history approach', *Physical Education Review,* **16**, 2, pp. 107–21.

TINNING, R. (1985) 'Physical education and the cult of slenderness: A critique', *ACHPER National Journal,* **107**, autumn, pp. 10–14.

TINNING, R. (1987a) *Improving Teaching in Physical Education,* Geelong, Deakin University Press.

TINNING, R. (1987b) 'Beyond the development of a utilitarian teaching perspective: An Australian case study of action research in teacher preparation' in BARRETTE, G.T., FEINGOLD, R.S., REES, C.R., and PIERON, M. (Eds) *Myths, Models and Methods in Sport Pedagogy,* Champaign, IL, Human Kinetics, pp. 113–22.

TINNING, R. (1990) *Ideology and Physical Education: Opening Pandora's Box,* Geelong, Deakin University Press.

TINNING, R. (1991) 'Teacher education pedagogy, dominant discourses and the process of problem setting', *Journal of Teaching in Physical Education,* **11**, 2, pp. 1–20.

TINNING, R. (1992a) 'Teacher education and the development of content knowledge for physical education teaching', keynote address prepared for the Conference on The Place of Subject Specific Teaching Methods in Teacher Education, Santiago de Compestela, Spain.

TINNING, R. (1992b) 'Action research as epistemology and practice: Towards, transformative educational practice in physical education' in SPARKES, A. (Ed) *Research in Physical Education and Sport: Exploring Alternative Visions,* London, Falmer Press, pp. 188–209.

TINNING, R. (1993) 'We have ways of making you think. Or do we?: Reflections on "training" in reflective teaching', invited address to the International Seminar on the Training of Teachers in Reflective Practice of Physical Education, Trois Rivieres, Quebec, July.

TINNING, R., KIRK, D. and EVANS, J. (1993) *Learning to Teach Physical Education*, Sydney, Prentice Hall.

VAN MANEN, M. (1977) 'Linking ways of knowing with ways of being practical', *Curriculum Inquiry*, **6**, pp. 205–28.

WALL, J. and MURRAY, N. (1990) *Children and Movement*, Dubuque, Wm. C. Brown Publishers.

WILSON, S.M., SHULMAN, L.S. and RICHERT, A.E. (1987) ' "150 different ways" of knowing: Representations of knowledge in teaching' in CALDERHEAD, J. (Ed) *Exploring Teachers Thinking*, London, Cassell, pp. 104–24.

WRIGHT, J.E. (1990) 'Remember those skirts: The constitution of gender in physical education' in SCRATON, S. (Ed) *Gender and Physical Education*, Geelong, Deakin University Press, pp. 63–77.

ZEICHNER, K. and LISTON, D. (1987) 'Teaching student teachers to reflect', *Harvard Educational Review*, **57**, 1, pp. 1–22.

ZEICHNER, K. and TABACHNICK, B.R. (1991) 'Reflections on reflective teaching' in TABACHNICK, B.R. and ZEICHNER, K. (Eds) *Issues and Practices in Inquiry Oriented Teacher Education*, London, Falmer Press, pp. 1–21.

*Part Four*

*An International Perspective*

# 12 Mentoring in the Australian Physical Education Teacher Education Context: Lessons from Cooking Turkeys and Tandoori Chicken

*Richard Tinning*

This chapter is not an advocacy for mentoring. Rather it is an attempt to problematize the notion within the context of current happenings in Australian physical education teacher education. Mentoring is not a common term in the context of Australian teacher education generally or physical education teacher education (PETE) specifically. That is not to say, however, that some of the same trends in terms of educational discourse which have shaped change in the UK (see Furlong, 1994) have not been impacting on the Australian teacher education 'industry' (that's one of the new terms). In this chapter I will present firstly a brief overview of such trends and discourses which will set up the background for a more specific look at PETE and mentoring. I will then discuss the potential for the practicum to actually 'deliver' on what is asked of it in the context of developing reflective teachers.

## The Australian Teacher Education Context: Change and Turmoil

In Australia recent changes include the development of explicit practicum curriculum, changes in the nomenclature of practicum participants, clearer delineation of the roles of these participants and changing responsibilities for practicum supervision by university and school-based personnel. (Gaffey and Dobbins, 1995, p. 2)

According to Gaffey and Dobbins the move to school-based initial teacher education with increasing responsibilities assigned to school-based teacher educators (who are more often called supervisory or co-operating teachers) has followed the current trend in the United Kingdom. As John Furlong (1994) has graphically described, the rise of the mentor in the British initial teacher training context has been an outcome of the new right discourses in education in general and teacher education specifically.

> By far the most significant change to initial teacher education in the
> last ten years has been the growing insistence by the government that
> schools take on a greater and more consistent involvement in the
> training process (of student teachers). (Furlong, 1994, p. 6)

Actually I think that the influence of the new right discourses which have
called loudly for the abolition of university-based teacher education in the
UK (see Evans, 1995) have been largely missing from the Australian context.
However, while there may not have been a direct call for the abolition of
university-based teacher education in Australia, there have been other influences which have resulted in the rise of school-based initial teacher education.
In particular, the creation of the Unified National System of universities in 1987
has been accompanied by massive reductions in the size of teacher education
faculties and a wholescale reduction in the number of student places in teacher
education. Such downsizing, and the corresponding expectation for teacher
educators to be active researchers in the university context, has created the
conditions in which reduced involvement in the practicum by the university
personnel is seen as a 'necessary evil'.

Gaffey and Dobbins (1995) claim that in some Australian institutions the
university personnel have withdrawn from the practicum to such an extent
that they only provide a liaison role in which the lecturers merely contact the
school to let them know that they have been assigned as the university contact person and if there are any points of clarification regarding the university
requirements to 'give them a call'. I can testify that this is the current situation in my own university program.

Somewhat ironically, however, there is an increasing expectation articulated by reports such as the *Draft National Guidelines for Initial Teacher
Education*[1] (1995) which explicitly advocate a more active partnership between the 'stakeholders' in the teacher education enterprise. 'In a partnership
model, the practicum would be seen as a co-operative undertaking allowing
school-based and tertiary teacher educators to work as a team guiding the
professional development of student teachers . . .' (Gaffey and Dobbins, 1995,
p. 3). How university teacher educators are meant to cope with the multiple
demands of increased student numbers, attracting research monies, publishing
in refereed academic journals, as well as working in co-operative partnerships
with local schools for the purposes of the practicum is one of the dilemmas
facing many teacher educators.

I think that there is little doubt that a new concept of teacher education
is currently being created in Australia. According to Knight, Lingard and Bartlett
(1993),

> . . . the earlier evolution of liberal-progressive forms of teacher educa-
> tion has been displaced by a new, more prescriptive managerialist and
> economic rationalist position on teacher education. It is as if a new
> paradigm for teacher education is emerging. (p. 25)

Bates (1994a) discusses the new paradigm in terms of a move towards (or rather back to) competency-based ideology. 'The move towards the subordination of the social to the economic, the cultural to the vocational and broad-based education to the narrow confines of competency-based vocational education is strong in Australia' (p. 6).

At the root of much of this debate over the future of teacher education within the university is the nature of a university education. MacIntyre (1988) has suggested that the university is a '. . . place of constrained disagreement, of imposed participation in conflict, in which a central responsibility of higher education would be to initiate students into conflict' (p. 231). For Kemmis (1994) the advocacy of a competency-based teacher education within the university context is entirely problematic. He claims that 'A framework of competencies . . . is intended to provide an *answer* to all the crucial questions of what and how to teach, not *pose* them' (p. 7). However, Kemmis believes that '. . . it is our task as university educators to engage in debate, not to suppress it. It is our role too, to disagree productively and constructively with those who take different views of teacher education from our own' (p. 10). But this idea '. . . taken into teacher education, is literally inconceivable from the perspective of the advocates of competency-based teacher education' (p. 10).

Bates (1994a) says it well when he claims that

> . . . what constitutes evidence of competent performance is also unclear. Performance of tasks are the ostensible measure of competency-based education but how *many* performances under what variety of situations are needed in order to demonstrate competence? A cook, who can produce a wonderful — indeed perfect — sponge on one set of equipment, may not be able to do so immediately on other equipment — nor be expert in cooking Tandoori chicken. (p. 7)

The recent resurgence of the competency-based education (CBE) discourses in teacher education (read training) represent a dimension of the new paradigm for teacher education that provides the context in which Australian PETE is located. It is a context that has profound implications for the notion of mentoring within the practicum.

### Australian PETE Context

What constitutes a PETE course or program in the Australian context needs some explanation. Over the past two decades or so PETE has come to be located in universities since the creation of the Unified National System of Universities which saw, among other things, all the colleges of advanced education reconstituted and renamed as universities. In essence there are two components of PETE programs: studies in the disciplines of human movement studies; and professional studies in education/physical education. In some institutions these components might take the form of separate degrees such as a Bachelor of Applied Science (Human Movement) and a Bachelor of Teaching or they might be combined within the one degree such as a Bachelor of Education. Unfortunately, the way that most PETE programs are set up, the professional studies and the discipline studies components are seldom integrated and often placed in an adversarial relationship to each other.

The last two decades has also seen the rise of human movement studies as a field of academic endeavour (see Kirk, 1990) and an accompanying privileging of the science as the dominant form of inquiry within the field. In most PETE programs now there is greater emphasis on learning about biomechanics, exercise physiology, motor control and the like than on practical activity (see Macdonald, 1992; Swan, 1993). This has led to a situation where recent graduates of our universities who are trained as teachers of physical education know more about the discipline knowledge of the field but less about their subject as a practical endeavour.

John Evans (1995), in an analysis of the teacher education context in the UK, claims that the various new right think tanks have had a considerable influence on policy development with respect to initial teacher education. He suggests that

> Amongst their various arguments are that initial teacher training courses place too little emphasis on the learning of subject knowledge, too much emphasis on educational theory, are obsessed with race, gender and inequality, produce students who have no respect for traditional values, are too expensive and are ineffective. (p. 11)

Within the Australian context similar criticisms would be levelled at the teacher education component of a PETE degree. Certainly many human movement academics would have a sympathy for these new right criticisms of teacher education because their work in human movement is underpinned by ideologies which support elitism, meritocracy, individualism, sexism and racism (see Bain, 1990; Tinning, 1990; Mc Kay, Gore and Kirk, 1990).

The claim that there is too little emphasis on learning subject knowledge is worth exploring further. What does it mean to know the subject of physical education in 1996? Part of the answer to this question lies in the definition of physical education as a school subject. In Australia there are now essentially two versions of school phys ed . . . one is practical in nature and usually the substance of what is taught through primary and lower secondary school. The other is theoretical and based on the disciplines of human movement studies. This version is typically the focus of physical education as an examinable subject in the final years of secondary school. This development has had profound affect on the teaching of physical education in Australian secondary schools. It is rather ironic that the increased popularity of Physical Education as an examinable subject in secondary school has been accompanied by a reduction in the popularity of physical education in years 7–10 (an essentially practical, games- and sports-oriented subject). Whether this is mere coincidence or causally related is at this stage unknown.

Possible reasons for this phenomenon have been proffered elsewhere (see Tinning and Fitzclarence, 1992; Tinning *et al*, 1994) but certainly what has been termed crisis of meaning' in physical education (Kirk, 1994) is a central problem. If Australian physical education is wrestling with the meaning of the subject in schools then this will impact on the nature of the practicum experience that is possible for student teachers. Also, how particular mentors at particular schools define their subject and the corresponding discourses they privilege in their work will impact on the possibilities of the practicum as a site for learning to teach.

## The Development of Reflective Teachers: Flavour of the 1990s

The *Draft National Guidelines for Initial Teacher Education* (1995) calls for the development of critical reflection in teachers. What is meant by critical reflection is unclear, except a teacher's critical reflective role is positioned as needing to be balanced with the system maintenance role. Presumably critical reflection is linked with a social reconstructivist position as against a social reproduction position. However, the agenda is different regarding the personal professional development of student teachers. Under the heading of 'Program and Curricula: Teaching and Other Practical Experiences' it is said that experiences designed to allow for professional and personal growth in student teachers '. . . should also be designed to ensure that teacher education students adopt a critically reflective rather than a reproductive approach to their professional growth as teachers' (p. 12).

John Smyth's (1992) work on the politics of reflection is informative here. He claims that there are four problems associated with the concept of reflective teaching as it appears in educational discourse today. I share these concerns. First, he contends that reflection is such a commonsensical notion that '. . . who could possibly be against reflection; it's an indisputable notion like "quality" and "excellence"' (p. 285). Second, and because of its universal appeal, reflection can mean all things to all people and, accordingly, 'it runs the risk of being totally evacuated of all meaning' (p. 285). Smyth suggests that '. . . we are witnessing . . . a kind of conceptual colonization in which terms like reflection have become such an integral part of the educational jargon that not using them is to run the real risk of being out of educational fashion' (p. 286). Martinez (1990) was concerned that even by the end of the 80s critical reflection was becoming 'the patchwork panacea of teacher educators of all theoretical persuasions' (p. 20).

His third concern relates to the issue of power. According to Smyth (1992) '. . . processes like reflection, which give the outward appearance of modernity and teacher autonomy, can in fact be used as rhetorical flourishes and a very effective cover with which to acquire even greater control over teachers' (p. 286). Smyth claims that reflection as a notion evolved from a largely individualistic/psychologistic origin and has been appropriated as a individualist solution to the problems of education and schooling.

Smyth's fourth concern is that the kind of reflection most appealing to many teachers is one grounded in pragmatism. The tendency in such pragmatism is for reflection to be an individualistic process which can very easily lack any understanding of the wider social/structural influences on schooling and teaching. One wonders how a teacher education program that pursues such a conception of reflection can develop a commitment to a social reconstructivist education in students teachers.

Although the development of reflective teachers is the flavour of the 1990s in most Australian teacher education documents (for example, the *Draft National Guidelines for Initial Teacher Education*), the process for such development is more difficult than it might at first seem (see Tinning, 1995). PETE has also responded to the rising popularity of reflective teaching and in 1993 conducted an international conference at Trois-Rivières in Canada that focused on the question, how can we train teachers to be reflective teachers? Such a question, however, presents further questions such as, what exactly is reflective teaching? What is the purpose of reflective teaching? On what shall teachers reflect? Importantly, as Bart Crum (1995) argues 'How we conceptualize teaching and what we are ready to take for granted, hold important implications for the kind of reflective stance we adopt' (p. 8).

Grossman (1992), claimed that reflective teachers are those who 'ask worthwhile questions of the teaching (and) continue to learn from their practice' (p. 176). Unfortunately this claim leaves the nature of a 'worthwhile' question unasked, and unanswered. For some, (for example Siedentop, 1991) worthwhile questions relate to the development of teaching skills as defined by the research evidence concerning effective teachers. For others, for example those who advocate a critical inquiry orientation to reflective teaching (see Kirk, 1988; Fernandez-Balboa, 1995; Prain and Hickey, 1995), what is considered a worthwhile question (on which to reflect) would be very different indeed.

So while the development of reflective teachers is something explicitly advocated for teacher education, the achievement of the ideal is highly problematic and no more so than in the practicum as a site for learning to teach. It was Ken Zeichner (1986), in addressing the Third National Conference on the Practicum in Teacher Education in Australia, who first articulated the notion of the practicum as an occasion for learning to teach. In his analysis he focussed on the obstacles to such learning such as the lack of an explicit practicum curriculum, the uneven quality of practicum supervision, the lack of formal preparation for supervisors, and the dominant view of the practicum as an exercise in apprenticeship. Most of the same criticisms are still valid today. In what follows I will explore the notion of the practicum as an occasion for learning to teach by considering what I will call the pedagogy of the practicum.

## The Practicum as a Site of Pedagogy and the Possibilities of Teaching Critical Reflection

I think it is useful to think of the practicum as a special case of pedagogy. Given the importance of this practicum as a site for learning to teach, considering the pedagogy of the practicum itself would seem necessary. Lusted (1986) offers a notion of pedagogy which I consider to be particularly generative. According to Lusted, how one teaches is inseparable from the nature of the subject matter and the nature of the learner. Thought of in this way, the practicum pedagogy involves the student teacher as the learner, the mentor(s) as the teacher (the one in 'how one teaches'), and the practicum curriculum as the actual 'subject matter' to be learned.

### *What Must be Learned in the Practicum?*

Teacher educators from universities and mentors from schools, not to mention politicians, parents, church groups and others with a vested interest in education, often disagree with respect to what should be the ingredients of a teacher education program. They will also disagree on what should be learned in the practicum. Notwithstanding such differences of opinion, there are recent moves in Australia (following the UK and the USA) to develop a national set of competencies for teacher education (for example through the National Project for Quality Teaching and Learning [NPQTL]). Such developments are part of the general focus on reform of which Bartlett (1992) has this to say 'The current reforms, including those seen in the drive to establish competency-based standards in the professions, lead to a mode of policy-making attempts to comply with existing world and national economic trends' (p. 61). So reforms in teacher education (including the role and function of the practicum) are themselves part of a meta-reform agenda driven by a framework of economic rationalism. There is not much cause for celebration here.

An example of the Competency Framework for Beginning Teachers developed by the NPQTL (August, 1994) is as follows:

Using and developing professional knowledge and value
    Knows content and its relationship to educational goals
    Understands how students develop and learn
    Understands the relationship between processes of inquiry and content
        knowledge
    Operates from an appropriate ethical position
Communicating, interacting and working with students and others
    Develops positive relationships with students
    Communicates effectively with students
    Recognizes and responds to individual differences

Planning and managing the teaching and learning process
    Plans purposeful programs to achieve specific student learning outcomes
    Structures learning tasks effectively
    Demonstrates flexibility and responsiveness
    Fosters independent and co-operative learning
Monitoring and assessing student progress and learning outcomes
    Knows the educational basis and role of assessment in teaching
    Monitors student progress and provides feedback on progress
    Maintains records of student progress
Reflecting, evaluating and planning for continuous improvement
    Critically reflects on own practice to improve the quality of teaching and
        learning
    Evaluates teaching and learning programs

We should note at this point that the NPQTL is a 'corporatist arrangement between Commonwealth and State governments and unions' (Bates, 1994b, p. 7) and that it failed to include representatives of the teaching profession, the university teacher education sector or any professional subject association.

Clearly, not all these competencies are intended to be developed through the practicum, but presumably the mentor is meant to be 'on a similar wavelength' to the university in relation to supporting the development of such competencies where possible through the pedagogy of the practicum. While most of us would agree broadly with most of these competencies, they are so broad as to tell us little. They are certainly not specific enough to tell us how to cook tandoori chicken. In the context of the practicum in PETE, both personal experience and research indicate that expectations are seldom articulated in explicit terms or competencies. Indeed many of the expectations of student teachers are implicit rather than explicit.

There is little doubt that the dominant expectations of student teachers is that they will learn to manage and control a class. In addition, they must learn to plan their work, act in a 'professional' manner and generally show an interest in the life of the school. Perhaps a little more might be expected of those same student teachers when they teach the theoretical aspects of physical education (e.g. motor learning, exercise physiology, biomechanics etc) but even in the theory class, the need for management and control are foregrounded.

One way of thinking about what is to be learnt in the practicum (in other words the subject matter of the practicum) is via an analysis of the characteristics of the 'task systems' in student teaching. This form of analysis is based on Doyle's (1980) conception of a task which he defined as a 'set of implicit or explicit instructions about what a person must do to successfully cope with a situation' (p. 2). When a number of tasks have a common focus they can collectively be called a task system. Importantly, the use of task systems as a framework of analysis, while tapping into some of the discourses of behaviourism is not meant to be an account of what ought to happen in the practicum. Rather it is an analysis of what is happening. As such a task systems framework avoids the possible ideological association with the competency-based education movement.

In a study by the author (Tinning and Siedentop, 1985) into the nature of task systems in student teaching, it was found that student teachers have to engage three different types of tasks on the practicum. There are the tasks comprising the *teaching task system* that relate specifically to situations in which the student teacher has direct contact with pupils in order to facilitate their involvement in physical education activities. They include teaching swimming, ball handling etc, and also the specific teacher behaviours of instruction and management. The *organizational tasks system* comprised those tasks that are engaged in during preparation for teaching. They include planning lessons or units of work, physically setting up the gymnasium or playing field and anything else done 'off paper' to prepare for teaching. Those tasks which in some way function to create and maintain cordial social relations between student teacher and significant others in the school experience setting (such as the supervising teacher, the university lecturer, other teachers and the principal) comprise the *social task system.*

A student teacher must satisfactorily engage in tasks from all three systems if a 'successful' practicum experience is to be achieved. The ability to manage and control a class, while important and necessary is only part of the story. Student teachers are also expected to plan in advance of the lesson and to 'get on' with numerous people.

Some mentors and university supervisors take a very hierarchical view of their relationship with student teachers. They believe they are the experts, and the students are the novices. As 'experts' they don't welcome being questioned or challenged with regard to the advice they give. In such situations, displaying an interested, non-argumentative, receptive, non-defensive manner in post-lesson discussions is judged to be a sign of maturity and professionalism. Most student teachers recognize the social task of maintaining cordial social relations in order to receive a good grade for their teaching practicum and accordingly defer to the 'experts'. Such are the lessons of survival. The extent to which a reconceived practicum with a partnership between school-based and university personnel will change these dynamics is problematic.

Of course there are teacher education programs which work hard to develop less hierarchical, more collegiate relationships between the mentor, the university lecturer and the student teacher (the triad as it is sometimes called). But even in such programs the student teacher must still engage all task systems. It's just that the nature of the social task system will be different.

Perhaps deferral to authority is an implicit learning for most student teachers in the practicum. Dodds' (1985) notion of the functional curriculum provides a useful framework to analyze the practicum as a site for learning to teach. Using such a framework we would need to consider the nature of the explicit, implicit, null and hidden curriculum of the practicum. There may be tensions between what is explicitly stated as outcomes of the practicum and what is learned through the hidden curriculum. For example, it is often stated that the practicum should be a place for the testing out of particular ideas about teaching. If however, some of these ideas are considered inappropriate or 'wrongheaded' by the mentor, then the student teacher is placed in a rather delicate position. To question the current practice of the mentor, to display in inquisitive manner, or to insist on 'trying out different ideas' might incur the disapproval of the mentor. Given the power relations in the practicum and the fact that the mentor must make a judgment with respect to the performance of the student teacher, there are strong forces on the student not to 'rock the boat'.

However, notwithstanding these significant obstacles, learning to teach should be considered as an opportunity to engage and appreciate the prob-lematic nature of teaching, rather than as an exercise in simply modelling what seems to work in practice. For the question must be asked, what does 'work' actually mean in this context? Does it mean merely keeping the class busy, happy and 'good' (Placek, 1983)? Indeed, what are the hidden learnings of the practicum and how should/would a mentor deal with them?

### The Nature of the Learner

There is an abundant literature that supports the claim that student teachers are usually chiefly concerned with complying with what works. The research of Iannaccone (1963), although over thirty years old, still reflects the situation of most student teachers. Iannaccone found that when student teachers fol-lowed the advice of the co-operating teacher, 'it worked', and 'getting through the lesson' became the primary objective. It was claimed that in the final ana-lysis the rationale of 'does it work to solve the immediate problem at hand?' became the chief criterion for student teachers in accepting or rejecting a par-ticular teaching procedure. Zeichner (1980) called this feature the development of a utilitarian teaching perspective and similar practices have been noted by Tabachnick *et al* (1978), Popkewitz (1977) and Zimpher *et al* (1980).

In the PETE context, the research of Tinning (1984) and Schempp (1983) support the fact that student teachers in physical education behave similarly. Moreover, Macdonald (1992) has found that PETE students' preference for utilitarian type knowledge extended beyond the practicum and in fact char-acterized their preference in the entire PETE program. Swan's (1995) study of student resistance and oppositional behaviours vividly demonstrates how PETE students respond to forms of knowledge and pedagogy which challenge such perspectives. In this case the nature of the learner is a serious limiting factor in the development of reflective student teachers.

### The Nature of the Mentor

Being chosen as a mentor in the Australian system is not necessarily a testa-ment to one's ability to facilitate the learning of student teachers. In the

Australian context mentors are typically not trained for their role. Traditionally, because of strong union influence, Australian teachers acting as co-operating teachers to supervise student teachers have been paid by the state for their efforts. While this should have been a strong controlling factor in selection, usually it failed to be so. Often universities were happy to get whoever they could, such was the competition to find places for student teachers in local schools.

Generally there has been little systematic training of such teachers and the role has had ambivalent status. Although there has been some advocacy of training for physical education co-operating teachers (see Tinning, 1984), for various reasons, including the low status of the practicum in the academic 'bun fight' for resources in the training institutions, such training has not been provided in any systematic or widespread manner.

This is particularly relevant in a context which is expecting co-operating teachers (mentors) to accept a greater responsibility for the training of student teachers. Remember that the *Draft National Guidelines for Initial Teacher Education* (1995) advocates the development of critically reflective student teachers and the practicum is an important site for such development. How is this to happen if the dominant ethos, expressed explicitly and implicitly by the mentor physical education teacher is one that favours reproduction rather than reconstruction?

## Mentors as reflective teachers?

In order to facilitate the development of critical reflection in student teachers one might expect that the mentor would both understand what is meant by the concept and hopefully even model such practice in their own teaching. What evidence is there that such is the case? Basically none! There is, however, strong evidence that teachers and university lecturers value different types of knowledge. Teachers' knowledge is described as *ideographic* or particular-istic (relating specifically to the context in which teachers' work). For instance, they possess specific knowledge of how certain strategies and approaches will work with *particular* children in *particular* classes. The knowledge valued by some university lecturers is claimed to be *nomothetic* or generalistic. Nomothetic knowledge relates not to a particular child in a particular class, but rather to children in *general* and classes in *general*.

The research of Chism (1985) revealed that in terms of professional development, teachers most value knowledge that is relevant to their own teaching lives (particularistic rather than generalistic), is utilitarian, in that it has clear implications for action, and has the capacity to actively engage them. The generalist knowledge of the theorist is considered to be of little relevance to the teacher. That said, however, it is important to recognize that the fact that many teachers don't have a high regard for theorizing is not to say that their practice is not informed by theory.

In the last decade it has been recognized that teachers do operate on the basis of their own 'theories-of-action', (see Schon, 1983; Smyth, 1984; McCutcheon, 1985). According to McCutcheon (1985), these theories-of-action

> ... are a set of constructs, beliefs, and principles on which the prac-
> titioners base decisions and actions. Practitioners develop these the-
> ories through their experiences and reflections, and to a lesser extent
> through reading or hearing about generic theory. Such theories illu-
> minate and guide practice because they comprise interrelated sets
> of interpretations about what should be taught and learned, how to
> improve and evaluate teaching and learning, and how to deal with
> daily tasks of managing curriculum development, classes, and work.
> (p. 47)

Importantly, however, these theories-of-action are usually part of the teacher's tacit world. They tend to be invisible in much the same way as the hidden curriculum is invisible. They are seldom articulated and are most often unrecognized by the teachers themselves. Often it needs considerable reflection on one's own teaching to begin to bring to the surface these theories which underpin our teaching.

So while teachers are, in the words of Doyle and Ponder (1977), 'pragmatic sceptics' when it comes to incorporating the ideas of theorists, they are themselves also theorists. Their theorizing, however, is not the nomothetic, law like type but rather the ideographic particularistic type. However, in the culture of teaching and schools there is often an artificial dichotomy maintained between teacher-practitioner and lecturer-theorist that reinforces a hierarchy in which the theorist is placed above the practitioner. Such a hierarchy severely limits the ability of those responsible for the education of student teachers to work collaboratively together. It is another dimension of the triad relationship which can often cause stress for the student teacher in trying to make sense of whose knowledge is most important, relevant and appropriate to a given situation, and trying to decide how to make such a judgment, given all the competing demands and dynamics.

In this sense then, moves to make the practicum experience a more collaborative endeavour between school-based and university-based personnel might be an important step in breaking down the dichotomous perception of theory and practice. On the other hand, however, depending on the nature of the mentor, the experience the student teacher receives on the practicum may merely reinforce the artificial disjunction between theory and practice and an unreflective approach to learning to teach.

### *Mentor as model or student teacher as master's apprentice*

#### *A story*
Nadine was watching her mother prepare a roast turkey. She watched her cut the legs off the turkey and then place them beside the body

of the bird in the large baking dish. The turkey was then stuffed, basted, and placed in the oven for cooking. Nadine looked puzzled and asked her mum why she cut the legs off. Her mum told that she learnt to do that by watching her mother cook turkeys and she always cut the legs off.

Blessed with a rare native curiosity, Nadine pursued the issue the next time she saw her grandmother. 'Why do you cut the legs off the turkey before roasting it?' she asked. Her granny smiled and told her that when she first began to cook roasts she only had a small baking dish and unless she cut the legs off she could not fit a large bird in the dish. Nadine then realized that her mum had simply copied a way of preparing the roast that was no longer necessary since she had a baking dish large enough to accommodate a large turkey without its legs chopped off. Nadine learned something of the limitations of the apprenticeship model.

There are lessons in this story for mentors and the practicum in teacher education. There is no doubt that we all learn a great deal about teaching from being a pupil ourselves. Dan Lortie (1975), in his book *Schoolteacher*, first argued that personal history, as opposed to formal training or teaching experience, was the most powerful socialization influence on student teachers. Larry Locke (1979) said that all student teachers have something like 20,000 hours of observation and involvement as a school pupil which serves as a somewhat 'invisible apprenticeship' into teaching. But sitting at the feet of Nellie, as apprenticeship is sometimes pejoratively called, can lead to a mindless copying of current practice. It can lead to chopping off legs unnecessarily.

### Mentor as an 'Extended Professional'

As a result of a shift in the conception of the supervision process within the practicum from one of 'direct, overt surveillance' (Smyth, 1993) to a more facilitatory role (Gaffey and Dobbins, 1995) teacher educators now 'have to grapple with a changed role . . . (which) becomes one of helping insiders to make sense of experience . . . rather than telling them what these experiences ought to look like' (Smyth, 1993, p. 42). According to Gaffey and Dobbins (1995) the role of the teacher educator in the 90s 'is one of facilitator and *mentor*, working in partnership with school-based personnel, to optimise student teachers' learning from the practicum' (p. 13, my emphasis). This means that teacher education requires a new conceptualizing of the co-operating teacher or mentor. Such a concept is embodied in Stenhouse's (1975) notion of teacher as extended professional.

The late Lawrence Stenhouse coined the term 'extended professionalism' which he claimed was characterized by: the commitment to systematic questioning of one's own teaching as a basis for development; the commitment and the skills to study one's own teaching; and the concern to question and to test theory in practice by the use of those skills (*ibid*, p. 144). This notion of 'extended professionalism' is, in essence, a redefinition of what it means to be a professional teacher and it distances itself from the applied science notion of professionalism. Extended professionalism requires that teachers reflect on their educational practice.

Basic to Stenhouse's notion is that while much day-to-day teaching is habitual in the sense that little time is spent in conscious reflection or analysis with respect to key questions such as 'What are the implications of what I teach and the way I teach?' (Tinning, 1987), improving one's own educational practice is actually an intentional activity.

Obviously, some of our teaching must, of necessity, be habitual in the same way that a golfer must have a swing which is performed automatically, habitually. For the golfer, however, the habitual nature of his swing is put to the test with every shot. Errors in the habitual swing will be readily seen as errors in the performance — the topped nine iron will fail to hold the green — the sliced drive will finish in the rough. For the teacher such is not quite the case. Ill-informed or bad teaching practices often go unnoticed, perhaps because their consequences are more deferred and therefore harder to see.

All teaching practices, whether habitual or not, should be able to be defended or justified, should be open for scrutiny in order that they can be analyzed. We saw earlier that teachers' educational practices do embody theories-of-action (McCutcheon, 1985), and that mostly they are tacit and need conscious reflection in order to bring them to the surface for analysis. For most student teachers less of their teaching will be habitual, in that most of it is new, and hence requires conscious attention. In this sense the task of reflection might be easier for a student teacher than for an experienced teacher who may do things habitually without any conscious thought.

It is important to realize that when we talk of reflective teaching we are not referring to what teachers normally do in the act of teaching. Being a reflective teacher is more than simply thinking about one's work. It involves, as Stenhouse (1975) pointed out, 'a capacity for autonomous professional self-development through systematic self-study, through the study of the work of other teachers and through the testing of ideas by classroom research procedures' (p. 144). Tony Rossi (chapter 11 of this volume) introduces the possibility of a different role for a mentor in the context of action research. The problem is, as has already been discussed, the typical practicum experience does not facilitate such systematic self-study, especially since the mentor will not usually model such extended professionalism.

By considering teaching and education to be essentially problematic (open to different opinions and interpretations) the way is clear to conceive of learning to teach as a process of learning certain skills as well as learning to critically reflect on one's own practice. According to Tom (1984), to make teaching problematic is to raise doubts about what, under ordinary circumstances, appears to be effective or wise practice (p. 37). Again, as we saw earlier, the practicum is generally not a place where the student teacher can raise such doubts and queries about 'effective or wise practice' especially if it is challenging the mentor's educational practice.

However, a view of learning to teach which is predicated on the problematic nature of truth about teaching is not universally popular in PETE. In physical education, there is a popular view that improving one's educational practice is best achieved through the application of certain research derived nomothetic knowledge to specific teaching situations. This is the view of those who argue that teaching should be thought of as an applied science (for example, see Siendentop, 1991).

Donald Schon (1983) argues that contemporary professionals in such diverse fields as education, architecture, and engineering are failing to deal with practice which is increasingly unpredictable, complex, situation specific and value laden. Increasingly professionals have tried to create law-like generalizations which apply to all situations of a particular kind. According to Schon, this model for the professions has shown itself to be bankrupt.

Relating to the teaching of physical education, Schon's message would be that generalizations about how to teach physical education will often fail when applied to particular situations which are complex, unpredictable and value laden. As mentioned above, generalistic type knowledge of the kind created by the 'outside expert' or theorist is limited in its applicability to particular situations. The way that individual teachers go about their teaching of physical education is going to be largely affected by the characteristics of the particular setting (the location of the school, the faculty support for physical education, the children themselves, the time of day or time of year etc). Therefore professional knowledge needs to be seen as problematic and needs to be actually tested out in the particular situation in which the teacher works. Ideas about practice can only be validated by practitioners themselves.

If we conceive of teaching as an educational craft (Tinning *et al*, 1993) in which knowledge about teaching is derived from collective wisdom, from research findings, and from observation and experiment of teaching itself, then we begin to move beyond the blind acceptance of 'experts' and towards a new notion of what professional knowledge means. Fundamental to this concept of a teacher as an educational craftsperson is the notion of reflective teaching.

The American Larry Locke (1977) once claimed that in physical education in the USA was not so much bedevilled by bad teaching as it was by mindless teaching. That same criticism has relevance for Australian physical education as well. The practicum and the role of the mentor in the pedagogy of the practicum could play a crucial role in challenging such mindless teaching. It is possible, through a process which stresses reflective teaching, to so problematize physical education teaching that graduating student teachers will view school physical education through a set of lenses which recognizes pre-service teacher education as merely the beginning of the development as an educational craftsperson with respect to teaching physical education.

Importantly, however, reflective teaching is something that is not done in addition to, or as well as, the development of pedagogical skills and curriculum knowledge in a PETE program. Rather, it must be embedded within the pedagogy of the program itself including the practicum. It should be the pedagogical process through which the student teachers learn about pedagogical and curriculum knowledge, and it should facilitate a reflexivity towards not only the student teacher's own teaching but also of the practicum, the 'methods' course and PETE program as well.

### *The Possibilities for Optimism?*

There are two fundamentally different positions with respect to the teacher education which have relevance to the issue of mentoring and the practicum. Spodek (1974) represents the view that I hold when he claims:

> All teacher education is a form of ideology. Each program is related to the educational ideology held by a particular teacher educator or teacher education institution, even though the relationship may not be made explicit. There is no such thing as a value-free education for children. (p. 9)

The other point of view is represented forcefully by the words of B.O. Smith (1980)

> The pre-service student should not be exposed to theories and practices derived from ideologies and philosophies about the way schools should be. The rule should be to teach thoroughly, the knowledge and skills that equip beginning teachers to work successfully in today's classrooms. (p. 3)

In Australia to date we have been sending student teachers into practicum contexts in which the views of Smith are more common than those of Spodek. We are also seeing the call by government-oriented bodies, for a new paradigm for teacher education which includes competency standards for graduating student teachers, included in which is the development of a critical reflective perspective on one's own educational practice. Although not prescribed with the degree of precision such as that necessary to demonstrate competence in cooking tandoori chicken, the explicit support for competencies of critical reflection is clear. There is, however, a fundamental tension at work here. The discourses underpinning competency standards are found in the words of Smith, whereas those underpinning critical reflection are found in Spodek's position.

In the face of what is known about the significance of the practicum as a site for learning to teach, and about the significance of the mentor in the pedagogy of the practicum, the Australian context remains one in which the lessons from cooking turkeys and tandoori chickens still tend to be ignored by all but a few. Critical reflection in Australian PETE remains an elusive practice, and pronouncements that teacher education should develop student teacher competencies in critical reflection, are at present merely an appropriation of discourse stripped of real meaning. It is clear that neither the mentors in schools nor the teacher educators in most PETE institutions are well positioned to 'deliver' critical reflection. As Macdonald and Tinning (1995) have shown, there is a trend towards proletarianization in Australian PETE which effects both student teachers, mentors and teacher educators. Since the discourses of practice in physical education are dominated by technical and utilitarian considerations, the space for critical reflective discourses in PETE programs is limited. More specifically, within PETE the practicum and the role of the mentor in the learning to teach process, are considered to be essentially unproblematic. Accordingly the possibilities for student teachers to develop the abilities and ideological frameworks to critically reflect on their teaching, and on education more generally, are also limited. Mentors, it seems, are unlikely to inspire (let alone 'train') student teachers to consider their future role as one of social transformation rather than reproduction. In this sense, the more things change the more they stay the same.

## Note

1   This is a paper prepared and endorsed by representatives of the following bodies: Australian Teaching Council; Australian Council of Deans of Education; Australian Teacher Education Association; Queensland Board of Teacher Registration; Teachers Registration Board of South Australia.

## References

BAIN, L. (1990) 'Vision and voices', *Quest*, **42**, pp. 2–12.

BARTLETT, L. (1992) 'Vision and revision: A competency-based scheme for the teaching profession', *Journal of Teaching Practice*, **12**, 1, pp. 58–81.

BATES, R. (1994a) 'Quality education for all', paper presented at the annual conference of the Australian Council of State School Organisations, Adelaide.

BATES, R. (1994b) 'Teacher education: An international perspective', paper presented at the New Zealand Council for Teacher Education National Conference, Wellington.

CHISM, N. (1985) 'The knowledge that teachers value: Findings from a case study', paper presented at the annual meeting of the American Educational Research Association, Chicago.

CRUM, B. (1995) 'The urgent need for reflective teaching in physical education' in PARE, C. (Ed) *Training of Teachers in Reflective Practice of Physical Education*, Trois Rivieres, Quebec, Universite du Quebec a Trois-Rivieres, pp. 1–21.

DODDS, P. (1985) 'Are hunters of the functional curriculum seeking quarks or snarks?', *Journal of Teaching in Physical Education*, **4**, pp. 91–9.

Dodds, P. (1995) 'Reflective teacher education (RTS): Paradigm for professional growth or only smoke and mirrors?' in Paré, C. (Ed) *Training of Teachers in Reflective Practice of Physical Education*, Trois-Rivières, Quebéc, Université du Quebéc à Trois-Rivières, pp. 65–83.

Doyle, W. (1980) 'Student mediating responses in teaching effectiveness', unpublished manuscript, North Texas State University.

Doyle, W. and Ponder, G. (1977) 'The practicality ethic in teacher education', *Interchange*, **8**, 3.

*Draft National Guidelines for Initial Teacher Education* (1995) June. Document 1: A companion document to the Australian Teaching Council's Program Recognition Procedures.

Evans, J. (1995) 'Teachers' professional knowledge, pedagogy and the future of teacher education', paper presented at the AIESEP International Conference, Wingate Institute, Israel.

Evans, J., Davies, B. and Penny, D. (1995) 'Pedagogy, identity and difference in physical education', paper presented at the European Educational Research Association Annual Conference, Bath.

Fernandez-Balboa, J.-M. (1995) 'Reclaiming physical education in higher education through critical pedagogy', *Quest*, **1**, pp. 91–115.

Furlong, J. (1994) 'The rise and rise of the mentor in British initial teacher training' in Yeomans, R. and Sampson, J. (Eds) *Mentorship: The Primary School*, London, Falmer Press, pp. 6–18.

Gaffey, C. and Dobbins, R. (1995) 'Tertiary teacher educators: Do they make a difference in the practicum?', paper presented at the Second National Conference in Practical Experiences in Professional Education, Gold Coast, Queensland.

Grossman, P. (1992) 'Why models matter: An alternative view on professional growth in teaching', *Review of Educational Research*, **62**, 2, pp. 171–9.

Iannacone, L. (1963) 'Student teaching: A traditional stage in the making of a teacher', *Theory into Practice*, **19**, pp. 73–80.

Kemmis, S. (1994) 'Control and crisis in university teacher education' Penny Lecture, University of South Australia.

Kirk, D. (1988) *Physical Education and Curriculum Study*, London, Croom Helm.

Kirk, D. (1990) 'Knowledge, science and the rise and rise of human movement studies', *ACHPER National Journal*, **127**, 18, pp. 8–11.

Kirk, D. (1994) 'Making the present strange: Curriculum history and the invention of Australian physical education', *Discourse: The Australian Journal of Educational Studies*, pp. 45–67.

Knight, J., Lingard, R. and Bartlett, L. (1993) 'Re-forming teacher education: The unfinished task' in Knight, J. Bartlett, L. and E. McWilliam (Eds) *Unfinished Business: Reshaping the Education Industry for the 1990s*, Rockhampton, UCQ Press, pp. 21–65.

Locke, L. (1977) 'Research on teaching physical education: New hope for a dismal science', *Quest*, **28**, pp. 2–16.

Locke, L. (1979) *Supervision, Schools and Student Teaching: Why Things Stay the Same*, New Orleans, LA, American Academy of Physical Education.

Lortie, D. (1975) *Schoolteacher: A Sociological Study*, Chicago, IL, University of Chicago Press.

Lusted, D. (1986) 'Why pedagogy?', *Screen*, **27**, 5, pp. 2–14.

Macdonald, D. (1992) 'Knowledge, power and professional practice in physical education teacher education: A case study', PhD, Deakin University.

MACDONALD, D. and TINNING, R. (1995) 'Physical education teacher education and the trend to proletarianization: A case study', *Journal of Teaching in Physical Education*, **15**, 1, pp. 987–1019.

MACINTYRE, S. (1988) *Whose Justice, Which Rationality?* London, Duckworth.

McCUTCHEON, G. (1985) 'Curriculum theory/curriculum practice: A gap or the Grand Ganyon?' in MOLNAR, A. (Ed) *Current Thought on Curriculum*, Alexandria, VA, Association for Supervision and Curriculum Development.

McCUTCHEON, G. and JUNG, B. (1990) 'Alternative perspectives on action research', *Theory into practice*, **24**, 3, pp. 144–51.

McKAY, J., GORE, J. and KIRK, D. (1990) 'Beyond the limits of technocratic physical education', *Quest*, **42**, pp. 52–76.

MARTINEZ, K. (1990) 'Critical reflections on critical reflection in teacher education', *Journal of Teaching Practice*, **10**, 2, pp. 20–9.

PLACEK, J. (1983) 'Conceptions of success in teaching: Busy, happy and good?' in TEMPLIN, J.O.T. (Ed) *Teaching in Physical Education*, Champaign, IL, Human Kinetics.

POPKEWITZ, T. (1977) 'Ideology as a problem of teacher education', paper presented at the annual meeting of the American Educational Research Association, New York.

PRAIN, V. and HICKEY, C. (1995) 'Using discourse analysis to change physical education', *Quest*, **47**, 1, pp. 76–91.

SCHEMPP, P. (1983) 'Learning the role: The transformation from student to teacher', paper presented at the AAHPERD Annual Convention, Minneapolis, Minnesota.

SCHON, D. (1983) *The Reflective Practitioner: How Professionals Think in Action*, New York, Basic Books.

SIEDENTOP, D. (1991) *Developing Teaching Skills in Physical Education* (3rd ed.) Palo Alto, CA, Mayfield Publishing Company.

SMITH, B.O. (1980) 'On the content of teacher education' in HALL, E., HORD, S. and BROWN, G. (Eds) *Exploring Issues in Teacher Education: Questions for Future Research*, Austin, TX, University of Texas Research and Development Centre for Teacher Education.

SMYTH, J. (1984) 'Teachers as collaborators in clinical supervision', *Teacher Education*, **24**, pp. 60–8.

SMYTH, J. (1992) 'Teachers' work and the politics of reflection', *American Educational Research Journal*, **29**, pp. 267–300.

SMYTH, J. (1993) 'Reflective practice in teacher education and other professions' in *Fifth National Practicum Conference*, Sydney, Macquarie University.

SPODEK, B. (1974) 'Teacher education: Of the teacher, by the teacher, for the child', *Journal of Teacher Education*, **31**, 6, pp. 45–55.

STENHOUSE, L. (1975) *An Introduction to Curriculum Research and Development*, London, Heinemann.

SWAN, P. (1993) 'Hierarchies of subject knowledge within physical education teacher education' in unpublished research project for the Deakin EdD program.

SWAN, P. (1995) 'Studentship and appositional behaviour within physical education teacher education: A case study', EdD, Deakin University.

TABACHNICK, B., POPKEWITZ, T. and ZEICHNER, K. (1978) 'Teacher education and the professional perspective of teachers', paper presented at the annual meeting of the American Educational Research Association, Toronto.

TINNING, R. (1984) 'The student teaching experience: All that glitters is not gold', *Australian Journal of Teaching Practice*, **4**, 2, pp. 53–62.

TINNING, R. (1987) *Improving Teaching in Physical Education*, Geelong, Deakin University.

TINNING, R. (1990) *Ideology and Physical Education: Opening Pandora's Box*, Deakin University, Geelong.

TINNING, R. (1995) 'We have ways of making you think. Or do we?: Reflections on "training" in reflective teaching' in PARÉ, C. (Ed) *Training of Teachers in Reflective Practice of Physical Education*, Trois Rivières, Canada, Université du Quebéc à Trois-Rivières, pp. 21–53.

TINNING, R. and FITZCLARENCE, L. (1992) 'Postmodern youth culture and the crisis in Australian secondary school physical education', *Quest*, **44**, 3, pp. 287–304.

TINNING, R. and FITZCLARENCE, L. (1995) 'Physical education for adolescents in the 1990s: The crisis of relevance', *Aussie Sport Action*, **6**, 2, pp. 12–13.

TINNING, R., KIRK, D. and EVANS, J. (1993) *Learning to Teach Physical Education*, Englewood Cliffs, NJ, Prentice Hall.

TINNING, R., KIRK, D., EVANS, J. and GLOVER, S. (1994) 'School physical education: A crisis of meaning', *Changing Education: A Journal for Teachers and Administrators*, **1**, 2, pp. 13–15.

TINNING, R. and SIEDENTOP, D. (1985) 'The characteristics of tasks and accountability in student teaching', *Journal of Teaching in Physical Education*, **4**, 4, pp. 286–300.

TOM, A. (1984) *Teaching as a Moral Craft*, New York, Longman.

ZEICHNER, K. (1980) 'Myths and realities: Field based experiences in preservice teacher education', *Journal of Teacher Education*, **31**, 6, pp. 45–55.

ZEICHNER, K. (1986) 'The practicum as an occasion for learning to teach', paper presented at the Third National Conference on the Practicum in Teacher Education, Geelong.

ZIMPHER, N., de VOSS, G. and NOTT, D. (1980) 'A closer look at university student teacher supervision', *Journal of Teacher Education*, **31**, 4, pp. 11–15.

# 13 Mentoring within Physical Education Teacher Education in the USA: Research Trends and Developments

*Deborah Tannehill and Deborah G. Coffin*

## Introduction

Counsellor, confidante, master, inspector, role model, sponsor, coach, teacher, trainer, guide, protector, leader and helper are all used to describe the role of a mentor. Numerous definitions defining mentoring within an array of contexts reflect the lack of consensus on the intent, roles, and functions a mentor serves. Alleman, Cochran, Doverspike and Newman (1984) suggested mentoring is 'a relationship in which a person of greater rank of expertise teacher, guides, and develops a novice in an organization or profession' (p. 329). This definition represents a rather sterile view of mentoring devoid of personal commitment or caring on the part of the mentor. The ERIC thesaurus defines mentors as 'trusted and experienced supervisors or advisors who have personal or direct interest in the development and/or education of younger or less experienced individuals, usually in professional education or professional occupations' (Houston, 1990). While this comes closer to our view of what a mentor could be within an educational setting it still does not allow for the role of mentor to vary as a function of the context in which it is situated.

Gehrke (1988) relates mentoring and the mentor-protege relationship to a gift-exchange phenomenon where the mentor provides a gift of knowledge and the protege accepts the gift and ultimately passes it on to another. A definition of mentoring which encompasses these criteria has been provided by Carruthers (1993):

> Mentoring is a complex, interactive process, occurring between individuals of differing levels of experience and expertise which incorporates interpersonal or psychosocial development, career and/or educational development, and socialization functions into the relationship . . . To the extent that the parameters of mutuality and compatibility exist in the relationship, the potential outcomes of respect, professionalism, collegiality, and role fulfillment will result. Further, the mentoring process occurs in a dynamic relationship within a given milieu. (pp. 10–11)

This definition conforms more closely to our notion of mentoring as a helping relationship between two colleagues regardless of age, expertise, or position. It allows us to apply mentoring across the career span of a teacher and represents numerous contexts including preservice education, beginning teacher induction, and the professional development of practicing teachers. Acheson and Gall (1987) suggested extending role delineations that include an educator working with other educators promoting their growth and development without the hierarchial connotations associated with supervision and evaluation. From this perspective supervision can be equated with mentoring and be applied to pre-service and in-service education. Our view of a mentor includes a pre-service teacher providing guidance to a peer in an early field experience, a practicing teacher serving in the role of a co-operating teacher sharing professional expertise with a student teacher, or some of the new applications of the mentor/supervisor role as they are being designed in collaborative school-university development efforts.

Learning to function in this mentor/supervisor role requires training and practice for both the mentor and the teacher being mentored. 'It is reasonable to think that the individuals one would choose as mentors are similar to those one would choose as supervising teachers or clinical instructors' (Stroble and Cooper, 1988, p. 235). It makes sense that these same teachers or other educators be charged with supervising beginning teachers whether they be at the preservice or induction level. 'What is good for the first year of teaching is also good for the last year of preservice' (Stroble and Cooper, 1988, p. 235). This could also be extended to include training pre-service teachers to perform in this mentoring capacity. Accepting criticism and feedback as well as being able to observe a peer and provide appropriate input and feedback on the teaching situation would provide a useful learning experience. Thus pre-service teachers leaving the university would understand the implications and benefits of mentoring for their own and others professional development and be more eager and prepared to participate in this endeavor throughout their career. This supports Schweitzer's (1993) view that, 'for many individuals, the effects of a mentoring program continues to exist beyond the life of an undergraduate mentoring program' (p. 52).

Informal mentoring occurs daily in physical education across the United States with students, undergraduates, beginning teachers and professors, and those who have relocated to a different teaching level. In many cases this might actually be socialization into an educational setting with both positive and negative effects, while in other instances informal mentoring may be occurring with positive outcomes assumed. This informal mentoring takes place as teachers and colleagues help children, pre-service teachers, and new university colleagues become acclimated to the educational environment. Formal or planned mentoring occurs when programs are structured to select and match participants according to experience, knowledge, and need. Teacher education in physical education has utilized formal mentoring in early field experiences, student teaching, and internships to one degree or another since teacher training first began (Schweitzer 1993).

Recently, planned mentoring emerged as a popular collaborative effort between schools and universities, in professional development sites, and within several school districts in staff development efforts (Bey and Holmes, 1992). Unfortunately, formal mentoring programs in physical education tend to be limited to those school districts which have implemented programs for all teachers. Recent restructuring of schools committed to the acquisition and sharing of knowledge among all members of the education community has resulted in the creation of partnerships (professional development schools) linking public schools and university colleges of education. These professional development schools (PDS) have increased the possibility for mentoring situations yet most of the literature has focused on procedures for the collaboration process rather than the quality and scope of the mentoring which takes place within them.

In this chapter we have chosen to focus on four aspects of mentoring in physical education professional preparation in the United States: (i) peer mentoring within preservice education; (ii) co-operating teachers as mentors; (iii) recent mentoring developments within collaborative or professional development school efforts; and (iv) mentoring in beginning teacher induction. These sections will explore formal and informal mentoring strategies, as well as research-based and experimental mentoring programs in an attempt to characterize supervisory mentoring in the USA.

## Peer Mentoring within Teacher Education

While the preparation of teachers involves personnel from various contexts serving in distinct roles, little attention has been paid to the interactions among pre-service teachers themselves. Professional training programs have involved students in peer discussions, reflections and evaluations during methods courses and early field experiences yet reports on the role of peers during these field based, practical experiences have been limited. The contribution of peers in these settings has had limited attention (Dodds, 1975; Veriaboff, 1983) relative to what peers learn from one another, what advice they share, or the impact of these interactions.

It is necessary to define our interpretation of peer coaching as distinct from peer supervision. Peer coaching has been defined by Batesky (1991) as 'one teacher helping another teacher improve his or her instructional skills or develop a new teaching practice' (p. 15). It is intended to be a supportive, non-threatening, and collaborative process rather than evaluative in nature. Joyce and Showers (1988) suggest that peer coaching is intended to build a community of teachers who deliberate on teaching, develop a shared technical language, and provide the framework within which new skills can be learned. Peer coaching closely matches our earlier interpretation of mentoring. Peer supervision on the other hand involves evaluation and attempts to identify specific teaching skills or behaviors which need improvement. While it has yet to be demonstrated persuasively that peers have the knowledge to provide substantive feedback and direction to significantly contribute to the professional development of another, there is more controversy on whether student peers should be placed in positions to evaluate one another as implied in the latter term.

The extent to which peer teaching experiences are utilized in the preparation of teachers is widespread in the United States. A national survey conducted by Strand (1992) reported that the 131 institutions responding provided 7.9 peer teaching experiences on average prior to the final student teaching practicum. These peer experiences were generally offered in conjunction with either skill or pedagogy courses yet no description of the role played by participants was offered.

Early work by Dodds (1975 and 1989) suggested that peer teaching allows student teachers to gain extended practice observing and coding one anothers' teaching behaviors, analyzing teaching situations, and providing and receiving immediate feedback from more than one source. An extension of this design was employed by Veriaboff (1983) where three to five student teachers were placed in one site. Many programs have since expanded on this format in both early field experiences and student teaching by placing groups of students in one site to practice specific skills simultaneously under the tutelage of a single supervisor. These experiences allow preservice teachers at the same developmental stage to practice specific and similar instructional behaviors (Metzler, 1990).

A teaching center concept employed at Slippery Rock College which will be further clarified in the next section was reported by Jones (1993) and reflects some of the positive aspects of cohort teacher sites. These teaching centers were designed to allow five health and physical education student teachers to work within one school district at the elementary, middle and high school settings simultaneously. During this practicum experience student teachers were required to meet as a group to interact on teaching and professional issues. They also had the opportunity to communicate on a daily basis to provide support and act as a sounding board for one another.

While group experiences appear to be widespread in practice, some recent reports suggest that preservice teachers participating in these practica actually have a specific role in the professional development of their peers on a one-to-one basis. West Virginia University (WVU) has started a mentoring program which pairs pre-service teachers in several stages of their professional development. Students completing their student teaching practicum return to campus for their final quarter, take a supervision course, and serve as mentors for students at earlier stages in their training. The goals of the supervision course include: (i) reinforcing key curriculum concepts previously taught and related to their student teaching experiences; (ii) helping debrief the student teaching experience; (iii) providing practice in the observation and analysis of teaching; and (iv) affording opportunities for professional growth through developing collegial relationships with other professionals (for example, Hawkins, 1995a). During the supervision course, these pre-service teachers are assigned as mentors to three other students at different phases of the teacher training program; a first year student in the introductory practica, an intern assigned to team-teach a basic instruction course with a graduate student, and a student teacher. Their mentoring role ranges from socializing new students into the program, assisting students to relate to their graduate student supervisor, sharing and reflecting on teaching in the schools, and helping a student teacher negotiate the student teaching experience (for example, Hawkins, 1995a). Finally, as will be explained later, these pre-service teachers are assigned to mentor a WVU faculty member who is teaching elementary physical education in a local school. This experience provides undergraduates the opportunity to share ideas with faculty who have limited experience in schools and more importantly enhances development of a collegial relationship with an established professional in the field.

Another peer mentoring program has been established at Springfield College where third year students in the program mentor their first year colleagues who are teaching small groups of elementary pupils in an after school program (for example, Petersen, 1995). This elementary field experience is in conjunction with the first teaching methods course which focusses on generic instructional strategies. The goal of the course is to provide the conceptual foundation for teaching and to provide a field experience for students to practically apply their developing skills. These mentors are selected by faculty based on grade point average (academic standing), performance in pedagogy courses, and responsibility displayed throughout the program. Their role as mentors requires them to make four-six visits to the elementary school to observe and analyze teaching. Two faculty members meet with the mentors each week prior to their visit to the school to review the goals for the week and discuss the focus of the observation (for example, management, transitions, feedback). These discussions are based on faculty members conceptions of what each student needs at a particular time. During these peer observations the mentors take notes, provide feedback to the field experience student, interact with them about their teaching, and share written feedback on what was observed. While no efforts have been made to formally assess the success of this mentoring program, positive student feedback has suggested it is valuable to pre-service students in the mentoring partnership.

Developmental Movement Education (DME) is the first methods course and practical experience required of first year students in the Ohio State University physical education teacher preparation program. The goal of this course/ practicum is for pre-service teachers to use their developing skills and knowledge to design appropriate movement experiences for an individual child in swimming, gymnastics, and fundamental motor skills. Second year students who have successfully completed this DME experience have the opportunity to serve as mentors to their first year peers. Students applying for this mentoring role are selected based on their performance in DME, previous peer interactions and relationships, and teaching effectiveness. Once selected they work with a graduate teaching associate or faculty member in charge of one movement area. The mentor role includes observing their peer's performance, collecting feedback data (positive/negative, specific/general, and appropriate), and providing both objective (data based) and subjective feedback to their peer on what occurred. This mentoring experience provides first year students with support and feedback. Reports from these students suggest that they seem to be most comfortable receiving feedback from their peers in this early stage of development (for example, Herkowitz, 1995). For the mentors, it provides reinforcement of teaching concepts which were introduced previously and are being stressed in their second teaching methods course.

The nature of peer teaching experiences from one teacher training program to the next is variable and reflects numerous models and numbers of students working together to meet varied program goals. Metzler (1990) suggests that 'peer supervision benefits both the teachers who practice skills and those who monitor and analyze that practice' (p. 41). Questions on the viability of peer mentoring/supervision are prevalent yet there is some indication that using it as a supplement to faculty supervision and feedback is desirable. Randall (1990) suggests that attempting to involve pre-service teachers in substantive interaction throughout their training is appropriate. While these peer interactions may not produce lasting pedagogical effects they may result in other benefits such as; building a community of teachers, developing a shared language, and providing a structure for continued training to foster the acquisition of new skills (Joyce and Showers, 1982).

Recent work at Ohio State University has explored the extent to which pre-service teachers in an early field experience can provide one another with support, guidance, and specific feedback on various aspects of teaching through electronic communication (e-mail). In a pilot study, LaMaster (1995) assessed the feasibility of this idea and found that these pre-service teachers could provide support and some alternative suggestions to their peers through e-mail. They did not, however, feel comfortable providing criticism to one another and it was concluded that this may have been due to their own lack of personal teaching experience. Where pre-service teachers had similar experiences and comparable concerns, they were better able to share alternative ideas which they had attempted in their own lessons.

Poole (1994) supported Joyce and Showers' (1982) ideas related to the benefits of peer coaching when he stated that 'having a peer available to ask questions, provide observations, and provide feedback is, arguably, extremely beneficial for teaching improvement' (p. 53). In an attempt to arrange more teaching experiences for undergraduate physical education teacher education students at the University of Utah, majors were paired with instructors in a Basic Instruction Program. This mentor/protege relationship was designed to provide '(a) peer teaching support, (b) classroom or action research, (c) the development of a teaching case, and (d) qualitative data collection' (Poole, 1994, p. 53). Together, these pairs were responsible for developing teaching cases related to the components of effective teaching. Through questions, observation, trial and error, and interviews these undergraduates developed in-depth cases intended to promote reflection on the teaching process. At the conclusion of the term, these cases were presented to peers at which time similarities were identified and discussed.

While the literature suggests that there is merit in peer mentoring and its contribution to the professional development of pre-service teachers, it might be that the major benefit lies in the support it provides and collegiality it fosters. As we move to more school-based field experiences, the need to further explore the role and efficacy of peer mentoring in the professional development of teachers is necessary.

## Co-operating Teachers as Mentors

Student teaching as the culminating experience in most teacher preparation programs has been reported and discussed extensively in the literature. While the practicum from the co-operating teacher's perspective has received the least amount of dialogue, we do know that co-operating teachers can be trained to supervise (Coulon, 1988; O'Cansey, 1988; Siedentop, 1981; Tannehill and Zakrajsek, 1990), value the impact of this experience on their professional lives (Berry and Ginsberg, 1990; Lieberman and Miller, 1989; Tannehill, 1989), and have a sincere desire to make a difference through assisting the student teacher (Rikard and Veal, in press; Tannehill, 1989).

Veal and Rikard (1995) have suggested that if we are to maintain the traditional triad arrangement (student teacher, co-operating teacher, and university supervisor) for student teaching then initiating a form of shared supervision will allow all members of the triad to provide professional development to one another. This new model would set the stage for shared decision-making among the triad with each providing an equal voice in the practicum. If all members of the triad do indeed learn from one another as Veal and Rikard suggest then this new model of shared supervision would account for and facilitate this learning. 'We envision the three adults in the student teaching triad developing a partnership that creates three-way communication. These three-way interactions are designed for exploring teaching issues and innovations as well as discussing supervision techniques that can be used by all members in a true community of adult learners' (Veal and Rikard, 1995, pp. 20–1). This supervisory partnership supports the position proposed by Joyce and Showers (1982) that when teachers share the same experience instructional events, strategies, and perspectives can be transmitted and interpreted as a team.

This notion of shared supervision in the student teaching practicum can be viewed as a form of mentoring among colleagues although it may not conform to traditional conceptions of mentoring. However, as Howey (1988) stated, 'since beginning and experienced teachers are undifferentiated in their roles and responsibilities, the relationship between teachers and mentors is more collegial or equal than are most mentoring relationships' (p. 209). With training, teachers are ideal for providing feedback to colleagues yet both teachers themselves and teaching organizations (school districts and teachers unions) are hesitant to place teachers in what they consider an evaluator's role. It is possible and practical for teachers to play this mentor role through staff development efforts and it can be extended to other scenarios. Teachers trained to take on this responsibility can become collegial supervisors/mentors with veteran and novice teachers, teaching aides, and pre-service teachers alike. Thus, this collegial supervisor role may be viewed as a mentor type relationship with expanded role designations.

At the University of South Carolina, co-operating teachers are selected by their program and teaching reputations. They must submit an application to the program and a videotape of their teaching. They take a course on effective teaching which is intended to provide them with a shared technical language with the student teachers and university faculty and expose them to what faculty believe is 'good' teaching. They also take a supervision course which highlights generic supervision skills and is closely aligned with the goals and philosophy of South Carolina's teacher training program. This clinical supervision model which has been in place for a number of years is unique and effective yet anything but traditional. In this program, the co-operating teacher is the 'key' player in the practicum, setting the goals for the experience, determining appropriate learning experiences, and overseeing all aspects of student teaching including the grading of the student teacher. The university does not provide support in the form of a university supervisor, rather they have trained the co-operating teachers and upheld that trust by relinquishing their traditional monitoring of the experience. The university provides in-service days and social events in an attempt to maintain contact, keep lines of communication open, and ensure maintenance of the program. In describing this model, Rink (1995) suggests that 'there is real ownership and sense of belongness/partnership with these people. Ten of them spent the summer revisiting the evaluation materials for student teaching to make them consistent with the Beginning Teacher Standards, some stuff going on in the state, Goodlad, etc'.

While they have yet to complete research to determine if this clinical model makes a difference on the student teachers they do 'get almost 100 per cent satisfaction from the student teachers' and based on student teacher performance and co-operating teacher feedback consider it successful (for example, Rink, 1995). There is also a big advantage in that the faculty can best use their time in other clinical experiences occurring earlier in the program.

Oregon State University in Corvalis has implemented a clinical supervision program for pre-service teachers working on teacher certification at the graduate level through a Master's of Education (MEd). Mentor teachers are selected in much the same way as described at South Carolina although a dearth of model practice sites does not allow placement by program quality in every instance. Mentors are provided with a handbook which includes responsibilities for all parties involved in the student teaching practicum, strategies on mentoring, and an assortment of eclectic assessment forms (i.e., focussed on development of specific teaching skills). Quarterly meetings are held with mentor teachers to conduct a 'pulse check' on successes, challenges, and concerns with the program. These meetings provide the faculty with a forum to introduce new supervisory topics or issues which need to be attended to in the internships. These mentor teachers receive little remuneration and have infrequent opportunities for professional development yet commit themselves to this role for the professional reward it offers and the chance to meet with other physical education colleagues in a supportive environment. One additional opportunity that is offered through this program is the chance to serve on a graduate student's committee and be part of the final oral exam. This exam is aimed at providing masters candidates a chance to present their professional portfolio in a public meeting. This portfolio is intended to be reflective of their best work throughout this one-year program. In order for a mentor teacher to serve on such a committee they need to have a masters degree themselves and they must apply for adjunct faculty status. 'Those teachers who have participated in this capacity, find it a positive experience and usually will repeat as committee members' (for example, van der Mars, 1995). There has been an interest by the mentor teachers to team teach pedagogy-related courses with faculty on campus although there are no funds to encourage this type of effort.

Another mentoring opportunity due to begin at West Virginia University in the summer of 1996 is linked to the training of student teachers and labeled the directing student teacher certification program. This program will certify teachers to direct student teaching placements and provide them with the opportunity to become adjunct faculty, qualify for a faculty/teacher exchange program, apply for summer university teaching, and serve in a more direct way as teacher educators. To prepare teachers to take on this directing student teacher role and become skilled in mentoring pre-service teachers they will be required to take a series of courses which are offered over a three-year period. The university will provide tuition waivers during the year and the school districts will pay for summer enrollment. The series of courses will include coursework on professional issues, effective teaching, supervision and a teaching practicum. In the practicum teachers will deliver a unit of instruction to their own pupils and employ principles of teaching effectiveness. As a result, it is believed that directing teachers will have the teaching and supervisory skills to successfully mentor pre-service teachers.

The Slippery Rock Teacher Center described earlier in relation to peer mentoring, was originally implemented to increase student teachers interaction with the school, teachers, and students (Jones, 1993). The extended time in one community permitted in-depth observations and interactions with students and between university and school personnel committed to the development of pre-service physical education teachers. Teachers in these centers accepted shared responsibility for a group of student teachers and each used their expertise as teacher educators to guide the professional development of the interns. After discussion and observation, student teachers selected a mentor teacher who had lead responsibility for guiding them through training. Selection of the mentor is based on teaching specialization, instructional style compatibility and personal characteristics. In addition, each student teacher had two other co-operating teachers selected from among the mentor's colleagues at different educational levels. Once in this mentoring role, the responsibilities are similar to those of a co-operating teacher in a traditional site; observation, feedback, informal meetings between classes, and more extended conferences covering the total experience. Each student teacher is part of a team composed of mentor, two co-operating teachers, university supervisor, and other peers at the site. This extended personal community allows for more cohesive guidance and input from a number of perspectives.

While the question of what a mentor is has yet to be resolved, deciding how they will be trained is just as vexing. 'Just as becoming a teacher involves making a transition from being a student to being a professional, so becoming a mentor involves making a transition from classroom teacher to teacher educator' (Field, 1994, p. 67). Whether this is the same as being trained to be a co-operating teacher or determining if there are further expectations and responsibilities associated with the mentor role needs to be explored.

### Mentoring Within Collaborative Projects

Collaboration has been compared to marriage (Graham, 1988) in that it is voluntary and takes a lot of work. Using the same analogy, we propose that mentoring be described as a bridesmaid to, or more imperatively, an offspring of, collaborative efforts. In most cases, mentorship is voluntary, intensive, time consuming, and productive but generally not the primary purpose for collaboration. However, some type of role modeling, coaching, and/or supervising inevitably occurs when school and university colleagues work together.

While the benefits and burdens of collaboration have been explored, discovered, investigated and reported by many respected physical education professionals (Lawson, 1990; Martinek and Schempp, 1988; Sharpe, 1992) significant investigation regarding the mentoring aspect of collaboration has not been undertaken. Despite this lack of specific reference to, and research on, mentoring, however, there is an abundance of evidence that it does occur in physical education collaborative efforts. Collaborative relationships in the US typically involve university personnel working with public school practitioners. In most cases, undergraduate students are placed at school sites for field experiences and student teaching. Atypically, graduate students interact directly with public school and/or experienced teachers and serve as mentors to inductees, or new teachers. The mentor/protege relationship may vary according to the type of collaborative model guiding the partnership (i.e., program assistance, research-bonded, or professional development), yet the sharing of professional knowledge between colleagues, mentors, and proteges is an emphasis of all collaborative efforts.

In a 1988 *Journal of Teaching in Physical Education* monograph edited by Martinek and Schempp two collaborative models being used in physical education were presented and included Program Assistance and Research Bonded. More recently, and as a result of several educational reform efforts, a third model has been introduced as the Professional Development School model (Holmes Group, 1990). Program assistance models 'focus on ways in which technical, curricular, and evaluative assistance are provided to pre-service and in-service programs and their teachers' (Martinek and Schempp, 1988, p. 161). Collaborative endeavors within this model use problem-solving techniques as a method to improve the teaching of physical education (curriculum, evaluation, instruction). While research may be an outgrowth of collaborative efforts operating under the program assistance model, it is not an expectation. Research-bonded models on the other hand attempt to provide this same instructional assistance to preservice and practicing teachers yet are guided by research. 'An important motivational factor underlying the use of these models is that teachers share in the responsibility of deciding what research questions to ask as well as how to answer them' (*ibid*). This move toward action research conducted with, not on, practising teachers allows practical application in a school setting.

Professional development schools (PDS) allow pre-service teachers the opportunity to experience portions of their teacher training in public school teaching sites under the guidance of practicing mentor teachers and university faculty. These schools also serve as inquiry sites for educational research conducted by teachers and faculty, graduate students, and in some cases undergraduates themselves. The Holmes Group (1990) defined the purpose of the Professional Development School:

> ... to bring the practicing teachers and administrators together with university faculty in partnerships that improve teaching and learning on the part of their respective students ... They would provide superior opportunities for teachers and administrators to influence the development of the professional relevance of their work through 1) mutual deliberation on problems with student learning and their possible solutions; 2) shared teaching in the university and schools; 3) collaborative research on the problems of educational practice; and 4) co-operative supervision of prospective teachers and administrators. (p. 56)

### Program Assistance

The School College Operation in Physical Education Project (Project SCOPE) at Queens College is best classified under the program assistance model with its emphasis on teacher development. Project SCOPE is one of the oldest (fifteen years) school-university partnerships in the US and prides itself as one of the few partnerships which 'takes a comprehensive and holistic approach to integrating and improving education' (Catelli *et al*, 1995, p. 8). Similar to the professional development school model, teachers in this program work with professors to develop and teach pre-service methods courses, serve as co-operating teachers, develop curriculum, and serve as role models and change agents for pre-service teachers and colleagues. Mentoring relationships grow each year as Queens College graduates are employed by the New York City School District and become the mentors for new proteges matriculating in the program. Action research has been an outgrowth of Project SCOPE as teachers have learned to collect and analyze data to critically reflect on particular aspects of their teaching (Catelli, *et al*, 1995.)

The Physical Education Program Development Center at Teachers College, Columbia University, encompasses six school districts, is housed at an affiliated school district with easy access for all participants, and is co-directed by a school and a university representative. The goal of this center was 'to build a collaborative relationship that would both develop and maintain effective physical education programs' (Anderson, 1988, p. 177). This project, which does not have a pre-service component, has been operating for fifteen years and was developed to benefit the school programs with the college involved in servicing these programs. Mentoring has taken on a slightly different connotation with graduate students serving as facilitators to a variety of curriculum projects determined by program directors and carried out at the Project Center. Teachers on the other hand perform the role of mentor to their teaching colleagues by sharing their experiences with curriculum development. The focus for this collaboration has been on in-service program improvement at the district level and within individual schools rather than interaction between teachers and pre-service students. While research has not been a focus of this effort, it has resulted through graduate student involvement in facilitating aspects of the center's work. As project co-ordinators at various school sites, several doctoral students have conducted extensive case studies culminating in dissertations (Schwager, 1986; Doolittle, 1987). Reflecting on the efficacy of the teaching center, Anderson (1988) noted that, 'College people learned to respect and value the priorities set by teachers. In turn, some of the alternatives put forth by the college representatives were eventually adopted . . .' (p. 183). In retrospect, the Physical Education Program Development Center at Teachers College, has been successful in meeting their goal of designing and maintaining a long term collaborative project.

### Research Bonded

Most collaborative projects are based on the assumption that participants will be equal partners and that decision-making processes will be shared. While mentoring specifically is rarely mentioned in collaboration, sharing ideas, developing collegial relationships, problem-solving, and advising are most often designated as primary intentions for entering into a partnership. Due to the specificity required by Operating under the auspices of a research question, research-bonded models do afford the opportunity to clarify formal mentoring roles yet these mentoring roles and functions may be determined by the context of the collaboration or by the research question being asked.

The SPARK (Sports, Play, and Active Recreation for Kids) Physical Education Program was originally developed at San Diego State University by Thomas McKenzie and James Sallis within the Encinitas Union and Poway Unified School Districts in California. Funded by the National Institutes of Health in June 1989, investigators worked with over 2000 students, classroom teachers, and administrators to design, implement, and evaluate a program of physical education for the twenty-first century. SPARK is a unique program which is decidedly research-based, includes collaboration among a variety of disciplines, and focusses on increasing and promoting regular physical activity for elementary children.

Texts and materials developed from the grant such as the SPARK Curricula, Staff Development, Measurement and Assessment Tools and Consultation are available to individual schools, districts, educators, researchers and professional organizations throughout the world on a non-profit basis. Mentoring occurs informally at the original schools through follow-up visits, or more formally through staff development, inservicing and consultation which may be arranged by contacting the SPARK organization.

*Professional Development Schools*

Recently instituted professional development schools at the Ohio State University, University of Nebraska-Lincoln, and West Virginia University are attempting to combine program assistance models with research in order to address the differences in experiences and perspectives which public school teachers and university faculty bring to the collaborative experience (Jones and Maloy, 1988; Coffin, 1991) and are frequently mentioned when building collaborative relationships. Clinical sites for teacher education have been advocated in the US since early in this century. John Dewey promoted the establishment of laboratory or campus schools as sites where research and practice could be combined to benefit the education of school children, university students, teachers, and professors. Although a lack of congruent expectations and support lead to their eventual decline, (Stallings and Kowalski, 1990) laboratory schools became a valuable precursor to current school/university partnership efforts. The most recent efforts at school university partnerships, professional development or clinical schools, were recommended in both the Carnegie Forum (1986) and Holmes Group (1986) reform reports.

Clinical schools would link faculties in elementary and secondary schools, colleges of education, and colleges of arts and science to

provide the best possible learning environment for teacher preparation
. . . The clinical school was seen as analogous to a teaching hospital
. . . Participants in this partnership would have opportunities to reflect
upon teaching and learning within the clinical school environment.
(Stallings and Kowalski, 1990, p. 255)

Again, while mentoring *per se* is not defined as a primary purpose for establishing a PDS or clinical school, recommendations for co-operative supervision and the analogy to a teaching hospital reflect the expectation that mentoring will indeed occur. Examples of mentoring within school-university partnerships have been or suggested at several sites in the US and discussed at the recent National Association of Sport, and Physical Education (NASPE)-sponsored National Teacher Education Conference.

Among the mentoring and collaborative activities underway at West Virginia University is the Cass Program being implemented at a local elementary school. At the present time, someone from WVU teaches every physical education class at Cass Elementary School. This arrangement has allowed the local school district to increase physical education instruction time for their pupils by releasing the physical educators from Cass to teach at other schools in the district, and expanding the number of physical education classes offered to Cass students. Classes at Cass are taught primarily by a WVU graduate student and PETE faculty members with some assistance from undergraduates enrolled in methods courses. In addition, those pre-service teachers participating in their post-student teaching practicum discussed earlier in relation to peer mentoring are involved teaching at Cass. A unique aspect of this situation is that every PETE faculty member (seven) must teach at least one class twice per week and some experienced undergraduate physical education majors have become mentors to the faculty. As Andrew Hawkins (1995b) related . . .

I know this it probably seems strange, but the mentoring part of this project is the undergraduate students, in the post-student teaching semester, mentoring the faculty as they teach at Cass . . . this seems like role reversal, but it seems to have some positive benefits to the faculty, most of whom have not frequently taught elementary PE. There are obvious benefits to the students who are mentoring as well. They begin to develop a real collegial relationship with the faculty whom they are observing. There is a great deal of give and take, sharing of ideas and experiences, explaining purposes and goals. So, strange as it may seem, the students in this case, really are mentors in a sense, for the faculty. That is not to say that the only ones to benefit are the faculty. I think it's a two-way street in this case.

While they have yet to complete any research in this new program they are currently collecting a 'boatload' of data to assess benefits of the program and its impact on their pre-service teachers and pupils it is designed for. The WVU faculty does believe that they have increased their credibility with pre-service teachers as they observe them trying to practice what they preach. An additional benefit of this project has been an increased understanding of the different roles played by practising teachers and university faculty. As teacher education faculty move into the schools in this teaching role, it has increased the respect they have gained from public school personnel.

At the University of Nebraska-Lincoln (UNL) the mentor roles have been described as co-operating teachers serving as models of good teachers, guest speakers in the academic portions of student coursework, collaborative action researchers, and initiating pre-service teachers to the public school experience (for example, Lounsbery, 1995). UNL professors serve with the teachers as 'joint instructors/mentors of daily deliberate practice, tying research and theory directly to daily instructional practice'. This relationship allows both in-service and pre-service teachers to gain multiple opportunities to incorporate systematic observation techniques with the goals and strategies incumbent in effective teaching in physical education. When practicing teachers work with undergraduates it becomes a rejuvenating process for them. As these teachers take a leadership role in their gymnasiums, this working relationship also facilitates teachers becoming mentors to their teaching colleagues. Lounsbery (*ibid*) stated that '. . . one possible roadblock to teachers mentoring teachers is relationships. Teachers must move toward a much more collegial working relationship'. In response to an inquiry about teachers mentoring graduate students, Lounsbery (*ibid*) responded that this does occur on an informal basis when graduate students serve as PDS co-ordinators/supervisors; 'not officially, but if you think of mentoring as learning from one another, then most definitely teachers mentor graduate students at least indirectly. When the PDS co-ordinator/supervisor, the teacher, and the undergraduate student teacher, sit together and provide feedback and insights on the undergraduate's teaching episode, I know the PDS co-ordinator/supervisor learns from the teacher's feedback and perspective as I hope the teacher learns from the PDS co-ordinator/supervisor through this process'. This suggests that there is a dual directional mentoring exchange between practicing teacher and graduate student.

At Ohio State University, plans are being made to implement mentoring into a new MEd program with teacher certification in the summer of 1996. Winter 1996 will see faculty, graduate students, and practising teachers coming together in a seminar with the intent of planning the field work and teaching methods courses associated with this new program. Practising teachers that have chosen to take part in this effort are those who have been actively involved in the present professional development school, The Franklin County Academy of Physical Educators. Several of these teachers have worked as clinical educators for the PDS, teaching a career seminar and curriculum clinics to pre-service teachers, offering workshops to practising teachers and undergraduates, and serving as liaisons between the University and public schools. Others have been trained in supervision and have served as co-operating teachers in the student teaching practicum for many years. Ohio State will be maintaining many of the positive aspects of the PDS as it now exists while attempting to strengthen their collaborative efforts directed toward the training of preservice teachers in realistic settings.

> Based on ideas that have surfaced at this time, we are looking to moving away from one clinical educator to working with four-five cohort teachers per year who will do a part of the elementary or secondary method work in their schools. We have excellent teachers with expertise in a variety of areas who are interested in having discussions about what this would mean for them, their schools and their students. Using the money previously provided to support a clinical educator, these teachers could potentially be compensated with a financial contract for: teaching on campus in August, preparing students to enter their classrooms throughout the year in cohort groups; supervision work during the year of small cohorts of students in their PE program at the school setting; work in after school teaching/advising of students on issues related to teaching . . .' etc. (Stroot, 1995, p. 3)

It is the belief that the practicing teachers associated with the Ohio State program have the skill and expertise to be effective teacher educators that is propelling this effort forward. Their role as mentors to the pre-service teachers in the new graduate certification program is a critical component that is to be fostered as this program is developed.

One of the six principles extolled by the Holmes Group (1990) to guide the genesis of PDS's encourages 'all adult participants, teachers, teacher educators, and administrators . . . to continue their professional growth both for its own sake and to model lifelong learning for their students' (Winitzky, Stoddart and O'Keefe, 1992). This guiding principle epitomizes many of the efforts of collaborators in physical education in the US to combine the expertise, experience and opportunities available from both teachers and professors at both school and university sites.

## Beginning Teacher Induction

Beginning teacher induction programs have received increased dialogue in the general education literature over the past decade yet are only just beginning to surface in reports from physical education. While there is a dearth of research on beginning physical education teachers, we do have some notion of the number of physical education teachers who leave the profession within the first five years or transfer to different teaching fields (Paese, 1986). As the teacher socialization literature begins to identify some of the issues and concerns faced by physical education teachers (Freedman, 1985; Paese, 1986; Stroot and Morton, 1989; O'Sullivan, 1989; Smyth, 1992) we will be in a position to design and implement induction programs to meet the needs of these novice teachers (Stroot and Williamson, 1993). As pointed out by O'Sullivan (1989), 'we have neglected our beginning teachers, and unless we know what realities they face on the job in their first few years, we cannot hope to provide the pre-service or in-service preparation to support successful transitions to teaching' (p. 242).

Attempts to confront and alleviate the problems being faced by beginning teachers are being addressed. Both the Holmes Group (1986) and Carnegie Forum (1986) recommended the notion of induction programs to assist and support the beginning teacher. In physical education, these mentored induction programs are only just beginning to take hold and in some cases are a part of a larger commitment to the development of all teachers across all subject areas.

Project Scope at Queens College previously described in the collaborative mentoring section has been so successful that graduates who were mentored by teachers in the New York City school system have been hired as first year teachers to fill vacancies in the district and continue in their mentoring relationship. Experienced teachers who have worked with the inductees as undergraduates, voluntarily serve as mentors within the school system as the novice teachers join the district. Already established as mentor and protege, the relationship has continued during the first year of teaching and beyond. As this project has been ongoing for fifteen years, the original proteges have now become mentors to the Queens College undergraduates.

Napper-Owen and Phillips (1995) have recently reported on their efforts to provide induction assistance to first year physical education teachers and to examine the impact of that assistance. Weekly teaching observations and follow-up conferences were held throughout the year between the researcher/ mentor and the teachers. During weekly conferences, feedback and ideas for modifying the lesson were provided by the mentor followed by discussion on why the lesson had been planned as delivered and how the alternative strategies might be incorporated. Reactions from the two teachers involved in this study, while different, were both positive relative to the mentoring they received. In one instance the teacher felt that induction assistance strengthened and reinforced what he had been taught in his pre-service training while the other teacher felt that it encouraged her to be more reflective about her own teaching (*ibid*). These researchers concluded that mentoring is more effective if the mentor is available to observe teaching at least once per week, does not serve in an evaluator role, and mentoring may reduce the feelings of isolation reported in the literature. They also concluded with the thought that continued contact and support following completion of the induction period might continue to foster feelings of collagueship and a resource to support continued growth.

Stroot, Faucette and Schwager (1993) supported formal and informal mentoring programs to improve instruction and as a means of coping with the concerns and issues faced by the beginning physical education teacher. 'Formal programs seem to have an advantage of providing consistency for novice teachers and opportunities for regular collegial interaction. Informal processes provide opportunities for self-selection of colleagues who share perspectives regarding teaching and learning' (p. 385).

One formal mentoring program, while not specifically designed for physical education or restricted to beginning teachers, provides mentored induction for all new teachers in the Columbus City Schools. 'Initiated by the Columbus Education Association (CEA), the Peer Assistance and Review (PAR) program is a collaborative effort between the teachers and administrators to provide assistance and evaluation to teachers at all levels of experience' (Stroot, 1995, p. 7). The mentored induction phase of PAR is facilitated by a pool of mentor teachers selected for their teaching effectiveness, leadership skills, and perceived ability to provide guidance to their colleagues. When a physical education teacher is hired in the school district an attempt is made to match the new intern with a physical education mentor thus providing the best match to support their professional needs and concerns. Mentors observe and assess an intern's teaching once per week, provide feedback and suggestions for improvement, and identify how to access instructional resources within the district (Stroot, 1991). As their role also includes assessment, these mentors document the intern's progress and recommend a continuing contract with the district. A collaboratively developed graduate program designed by PAR consultants and faculty in Ohio State University College of Education is offered to all new teachers in conjunction with their mentored induction. Stroot (*ibid*) indicated that the design of this program was to 'address issues and concerns of intern teachers, and represent a balance of theory, research, and craft wisdom' (p. 7). Research on the impact of this program is ongoing with the impact on teachers being positive.

If Schweitzer (1993) is correct in her proposition that mentoring not be limited to pre-service teacher training then mentored induction programs must be developed to meet the more specific needs of the intern teacher. Efforts like those just described are a beginning and results of these early efforts will inform the design and implementation of specific programs for the beginning and veteran physical education teacher.

## Summary

While mentoring is not frequently used as a definition for roles played by physical education professionals in the United States, supervision, advising, coaching and training can be found throughout the research literature. Mentoring, however, occurs across the career span as a helping relationship between two colleagues regardless of age, expertise or position. If we assume that learning to teach is a process which extends across a teacher's career then each aspect of mentoring being explored in physical education in the United States will play a role in the development of effective teachers. Key components of successful mentoring programs, which have surfaced as a result of our examining the previously cited works, include focussed training, public recognition of all participants, respectful interaction, and frequent availability. As noted, neither mentoring or supervision are the same as teaching, and require the development of different skills (i.e., focused training); mentoring, to be effective is hard work and needs to be rewarded (i.e., public recognition); mentoring relationships can be challenging and provide growth for both members in the relationship (i.e., respected interaction); and mentoring requires one-on-one interaction at frequent intervals (i.e., frequent availability). While many of these components are still in the planning stages at institutions across the United States, physical education professionals are beginning to recognize and implement projects which incorporate the knowledge and experience of veterans to help novice teachers develop expertise and to allow novice teachers to enlighten some of the outdated traditions we hold onto.

## References

ACHESON, K.A. and GALL, M.D. (1987) *Techniques in Clinical Supervision of Teachers: Pre-service and In-service Applications* (2nd edition), New York, Longman.

ALLEMAN, E., COCHRAN, J., DOVERSPIKE, J. and NEWMAN, I. (1984) 'Enriching mentoring relationships', *Personnel and Guidance Journal*, **12**, pp. 329–32.

ANDERSON, W.G. (1988) 'A school-centered collaborative model for program development', *Journal of Teaching in Physical Education*, **7**, 3, pp. 176–83.

BATESKY, J. (1991) 'Peer coaching', *Strategies*, **4**, 6, pp. 15–19.

BERRY, B. and GINSBERG, R. (1990) 'Creating lead teachers: From policy to implementation', *Phi Delta Kappan*, **71**, 8, pp. 617–21.

BEY, T. and HOLMES, C.T. (Eds) (1992) *Mentoring: Contemporary Principles and Issues*, Reston, VA, Association of Teacher Educators.

CARNEGIE FORUM ON EDUCATION AND THE ECONOMY (1986) *A Nation Prepared: Teachers for the 21st Century*, New York, Carnegie Forum.

CARRUTHERS, J. (1993) 'The principles and practices of mentoring' in CALDWELL, B.J. and CARTER, E.M.A. (Eds) *The Return of the Mentor: Strategies for Workplace Learning*, London, Falmer Press.

CATELLI, L. (1992) 'Against all odds', *Action in Teacher education*, **XIV**, 1, pp. 43–51.

CATELLI, L., DeCURTIS, P., NIX, W., JOHNSTON, D., McLAUGHLIN, P., MONGIELLO, B. and MOSKOWITZ, K. (1995) 'Collaborate: Become a "new" professional', *Strategies*, **9**, 3, pp. 8–15.

COFFIN, D.G. (1991) 'Multiple realities can enhance school/university collaboration', *The Physical Educator*, **51**, 2, pp. 93–103.

COULON, S.C. (1988) 'The effects of self-instructional modules on the task statements of the co-operating teacher, the teaching behaviors of the student teacher, and the in class behaviors of the pupils', *Dissertation Abstracts International*, **48**, 9, pp. 2273A.

DODDS, P.A. (1975) 'A behavioral competency-based peer assessment model for student teacher and pupil behavior', *Dissertation Abstracts International*, **36**, pp. 3486-A. (University Microfilms No. 75–26570)

DODDS, P.A. (1989) 'Student teachers observing peers' in DARST, P.W., ZAKRAJSEK, D.B. and MANCINI, V.H. (Eds) *Analyzing Physical Education and Sport Instruction*, Champaign, IL, Human Kinetics, pp. 225–32.

DOOLITTLE, S. (1987) 'Curriculum writing in physical education: A multi-case study', paper presented at the AIESEP World Congress, Trois Rivieres, Canada.

ELLIS, N.H. (1993) 'Mentoring: Enhancing the experienced career'. *Kappa Delta Pi Record*, **29**, 2, pp. 130–5.

FIELD, B. (1994) 'The new role of the teacher — Mentoring' in FIELD, B. and FIELD, T. (Eds) *Teachers as Mentors: A Practical Guide*, London, Falmer Press, pp. 63–77.

FREEDMAN, M. (1985) 'Research on follow-up of teacher education: Promise for the future' in VANDEIN, C.L. and NIXON, J.E. (Eds) *Physical Education Teacher Education*, New York, MacMillan, pp. 156–62.

GEHRKE, N. (1988) 'Mentoring teachers', *Theory into Practice*, **XXVII**, 3, College of Education, Ohio State University, pp. 190–4.

GRAHAM, G. (1988) 'Collaboration in physical education: A lot like marriage?', *Journal of Teaching in Physical Education*, **7**, 3, pp. 165–77.

HAWKINS, A. (1995a) personal communication, 18 November.

HAWKINS, A. (1995b) personal communication, 28 November.

HERKOWITZ, J. (1995) personal communication, 21 November.

HOLMES GROUP (1986) *Tomorrow's Teachers: A Report of the Holmes Group*, East Lansing, MI, Holmes Group.

HOLMES GROUP (1990) *Tomorrow's Schools: Principles for the Design of Professional Development Schools*, East Lansing, MI, Holmes Group.

HOUSTON, J.E. (Ed) (1990) *Thesaurus of ERIC Descriptors*, (12th ed). Phoenix, AZ, Oryx Press.

HOWEY, K. (1988) 'Mentor-teachers as inquiring professionals', *Theory into Practice*, **XXXVII**, 3, College of Education, Ohio State University, pp. 109–213.

JONES, R. (1993) 'The teaching center: An alternative to traditional student teaching practice', *Journal of Physical Education, Recreation, and Dance*, **64**, 7, pp. 53–8.

JONES, B. and MALOY, M. (1988) *Partnerships for Improving Schools*, New York, Greenwood Press.

JOYCE, B.R. and and SHOWERS, B. (1982) 'The coaching of teaching', *Educational Leadership*, **40**, 1, pp. 4–16.

JOYCE, B.R. and SHOWERS, B. (1988) *The coaching of teaching; Student Achievement Through Staff Development*, New York, Longman.

LAMASTER, K.J. (1995) 'Pre-service teachers and their use of e-mail: Communication during an early field experience', unpublished second year study, Ohio State University.

LAWSON, H. (1990) 'Sport pedagogy research: From information gathering to useful knowledge', *Journal of Teaching in Physical Education*, 10, pp. 1–20.

LIEBERMAN, A., and MILLER, A. (1989) *Teachers, Their World and Their Work*, Alexandria, VA, Association of Supervision and Curriculum Development.

LOUNSBERY, M. (1995) personal communication, 9 November.

MARTINEK, T. and SCHEMPP, P. (1988) 'An introduction to models for collaboration', *Journal of Teaching in Physical Education*, **7**, 3, pp. 160–4.

METZLER, M.W. (1990) *Instructional Supervision for Physical Education*, Champaign, IL, Human Kinetics.

NAPPER-OWEN, G.E. and PHILLIPS, D.A. (1995) 'A qualitative analysis of the impact of induction assistance on first-year physical educators', *Journal of Teaching in Physical Education*, **14**, 3, pp. 305–27.

O'CANSEY, R.T.A. (1988) 'The effects of a behavioral model of supervision on the supervisory behaviors of co-operating teachers', *Journal of Teaching in Physical Education*, **8**, 1, pp. 46–62.

O'SULLIVAN, M. (1989) 'Failing gym is like failing lunch or recess: Two beginning teachers' struggle for legitimacy', *Journal of Teaching in Physical Education*, **8**, 3, pp. 227–42.

PAESE, P.C. (1986) 'A review of teacher induction: Are special programs needed for beginning physical education teachers?', *The Physical Educator*, **47**, 3, pp. 159–65.

PETERSEN, S. (1995) personal communication, 13 November.

POOLE, J.R. (1994) 'Finding more teaching opportunities for physical education teacher education', *The Physical Educator*, **51**, 1, pp. 53–6.

RANDALL, L.E. (1990) *Systematic Supervision in Physical Education*, Champaign, IL, Human Kinetics.

RIKARD, L. and VEAL, M.L. (in press) 'Co-operating teachers: Insights into their preparation, beliefs, and practices', *Journal of Teaching in Physical Education*.

RINK, J. (1995) personal communication, 14 November.

SCHWAGER, S. (1986) 'Ongoing program development: Teachers as collaborators', *Journal of Teaching in Physical Education*, **5**, pp. 272–9.

SCHWEITZER, C.A. (1993) 'Mentoring future professionals', *Journal of Physical Education, Recreation, and Dance*, **64**, 7, pp. 50–2.

SHARPE, T. (1992) 'Teacher preparation: A professional development school approach', *Journal of Physical Education, Recreation, and Dance*, **63**, 5, pp. 82–7.

SIEDENTOP, D. (1981) 'The Ohio State University supervision research program summary report', *Journal of Teaching in Physical Education, Introductory Issue*, pp. 30–8.

SMYTH, D. (1992) ' "The kids just love him": A first year teachers' perceptions of their workplace', paper presented at the annual meeting of the American Educational Research Association, San Francisco, April.

STALLINGS, J.A. and KOWALSKI, T. (1990) 'Research on professional development schools' in HOUSTON, W.R. (Ed) *Handbook of Research on Teacher Education*, New York, Macmillan, pp. 251–63.

STRAND, B.N. (1992) 'A descriptive profile of teacher preparation practices in physical education teacher education', *The Physical Educator*, **49**, 2, pp. 104–12.

STROBLE, E. and COOPER, J.M. (1988) 'Mentor teachers: Coaches or referees?', *Theory into Practice*, **XXXVII**, 3, College of Education, The Ohio State University, pp. 231–6.

STROOT, S.A. (1991) 'Formalized socialization into teaching: The induction process for first year teachers', paper presented at the annual meeting of AAHPERD, San Francisco, April.

STROOT, S.A. (1995) 'Lesson learned from a PDS: Looking toward the future', paper presented at the National Teacher Education Conference, Morgantown, WV.

STROOT, S.A., FAUCETTE, N. and SCHWAGER, S. (1993) 'In the beginning: The induction of physical educators', *Journal of Teaching in Physical Education*, **12**, 4, pp. 375–85.

STROOT, S.A. and MORTON, P.J. (1989) 'Blueprints for learning', *Journal of Teaching in Physical Education*, **8**, 3, pp. 213–32.

STROOT, S.A. and WILLIAMSON, K.M. (1993) 'Issues and themes of socialization into physical education', *Journal of Teaching in Physical Education*, **12**, 4, pp. 337–43.

TANNEHILL, D. (1989) 'Student teaching: A view from the other side', *Journal of Teaching in Physical Education*, **8**, 3, pp. 243–53.

TANNEHILL, D. and ZAKRAJSEK, D. (1990) 'Effects of a self-directed training program on co-operating teacher behavior', *Journal of Teaching in Physical Education*, **9**, 2, pp. 140–51.

VAN DER MARS, H. (1995) personal communication, 13 November.

VEAL, M.L. and RIKARD, L. (1995) 'Silent partners in the student teaching triad: Co-operating teachers speak out', unpublished.

VERIABOFF, L. (1983) 'The five-to-one student teaching experience', *Journal of Teaching in Physical Education*, **2**, 2, pp. 55–61.

WINITZKY, N., STODDART, T. and O'KEEFE, P. (1992) 'Theme: Professional development schools', *Journal of Teacher Education*, **43**, 1, pp. 3–18.

# List of Contributors

**Susan Capel** is Principal Lecturer and Director of the Academic Standards Unit at Canterbury Christ Church College, Kent.

**Deborah G. Coffin** is Assistant Professor in the Department of Physical Education, School of Education, University of Missouri-Kansas City.

**Colin Hardy** is Senior Lecturer in the Department of Physical Education, Sports Science and Recreation Management, Loughborough University.

**Joanne Hudson** is a Research Assistant, Chelsea School of Physical Education, Sports Science, Dance and Leisure, University of Brighton.

**Ann-Marie Latham** is Senior Lecturer, Chelsea School of Physical Education, Sports Science, Dance and Leisure, University of Brighton.

**Mick Mawer** is Lecturer in Physical Education, School of Education, University of Hull.

**Elizabeth Murdoch** is Professor and Head of School, Chelsea College of Physical Education, Sports Science, Dance and Leisure, University of Brighton.

**Ros Phillips** is Principal Lecturer in Physical Education, IM Marsh Centre for Physical Education, Sport and Dance, School of Education and Community Studies, Liverpool John Moores University.

**Tony Rossi** is Lecturer in Physical Education Pedagogy and Curriculum, Faculty of Education, University of Southern Queensland, Queensland, Australia.

**Patricia Shenton** is Head of IM Marsh Centre for Physical Education, Sport and Dance, School of Education and Community Studies, Liverpool John Moores University.

**Joan Stephenson** is Head of Department of Education, De Montfort University, Bedford.

**Emma Tait** is a Research Student at the Cheltenham and Gloucester College of Higher Education, Cheltenham.

**Deborah Tannehill** is Associate Professor in Physical Education Teacher Education, School of Health, Physical Education and Recreation, Ohio State University, USA.

**Michael Taylor** is a Research Student, Department of Education, De Montfort University, Bedford.

**Richard Tinning** is Professor of Physical Education, Faculty of Education, Deakin University, Australia.

**Chai Kim Yau** is Lecturer/Research Assistant, IM Marsh Centre for Physical Education, Sport and Dance, School of Education and Community Studies, Liverpool John Moores University.

# Index